Jewish Life

in the Industrial Promised Land, 1855–2005

·

Nora Faires and **Nancy Hanflik**

·

Michigan State University Press · *East Lansing*

 Celebrate 350
Jewish Life in America
1654~2004

Jewish Life in the Industrial Promised Land, 1855–2005, was published with the support of the Alfred P. Sloan Museum and the Flint Jewish Federation.

⊚ The paper used in this publication meets the minimum requirements of ANSI/NISO Z39.48-1992 (R 1997) (Permanence of Paper).

Michigan State University Press
East Lansing, Michigan 48823-5245
www.msupress.msu.edu

Printed and bound in the United States of America.

11 10 09 08 07 06 05   1 2 3 4 5 6 7 8 9 10

LIBRARY OF CONGRESS CATALOGING-IN-PUBLICATION DATA
Faires, Nora Helen.
Jewish life in the industrial promised land, 1855–2005 / Nora Faires and Nancy Hanflik.
p. cm.
Includes bibliographical references and index.
ISBN 0-87013-771-9 (cloth : alk. paper)
1. Jews—Michigan—Flint—History. 2. Flint (Mich.)—Ethnic relations.
I. Hanflik, Nancy. II. Title.
F575.J5F35 2005
977.4'37004924—dc22
2005021254

Cover and book design by Sharp Des!gns, Lansing, Michigan

Cover art is a combination of two photographs of the Vehicle City arches on South Saginaw Street in Flint, Michigan. The photograph of the original arches, ca. 1905, is used courtesy of the Crooks Collection, Scharchburg Archives, Kettering University. The photograph of the replica arches in 2003 is used courtesy of the *Flint Journal.*

green press Michigan State University Press is a member of the Green Press Initiative and is committed to developing and encouraging ecologically responsible publishing practices. For more information about the Green Press Initiative and the use of recycled paper in book publishing, please visit *www.greenpressinitiative.com.*

To the memory of
Nancy Faires Conklin
and to the Gruner Sisters,
Fay, Stella, Anna, and Mimi,
whose stories inspired us

Contents

Illustrations

Foreword

In 2005 we celebrate both the three hundred and fiftieth anniversary of Jews in America and the sesquicentennial of the city of Flint, Michigan. Fittingly, the two institutions we represent—the Flint Jewish Federation and the Sloan Museum in Flint—have worked together for nearly a decade to help bring this story of Jewish life in our community to a broad audience, first through a museum exhibit and now through this publication. *Jewish Life in the Industrial Promised Land, 1855–2005,* offers a unique perspective on the role of the Jewish community in the development of our city. It is a saga of people seeking the American dream, building lives in good times and bad. In many ways this is a book about people helping others. The stars of this story are our neighbors, friends, and co-workers.

We are very grateful to the more than one hundred community contributors who donated photographs and artifacts, and to the many individuals who shared their life stories through oral histories. We also thank the members and staff of both of our institutions, who helped in so many ways throughout this project. The partnership of our institutions has resulted in a close and lasting relationship, adding another episode to the chronicle of Flint and Flint's Jewish community.

GARY S. ALTER, *Executive Director, Flint Jewish Federation*
TIM SHICKLES, *Director, The Sloan Museum*

Preface

Surveying three hundred and fifty years of Jewish life in the United States, historian Hasia Diner concludes that "A constant process of negotiation shaped the history of Jews in America. Many—probably most—ordinary Jews wanted both to be good Jews and to be full Americans."[1] Our analysis of the small Jewish community in Flint, Michigan, shares this perspective, examining the many ways that community members and the community itself negotiated Jewish and American identities from the middle of the nineteenth century through the beginning of the twenty-first. Like their counterparts in large urban centers such as New York, Chicago, and Los Angeles and in a host of small towns across the nation, most of Flint's Jews "looked inward to Jewish tradition to shape the patterns of their lives, while looking outward to their American neighbors as they decided how to live and how to present themselves."[2] Many wished to be—and succeeded in being—both good Jews and active participants in the making and remaking of the city in which they lived. In its overall contours, our story of *Jewish Life in the Industrial Promised Land* mirrors that told in a rapidly growing literature that documents both the accomplishments, acculturation, and acceptance of Jews in America and a continued separateness, sometimes voluntary and sometimes involuntary, that together define the American Jewish experience.

Our book also follows the trend in the historiography of American Jewry to expand the focus from the immigrant experience of the nineteenth and early twentieth centuries to include more recent years, when these immigrants' descendants came of age and when another wave of Jewish immigrants came to the United States. Scholars adopting this larger time frame have begun to recast the narrative of Jewish experience in the United States and relocate the construction of a distinctly American Jewry. Jonathan D. Sarna, for example, sees the "years between World War II and the end of the 1960s" as the "crucible of American Jewish life," while Hasia Diner singles out these decades as a "golden age" for American Jewry.[3] In this respect the site of our study proves of special importance. For in both popular accounts and scholarly writings, Flint is an iconic city of postwar plenty. This manufacturing center's single industry, automobile production, and largest employer, the General Motors Corporation, symbolize the acme of American industrial might and abundant consumer goods. As this book shows, Jews participated in Flint's economic "golden age" but remained outsiders to the city's major industry and consequently from its most important corridors of power. Most Jewish families in Flint worked as storekeepers, entrepreneurs, and professionals, carving a niche in the interstices of a political economy over which, like the autoworkers who were their customers and clients, they had no control. Yet their economic fate, like that of others in this autotown, was tied irrevocably to the fortunes of the giant carmaker. As a result, the city's Jews suffered dire consequences when General Motors slashed jobs in the city. Flint Jewry thus was forged in a setting of economic boom, but has seen that white-hot prosperity turn to ash, as the city has become a portrait in rustbelt deindustrialization.

Jewish Life in the Industrial Promised Land provides a unique window to the religious, social, and communal structures created by Jews in a wildly turbulent environment. It traces a Jewish community made up of multiple strands of migrants, from those fleeing persecution in Southern and Eastern Europe at the end of the nineteenth century to those arriving from the Soviet Union at the end of the twentieth. It sees Flint Jewry as part of a global diaspora during a century of tumult, destruction, and international realignment. The book explores how a community established and maintained a space for itself; examines how its members fashioned lives and remade themselves and their community; and seeks to explain how in so doing they contributed to the evolution of aspects of American society and culture. With our study of Jewish community life in Flint we hope to stir memories and imagination, to engage as well as enlighten. We embrace Jonathan Sarna's sentiment that "To study the history of American Judaism is, among other things, to be reminded anew of the theme of human potential; in our case, the ability of American Jews—young and old, men and women alike—to change the course of history and transform a piece of their world."[4] For Jews in Flint, their piece of the world was America's autotown.

Acknowledgments

Even more than most coauthored works, this book represents the culmination of a collaborative enterprise. We are grateful to the individuals and institutions who have made this venture in community history possible and thank them for their good will, generosity, and patience. In part the idea for the book emerged from a 1997 project, jointly undertaken by the Flint Jewish Federation and Flint's Sloan Museum, to collect photographs and artifacts relating to the history of Jewish life in the region. More than a hundred members of the Jewish community participated in the project, which was directed by Nancy Hanflik. Working with the staff of the local Federation and the Sloan Museum, in 2001 we curated an exhibit entitled "A Century of Jewish Life in Flint" that brought a selection of the collected photographs and artifacts to a broad public. We owe a particular debt to Joel Kaplan, then Federation director, and Steve Germann, then Sloan Museum director, who helped launch the project. Their successors, Gary S. Alter and Tim Shickles, respectively, not only continued the project but made it their own; we thank them for their steadfast support and thoughtful suggestions. Our sincere thanks as well to staff members at both institutions, especially the Sloan Museum's Jeff Taylor, Andrew Clark, and Karen Clark; and to Cindy Ornstein, chief executive officer of the Flint Cultural Center Corporation; members of the board of the Friends of Sloan Museum; the officers of the Flint Jewish Federation, especially past president Jeffrey Himelhoch; David C. White, curator of the Scharchburg Archives at Kettering University; Paul Gifford, archivist at the Genesee Historical Center, Frances Willson Thompson Library, University of Michigan–Flint; and Reva Ratner, pioneering chronicler of Flint's Jewish history.

The research for this project began as part of Nancy Hanflik's Master's thesis in American culture at the University of Michigan–Flint. She thanks Neil Leighton for sparking her interest in community history and her thesis readers, Jacqueline Zeff and Bruce Rubenstein. She is especially grateful to Clifford Hart, Esther Price, and Gilbert Rubenstein, who always were eager to share their knowledge and insight into Flint

Jewish life. Nora Faires's work was supported in part by grants from the Faculty Research and Creative Activities Support Fund and other funds from the office of Research and Sponsored Programs at Western Michigan University, for which she expresses her appreciation. Cynthia B. Foor and Elaine Beckelic provided capable research and transcription assistance. For timely help in various ways, Nora Faires is grateful to current and former colleagues, particularly Robert Berkhofer, José Brandão, Michael Chiarappa, Janet Coryell, Fred Dobney, Marion Gray, Bruce Haight, Lynne Heasley, Mitch Kachun, Leslie Page Moch, John Norman, James Palmitessa, Carolyn Podruchny, Theodosia Robertson, Patricia Rogers, Judith Stone, and Kristin Szylvian. For valuable comments offered on conference papers presented on the project we thank Margo Anderson, Judith Endelman, Rick Halpern, John Hart, Frank Tobias Higbie, and Catherine Lewis. We also are grateful to Aimee Ergass, then editor of *Michigan Jewish History*, where an earlier version of chapter three appeared; to Wallace V. Genser for his suggestions regarding Flint's place in American culture; and to Tim Retzloff for generously sharing his research on Flint's history. We especially thank Kenneth Waltzer, whose incisive presentation at the exhibit guided our further research, and Linda Borish, Phyllis Leffler, and Michael J. Schroeder whose comments on the entire manuscript greatly aided in revision. At Michigan State University Press we received a warm reception for our project, especially from Martha Bates and Julie Loehr, who understood the book we wanted to write and helped us accomplish the task.

Our deepest gratitude is to all those community members who participated in the project through telling their stories, offering photographs and artifacts, and sharing their wisdom. The names of these participants are listed separately. We salute their dedication to preserving and continuing to make their own history. We assume responsibility for any errors, and offer this book in the spirit of collaboration that has buoyed us since the project's inception.

Each of us owes a special debt to those who, in sharing their lives with us, also lived with this project. Nancy Hanflik is immensely grateful to her husband Henry, who encouraged and supported her even when it meant the loss of a companion at the movies, and to her son Jason, whose constant enthusiasm inspired her over the course of this long endeavor. Nora Faires thanks Michael Schroeder for his appreciation of the project, support for her work, and good-natured, clear-eyed consideration of multiple drafts of text. Together we dedicate this book to women in our families from whom we have learned so much.

Project Participants

Our thanks to the following for their commitment, dedication, and invaluable contributions.

Alan Agree
Marian Agree
Rob Agree
Fay Laro Alfred*
Emily Bank Alter
Dorothy Barnett
Sara Beren
Florence Berner
Anna Berg*
Morley Biesman, D.D.S.
Harry Binder
Idelle Binder*
Pat Binder
Daryl Brenner
Kathy Ciccione
Debrah Chimovitz
Rabbi Karen Companez
Julie Colish
Bea Cossman*
Marshall Cossman, D.D.S
Sam Cossman*
Ruth Dodge
Charlotte Dubin

Bessie Feldman
Wendy Flamenbaum
Yuliya Gaydayenko
Paul Gifford
Steve Germann
Harold Glen
Evelyn Golden, M.D.*
Rabbi Mark Goldfarb
Mimi Goldstein
Hanna Goodstein
Peter Goodstein
Saul Gorne, M.D.*
Eugene Griffel
Rhina Griffel
Edith Gutow
Julius Gutow, M.D.*
Helaine Hamelstein*
Mimi Hanflik
Ilene Harris
Clifford Hart
Richard Heitzner
Charles Himelhoch
Jeffrey Himelhoch

Sue Himelhoch
Ted Himelhoch
Shelly Hoffman
Alma Hourvitz
Arthur Hurand
Bess Hurand
Joel Kaplan
Charlotte Kasle
Judy Kasle
Louis Kasle*
Noreen Kasle
Estelle Kaufman
Benjamin Kaufman, D.D.S.
Goldie Klein
Roz Kramer
Morton Krasner
Bess Krolik
David Larzelere
Sylvia Levenson
David Leyton
Max Linder*
Diane Lindholm
Eleanor Megdell
Leonard Meizlish
Michael Melet
Rabbi James Michael
David Miller
Sheila Morgan
Marilyn Natchez
Caroline Panzer
Milton Panzer, D.D.S.
Michael Pelavin*
Natalie Pelavin
Martin Podolsky
Esther Price
Reva Ratner
Diane Ring
Harvey Ring
Diane Roark
Jack Rosenberg

Gilbert Rubenstein
Dora Saltiel
David Schafer*
Faith Schafer
Joan Schafer
Arnold Schaffer, D.D.S.*
Jody Schaffer
Robert Schaffer
Charna Seide
Gloria Siegel
Gail Silverman
Ronald Silverman, Ph.D.
Jack Shaprow*
James Sharp
Gail Shulman
Morris Solomon
Berna Sorscher
Sam Sorscher, D.D.S.*
Jack Stanzler, D.O.
Deborah Steinman
Harold Steinman, O.D.
Leonard Teitelbaum
Florence Tucker*
Lisa Walker
Janet Warren
Shainie Weingarten
Rabbi Yisroel Weingarten
Charles Weinstein
Harry Weinstein
Mitchell Weiss, Ph.D.
Sue Weiss, D.D.S.
Jerome Winegarden Jr.
Irving Wiseman
David C. White
Myra White
Connie Winston
Sam Winston

*deceased

Introduction

On 1 November 1954 a portrait of Harlow Herbert Curtice, president of the General Motors Corporation, appeared on the cover of *Time*, the most widely circulated news weekly of the day. The magazine praised Curtice's leadership of America's largest industrial corporation and applauded his confidence in the continued expansion of the nation's postwar economy. Fourteen months later, his face reappeared on *Time*'s cover as the magazine declared him "Man of the Year" for 1955. Curtice was the first business leader in twenty-five years to receive this honor, typically bestowed on such international political figures as U.S. Secretary of State John Foster Dulles (1954) and French President Charles De Gaulle (1958). In 1955 the celebration of America's remarkable ascent as a global economic powerhouse was the lead story of the year. For *Time,* as for many of its readers, Curtice exemplified the equation of corporate profit and national welfare captured in the catchphrase "What's good for General Motors is good for America."[1]

Nowhere did the slogan seem more apt than in Flint, Michigan, the birthplace of General Motors (GM), the home of Harlow Curtice, and, according to *Time,* "the world's most General Motorized city."[2] The giant firm dominated Flint's economy, employing more than eighty-six thousand men and women, some two-thirds of the city's total workforce. GM's unionized workers earned hourly wages that exceeded the national per capita wage by more than a third.[3] Their union, the United Automobile Workers, had deep historical connections to the city, site of the world-famous Sit-Down Strike of 1936–37. Some two decades after this watershed event, hefty GM pay packets translated into a working class in Flint that could afford to purchase the cars they made and still have money left over to buy homes and furnish them with modern appliances and television sets. If in the 1950s Curtice and General Motors thus symbolized the triumph of American corporate capitalism, Flint and its autoworkers epitomized the attainment of a mass consumer society dependent on that corporation's continued economic growth. Flint-built cars, with their gleaming grilles,

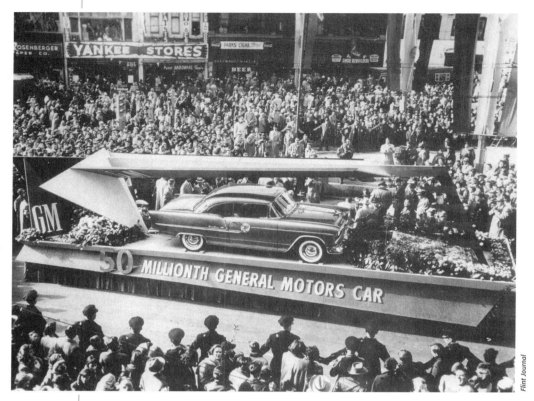

Flint Journal

Downtown Flint celebrates production of the fifty-millionth General Motors car, 1954.

shining tail fins, and roaring engines, became the icons of the age. Fittingly, in 1954 GM celebrated both its first year of billion-dollar earnings and the production of its fifty-millionth car by holding a giant parade in Flint. The final float featured neither smiling dignitaries nor waving celebrities, just a glittering, riderless gold Chevrolet.

That same year Flint also entered America's consciousness as a model of civic-mindedness, a community where people pulled together in the face of tragedy. In June 1953 a tornado swept through Flint's northern district, leveling houses, uprooting trees, tossing vehicles aloft, and leaving 116 dead. In the face of this devastation, the city launched a massive relief and rebuilding effort dubbed "Operation Tornado." Newspapers reported that thousands turned out to help stricken families and businesses, highlighting the work of young and old, poor and, especially, rich. A photograph of seventy-seven-year-old multimillionaire Charles Stewart Mott, a founder of GM, depicted him wearing a carpenter's apron and pounding a nail. In part because of Mott's brief stint as a relief worker, President Dwight Eisenhower named him "Big Brother of the Year" for 1954, while the National Municipal League and *Look* magazine, another popular national publication, hailed Flint as an "All-American City."

Just what this title signified, beyond a general concern for public welfare, remained appropriately vague, for, despite its victory in the Second World War and its booming economy, America experienced a crisis in defining its core values during the 1950s. The cold war, waged first with the Soviet Union, and then with China as well, provided the United States with identifiable enemies. Yet was America more than its antithesis? If virtually all Americans opposed "godless Communism," fewer agreed about what their nation was, or, given its professed ideals, what it should be. The Depression of the 1930s followed by the next decade's fight against fascism had forced into the open long-standing domestic issues about the boundaries of citizenship and the limits of equality. By the mid 1950s such controversies reverberated throughout the land. The unanimous 1954 Supreme Court decision in *Brown v. Board of Education* declared racial segregation unconstitutional, and the thirteen-month-long Montgomery, Alabama, bus boycott that ended the next year portended a future in which, through struggle, the walls of state-sanctioned racial separation would fall.

C. S. Mott participates in "Operation Tornado," 1953.

Flint Journal

The question of the extent of anti-Semitism in the United States also became a focus of national attention. The horror of the Nazi death camps had demonstrated to Americans, some firsthand, where government policies based on racial, ethnic, and religious hatred and exclusion could lead. Victims of Nazi genocide included millions of people of various creeds and nationalities, among them homosexuals, Christian ministers, political dissidents, labor activists, Gypsies, Poles, and Slavs. Yet Hitler's "Final Solution," set forth in 1942 after a decade of vicious anti-Semitism in the Third Reich, was designed specifically to resolve the so-called Jewish problem. The murder of six million European Jews and the destruction of European Jewish culture during the 1930s and 1940s resulted in the United States becoming the center of Jewry in the postwar world. In 1950 America was home to five and a half million Jews, a number larger than in any other nation and fully 40 percent of the world's Jewish population.[4] These developments, in the context of the growing civil rights movement and the ongoing national debate over intergroup relations and tolerance, provided the backdrop for a spate of scholarly and journalistic inquiries into the issue of anti-Semitism in America.

In 1955 William Attwood, the national affairs editor of *Look* magazine, decided to undertake his own examination of the topic. In the postwar years most Jewish Americans resided in those locations that had attracted the majority of Jews for a century, urban and suburban areas along the East Coast, especially New York, or in newer concentrations in Florida and California. In selecting a local study to add to his national overview, Attwood chose to ignore these centers of Jewish life, leaving his New York City office and traveling to the heartland of the nation, to a place of industrial might, consumer abundance, and civic pride. For his in-depth look at "The Position of the Jews in America Today" he came to the industrial promised land of Flint. The resulting article offers a window into how a well-known, informed, and sympathetic outsider interpreted Jewish American life during the postwar boom.[5]

Attwood began by identifying himself as "an inquisitive Gentile" with some questions he wished to have answered. The first was the most fundamental, and had a long, poignant, and contentious history: "What," he asked, "is a Jew?" Attwood replied with his own definition: "A Jew is a member of a historical community held together by common memories, religious tradition, and external pressure."[6] At the outset of his inquiry, then, Attwood viewed Jewishness more broadly than did those who maintained that being a Jew was overwhelmingly, or solely, a matter of religious belief and practice. Advocates of this position included Will Herberg, whose highly influential text *Protestant, Catholic, Jew: An Essay in Religious Sociology* had appeared earlier in 1955.[7] The equation of Jewish identity with adherence to Judaism was also central to the plot of the Academy Award winning 1947 movie *Gentleman's Agreement.* The film's main character, a Gentile journalist played by Gregory Peck, pretends to be Jewish in order to experience and then expose anti-Semitism.[8] He encounters shocking prejudice, depicted as religious animosity, presumably made more believable to the audience because suffered by a non-Jew.

In order to personalize his story, real-life journalist Attwood took a different tack. To engage the attention and sympathy of *Look*'s overwhelmingly Gentile readership, he wrote about actual members of the "historical community" of Jews, focusing on one "bustling," prospering, and religiously observant family, Art and Bess Hurand and their five children. Attwood placed the success of this and other Jewish families squarely in the context of the economic good times their hometown represented, beginning his profile by stating flatly: "Flint, Mich., is a good place for Americans to live. It is a prosperous automobile-manufacturing town of 165,000. Among its people are 800 Jewish families." Portraying the Hurands as close-knit, hardworking, and middle-class, Attwood also stressed the family's commitment to their city and nation. The son of an immigrant from Russia who settled in Michigan during World War I and opened a bakery, Art was "born, raised, and educated in Flint" and was "married to a local girl, Bess Bryer." According to Attwood, Art "came home after five years in the

Art Hurand helps young customers at one of his Buttercup Bakery shops, 1955.

Look, Nov. 29, 1955

Look, Nov. 29, 1955

Art Hurand and sons in the backyard of their home, 1955.

Army to continue his father's bakery business," expanded it to a chain of ten "Butter-cup Bakery" stores, joined the local chapters of the Chamber of Commerce and Civil Defense, and "[i]n the aftermath of the Flint tornado . . . put his bakery experience to community use to direct the feeding of the homeless." Similarly, Attwood highlighted Bess's service as a Cub Scout den mother, tacitly lauding her blending of domestic with public virtue. A photograph of Art and his three sons playing football in "the big back-yard of [their] five-bedroom brick house" further underscored the image of this fam-ily as upwardly mobile and all-American.

What, then, distinguished the Hurands as Jews? The article emphasized the role of religious faith, showing the Hurand children attending Hebrew school in their syn-agogue and celebrating the holiday of Hanukkah. At the same time, these pictures underscored that the Hurands upheld the same basic values as other Americans, vary-ing principally in the language they sometimes used and the specific rituals they prac-ticed. Perhaps it was their interactions beyond the family that distinguished the Hurands as Jewish? Attwood's article also featured a picture of Art and Bess Hurand at home entertaining three friends, another all-American depiction of the good life of the Eisenhower era. Yet the photograph's caption not only identified the guests by name, but indicated that all were Jewish, deftly implying what the article explicated in the social scientific terminology of the day: Flint's Jews had achieved "civic" but not "social" assimilation.[9] Atwood concluded that anti-Semitism still exerted "external pressure" on the Hurands, barring them from "country club social life." Like other Jewish families, they also experienced the more informal exclusion of the "five o'clock shadow." When the business day ended, so did social relations with Gentiles. This "last big barrier" to the full integration of Jews into American life, Attwood asserted, con-stituted a greater obstacle than most Gentiles recognized (or would admit). At the same time he believed it had a reciprocal quality. The Hurands and their friends tended to spend time with other Jews through inclination as well as necessity, enjoying the company of those who shared the "common memories" Attwood had defined as inte-gral to their Jewishness.

Clinical and condescending toward the subjects of his article, Attwood nonethe-less offered some thoughtful observations on "the position of the Jews in America" at midcentury, conveying his impressions in terms his readers could appreciate. By focusing on particular aspects of the life of one Jewish family in a bona fide all-Amer-ican city, Attwood encouraged *Look* readers to see the Hurands as neighbors. His explicitly outsider stance toward his topic may have helped other Gentiles feel com-fortable enough to extend this perspective to Jews more generally and to examine their own degree of anti-Semitism.

Attwood was already a prize-winning reporter and established political writer at the time he published this story.[10] A Princeton graduate, European correspondent for the *New York Herald Tribune* and *Collier's,* and speech writer for unsuccessful Democra-tic presidential candidate Adlai Stevenson, in 1955 he received the National Headliners

Look, Nov. 29, 1955

In Attwood's article the caption of this photograph began "At home with friends." Taken in the Hurands' living room, the photo includes (*left to right*) Art and Bess Hurand, Reva Ratner, Marcia Levy and husband Marvin Levy, 1955.

Award for outstanding journalism. The following year his reporting on contemporary American life for *Look* earned him the highly prestigious George Polk Memorial Award for magazine writing. Thereafter he became editor of *Look* and later publisher of *Newsday,* and also pursued a career in public service, acting as a delegate to the United Nations and ambassador to Guinea, then Kenya, during the Kennedy and Johnson administrations. His memoir, published two years before his death in 1989, reveals some softening of his most strident cold war foreign policy sentiments but an affirmation of his commitment to enhanced international understanding and closer intergroup relations, central tenets of the 1950s liberal credo that he personified.[11]

As a child Attwood had dreamed of becoming an explorer, a wish he fulfilled by visiting eighty-one countries and bringing back to armchair bound Americans stories about the peoples of the world beyond their living rooms. In these eyewitness accounts Attwood assumed the role of tour guide, domesticating the foreign, rendering the alien understandable, and emphasizing what he deemed the universal qualities of human experience, all judged from his particular vantage point of unacknowledged and unexamined privilege. Attwood's assessment of the state of Jewish life in America shared this quality of an urbane observer's account of a gratifyingly successful expedition

Flint Journal

Art Hurand, 88, holds a photograph taken in April 1945 that shows him and an unidentified Army nurse standing in front of human remains at Dachau. Hurand belonged to a field hospital unit that was one of the first to witness the horrors of the death camp after its liberation. Along with ten other Genesee County veterans, both Jews and non-Jews, in May 2005 he participated in a Holocaust Remembrance Ceremony held at Congregation Beth Israel and sponsored by the Flint Jewish Federation.

across an unknown landscape. His voice dominated the article. In discussing the national scene Attwood occasionally included observations from Jewish Americans themselves but he incorporated not one word of commentary from those at its center, Art Hurand and his family.

Attwood also ignored aspects of Art Hurand's biography that bore directly on his "position" as a Jew in Flint. Intriguingly, William Attwood and Art Hurand both had served in the U.S. Army during World War II and both had risen through the ranks to become captains.[12] Attwood had volunteered shortly after the 1941 Japanese attack on Pearl Harbor, but Hurand had joined the year before U.S. entry into the global conflict. More highly educated than Attwood indicated, Hurand held college and law degrees. In 1939 he had returned to his hometown as a graduate of Detroit's Wayne (State) University law school. As a newly minted attorney without close connections to the city's law firms, many of which were family–owned partnerships, Hurand had found it difficult to make a living practicing law. Meanwhile, across the Atlantic Jews endured fierce anti-Semitism. Hurand's decision in 1940 to volunteer to serve his country thus drew on a combination of sentiments common to many Jewish Americans: love for his country, despite the discrimination he faced there, and grave concern about the fate of Europe's Jews. During the war Captain Attwood served in the Pacific, while Captain Hurand saw action in Europe and at war's end observed the ghastly scenes of the Nazi death camps. Writing just a decade after the Holocaust ended, Attwood only briefly mentioned it, although its specter still loomed overwhelmingly for Jews. As a consequence of the calamity, many Jewish Americans, including Hurand, reconsidered their situation in their nation and their world. In 1999, at the age of eighty-two, Art Hurand recalled that what he witnessed in 1945 transformed his identity and his political priorities: "When I went into the service[,] believe it or not . . . I felt that if you were American, you could be [an] American Jew . . . and then I [saw] Dachau and Auschwitz."[13] Upon his return to Flint Hurand became a pillar of Jewish community life, serving as the president of the local Jewish Community Council, founded two years before to support relief efforts for European Jewry. Convinced that "Jews needed a State of Israel," he also became a leading fund-raiser for the Zionist cause.

Attwood's article omitted any mention of Flint's dense Jewish associational life, much less Art Hurand's place in it. Instead *Look*'s readers learned only of his participation in organizations like the Elks. Yet for Hurand and many other Jewish Americans such activism went hand in hand, their roles in Jewish communal affairs often leading them into collaborative efforts with Gentiles and affording them what limited entrée they had into the city's upper echelons. Good evidence for this pattern existed in Flint while Attwood visited there. In 1954 the local business and industrial elite launched a nationally heralded project to develop a "college and cultural center" consisting of a complex of institutions that included an art gallery, museum, planetarium, and theater. Spearheaded jointly by GM's Harlow Curtice and the editor of Flint's newspaper, this ambitious and costly effort reached high gear by 1955. Had Attwood examined the membership of the cultural center's all-male, all-white planning board he would have found that of its fifteen members, only one, Ellis Warren, was Jewish. A successful manufacturer, Warren owed his seat on this premier civic committee to his achievement in raising large sums to construct a new Reform temple as well as his presidency of Flint's Community Chest, an umbrella philanthropic organization.

Even these few details from the lives of Ellis Warren and Art Hurand suggest some key revisions to Attwood's depiction of Jewish life in Flint in the 1950s. His article downplayed the impact of anti-Semitism, overestimated the degree of Jewish integration into community organizations, and either ignored or failed to appreciate the vitality of a Jewish social life that extended beyond the boundaries of family and friends. With little explanation, at the end of the article Attwood abandoned the multifaceted definition of Jewishness he had proffered at the outset and endorsed the equation of Jewishness with belief in Judaism. Following Herberg, he prophesied that the "American melting pot" would do its work and that in the future "American Jews will no longer be regarded as 'different'—any more than Quakers are today." Dismissing as a passing phenomenon the anti-Semitism he had seen operating in Flint and elsewhere, Attwood

Flint Journal

Members of the Planning Board meet to chart the development of the Flint College and Cultural Center; Ellis Warren (*fifth from left*) 1954.

further predicted that "the American dream which says that any boy can grow up to be President will apply to Jews too." He imagined this day dawning soon, declaring that the continued "integration" of Jews into American life would occur so rapidly that "in another generation, there will be no purpose in a report such as this one."

Attwood's commitment to the goal of cultural assimilation and his stance as a well-meaning but confirmed outsider limited him as an observer of cold war–era Jewish America and rendered him a poor prognosticator of the development of Jewish-American life. Nearly half a century after Attwood published his article, many Americans neither believe in a melting pot nor wish for the bland cultural gruel it would produce. Anti-Semitism persists, in forms both similar to and different from those Attwood identified. While Jews are more prominent at all political levels than they were in the 1950s, no Jewish person—male or female—has held the nation's presidency. Yet if there is indeed "no purpose in a report such as th[e] one" Attwood wrote, there are good reasons to ground an understanding of Jewish-American experience in an examination of the lives of people like Art Hurand and to do so in the city that the *Look* editor chose for his case study five decades ago.

For in the late twentieth century Flint once more became a national icon. Boom had become bust, and the city that in the postwar era represented an expansive, buoyant America became an emblem of the deindustrialization and consequent demoralization that plagued manufacturing centers throughout the Northeast and Midwest. Over the course of twenty years the city lost some fifty thousand GM jobs, the giant automaker closing plant after plant in its birthplace. Massive unemployment triggered outmigration, causing a precipitous drop in the city's population. As lawns sprouted "for sale" signs and municipal services declined, the crime rate soared. The downtown street where in 1954 a throng had cheered as the empty golden Chevrolet glided by became dotted with boarded-up storefronts, its remaining businesses struggling to hold on to a dwindling number of customers. Stripped of its plenty, the postwar cornucopia became a "town abandoned," no longer a model of abundance and civic-mindedness but of fiscal crisis and racial strife.[14]

Flint's "dismal image" became firmly etched in the popular consciousness with the release in 1989 of self-described native-son Michael Moore's popular, acclaimed, and controversial documentary *Roger & Me*.[15] Moore's scathing portrait of GM's abandonment of his hometown drew further media attention to Flint, as did news stories of some of the solutions to the city's woes that its leaders pursued.[16] The most remarkable of these, phenomenal in the scale and cost of its failure and the misplaced boosterism behind it, was the construction of "Autoworld." Touted as an innovative and exciting amalgamation of theme park and automotive museum, this vast, odd would-be attraction closed shortly after opening, a sinkhole for desperately needed public funds.[17]

By 1992 a headline in the *New York Times* pronounced Flint "A City Where Hope Runs on Empty."[18] In less than forty years the "most General Motorized city," the site that drew William Attwood to witness all-American success, had become the nation's poster town for the widening rustbelt.

As we discuss in this book, throughout the twentieth century Flint's auto industry employed few Jews, either as workers or as managers. Yet the economic success of Flint Jewry depended in large measure on the health of the automotive industry that was the core of this one-company town. Reflecting their city's altered conditions, Flint Jewry consequently had entered a downward spiral by the 1990s, the community declining in overall numbers and its members dispersing from older neighborhoods to increasingly far-flung suburbs. In conjunction with the aging of some of its leaders, this crisis in the Jewish community sparked a sense of urgency to preserve its heritage. The result was a substantial public history effort in which more than a hundred individuals participated, locating, identifying, collecting, and, with aid of museum professionals, safeguarding photographs and artifacts of Jewish life in Flint. The idea for this book similarly has its genesis in this collective endeavor.

Our history of Flint Jewry consequently eschews the supposed neutrality and objectivity of Attwood and social observers like him. Instead we analyze the evolution of Flint's Jewish community through critically informed subjectivity, blending "insider" with "outsider" knowledge to produce a richer, more layered portrait of the group, its organizations, the individuals who comprise it, and the challenges and opportunities that have confronted it. In addition to more standard archival and secondary sources, the study draws both on oral history interviews we conducted and on the community's effort, in which we participated, to preserve the records of its past. The subjects of this book thus have participated in the creation of some of the major resources upon which it is based. We have sought throughout the study not only to incorporate their recollections and reproduce their photographs but to accord them "shared authority" in fashioning the narrative presented here.[19]

Our story unfolds in four chronological periods. Realizing that the familiar tale of Flint's meteoric rise and catastrophic decline obscures as well as reveals, we nonetheless see the city's economic trajectory as the central backdrop against which Jewish life has been played out over the last century and a half. Our account begins just before the Civil War with the first Jewish arrivals in Flint, then a small lumber town. Relatively few Jewish immigrants set down roots in the city until it entered the industrial era, emerging as a major center of automobile production after 1905. Thereafter a small but significant Jewish community, comprised mostly of Southern and Eastern European immigrants, became established in Flint. By the end of World War I, these settlers to the city had established a cluster of sometimes conflicting religious and social institutions.

Major expansion of Jewish social and economic life occurred during the 1920s, when the city's foremost product represented the good life in modern America. The Depression that brought the "Roaring Twenties" to an end dealt Flint's economy a particularly powerful blow. Demand for vehicles plummeted, leading to massive unemployment. Flint's Jews, many of whom owned small firms, shared in the city's travails and its dramatic moments. The "Great Flint Sit-Down Strike" in 1937 brought the city international attention and resulted in better wages for the autoworkers who made up the bulk of Jewish entrepreneurs' customers. Meanwhile, anti-Semitism flourished abroad. Some refugees from war-torn Europe arrived in Flint during the late 1930s, their flight a symptom of the horror that was spreading across the continent. We trace the story of Flint Jewry through the dreadful years of World War II and the beginnings of the postwar world. By 1948 the legacy of the Holocaust and the creation of the state of Israel were remaking Jewish identity throughout the nation, while in Flint wartime production had spurred the return of economic good times.

Our saga continues where William Attwood engaged it, focusing on the salad days of the 1950s through the mid 1970s, an era of industrial growth and demographic expansion in which the Jewish community participated. Crosscutting this account of progress toward American abundance and democracy, our account highlights the city's growing political, racial, ethnic, and religious antagonisms. In the 1950s and 1960s Flint led the nation in per capita income for working people and established a rich cultural life, but conflicts brewed in this all-American city. We detail the troubled leadership of the Jewish community as it struggled to address these strained relations in the postwar world.

Our narrative then turns to the past three decades. Beginning about 1973, Flint's faltering economy, shrinking and scattering population, and conflict-ridden civic life wrought new tensions. This period saw the bursting of the postwar bubble and the sad emergence of Flint as a symbol of rustbelt decline and civic decay. As General Motors abandoned the city of its birth, Jewish entrepreneurs and professionals, like their non-Jewish counterparts, left their downtown stores and offices, some relocating to the suburbs and others moving out of the area. During these decades international events also reshaped life for the city's Jewry. We examine the resettlement in Flint of hundreds of Jewish residents of the former Soviet Union and outline the ways in which controversies in the Mideast galvanized Jewish support for the state of Israel.

Returning to the powerful iconography of Flint as a site of American economic triumph and travail, an industrial promised land that has become a deindustrialized city, we close this book with observations by current Jewish community members about their lives in Flint and their hopes for the future. We intend *Jewish Life in the Industrial Promised Land* to contribute both to the history of Jewish America and to an analysis of the evolution of twentieth-century American culture. Our story affirms the assessment made recently by longtime city resident and attorney Gilbert Rubenstein. Looking back on the contours of Flint's civic life and contemplating the city's dire future, he reminded us that "There are many, many Jewish people who did things for this community—this Jewish and non-Jewish community."[20] Our book is for them, and for all those who seek to understand and enhance their world, starting where they live. We hope this history contributes to that effort.

CHAPTER ONE

Settlers to the City

NINETEENTH-CENTURY PIONEERS

In the spring of 1859 Henry Brown arrived in Flint, three years before the first locomotive entered the busy agricultural settlement of some three thousand. He thus became the town's first long-term, influential Jewish resident. Like many other Jews who settled in Flint throughout the next century, Brown first had settled elsewhere in the United States. Typical of smaller towns and cities away from the East Coast, Flint was often a destination of "secondary migration." Until its development as an automotive center, Flint also would prove a short-lived destination for many Jewish immigrants, as most arrived, stayed for a few months or years, then moved on, seeking a better livelihood or a more fully developed Jewish community life. This pattern of in- and out-migration would characterize Flint Jewry even after the city's rise as a manufacturing center. The railroads and later roadways that made Flint a transportation center and the very cars fashioned in the city's auto shops facilitated this movement. Brown proved an exception, residing there until his death in 1877. By that year a cluster of Jewish families lived in Flint, but the city still housed no Jewish social or religious institutions. Until the first decade of the twentieth century those observing traditional dietary laws or wishing to attend religious services had to travel seventy miles south to the growing Jewish community in Detroit or forty to fifty miles north to the smaller Jewish settlements in the logging centers of Saginaw or Bay City.[1]

Brown probably did not make such trips, for like many German Jewish immigrants at midcentury he seems neither to have observed Jewish law nor identified publicly as a Jew.[2] Born Heinrich Braun in 1821 in the small town of Walsdorf, Bavaria, he was subject to his native province's harsh code restricting the rights of Jews to marry or change residence and promoting their assimilation through education in state-run schools.[3] Accordingly young Heinrich attended the local school, where Roman Catholic clergy supervised his studies.[4] The hostile climate for Jews may have played a role in encouraging Braun to emigrate to the United States, but he joined thousands of other German-speaking men and women of diverse economic and religious backgrounds. In common with other provinces that became part of the German nation in 1871, Bavaria experienced massive out-migration from the 1840s through the 1880s.

Brown immigrated in 1840 at age nineteen. Anglicizing his name, he settled first in Richmond, Virginia, where he obtained a job as a dry goods clerk, climbing up the first rung of the ladder that led to his economic success. He married another Jewish Bavarian immigrant, Babette Rosenfeld, and opened a small shop, then moved to New York City, where he established a larger enterprise in wholesale boot and shoe sales. When he was thirty-eight Henry Brown and his wife resettled to Flint, drawn perhaps by the possibilities of a thriving agricultural settlement in the midst of becoming a booming lumber town. Brown quickly established a dry goods business, buying stock for his store from one E. Lieberman, whose name suggests that he, too, was Jewish. E. Lieberman had resided in Flint since at least 1855 and seems to have remained in the city for several more years, competing with Brown in the growing settlement. In October 1859 Flint's newspaper, the *Wolverine Citizen*, ran an advertisement for "ready made clothing" for purchase at an "old established stand" owned by "M. & N. Lieberman," located in the same downtown building where E. Lieberman previously had sold goods. German immigrants, the Liebermans may have been brothers or father and son; by 1861 both had left Flint.

> There are few Jewish people in Flint. . . . Jews will not live in Flint because there are no Kosher markets. Also, there are no synagogues nearer than Saginaw, Bay City and Detroit.
>
> —*Frank V. V. Swan, Secretary, Manufacturers Association of Flint, 1909*

A series of Jewish immigrants replaced the Liebermans as competitors to Brown in the retail clothing trade. In Flint as elsewhere in America, Jews carved out a niche in many aspects of clothing production and sales, sewing garments and shoes, peddling on city streets and in rural areas, selling ready-made apparel in small shops and extensive establishments, and expanding the array of merchandise carried in dry goods shops and, by the end of the nineteenth century, ordered through catalogues.[5] In the decade after the Civil War Jacob Aarons and Solomon Freedman owned small stores where they sold clothes "off the rack" to Flint-area farmers, lumberers, and townsfolk. Several other Jewish immigrants in the clothing business, such as Peter Mendelsohn, had non-Jewish partners, as did Brown himself after 1870. In that year Albert Myers became a co-owner of Brown's flourishing store on Saginaw Street, the city's main thoroughfare. By then Brown had become a well-known business leader and public figure, acquiring valuable parcels of downtown real estate and being elected a ward alderman and member of city council. As a charter member of the board of directors of the Genesee County Savings Bank, founded in 1872, he served with some of the area's most prominent men, including W. W. Crapo, son of lumber king, railroad baron, and former Michigan governor Henry Howland Crapo.[6]

Brown seemingly faced no social exclusion. Like many Jews of his standing during this era, he held membership in the Masons, an elite fraternal organization. When

Wolverine Citizen, 23 January 1858

An advertisement for E. Lieberman's dry goods store stresses the variety and low price of his ready-made goods and features a distinctive admonishment to his would-be customers: "Be Ye Clothed."

he died in 1877 the local chapter eulogized him as a man of "spotless" character, an "honorable, pure, kind-hearted, genial and cultured gentleman unsurpassed." The entire city council attended his funeral service, and he was buried near the grave of former governor Crapo in Flint's shady, gardenlike Glenwood Cemetery.[7] This was done despite the shocking cause and grisly manner of his death. Three days after he sold all the shares in his business to his partner, Myers, the fifty-six-year-old Brown committed suicide by opening a vein in his arm with a straight razor. Because he appeared to be healthy at the time he took his life, Brown violated both civil and sacred law. Still, family members may have recited the Kaddish, the prayer for the dead, at the burial service that his Masonic brothers conducted in the Brown residence.[8]

In the wake of her husband's death, Babette Brown moved her three children to Detroit. Given the opportunity of participating in an established Jewish community, the remaining Browns apparently did so. They transferred Henry's remains to the portion of Detroit's Woodmere Cemetery that the Temple Beth El, Michigan's oldest Jewish congregation, maintained.[9] In this resting place, as sylvan as that in Flint, the Brown family expressed their own religious allegiance, an identity Henry did not claim in life. Meanwhile the marriage of Henry and Babette's daughter Ida Gertrude Brown to Henry A. Krolik, partner in a leading Detroit wholesale enterprise, reconnected the family to the activity that may have lain closest to Henry Brown's heart: the dry goods business. With the marriage Ida also installed the Browns among the city's prominent

The Henry A. Krolik family

Ida Gertrude Brown Krolik was the daughter of pioneer Jewish settler to Flint Henry Brown. She put aside her plans to pursue medicine in order to follow her parents' wishes, teaching at the Michigan School for the Deaf, Dumb and Blind. After her marriage to wholesale grocer Henry Krolik she became a mainstay of Detroit Jewish life, ca. 1900.

Jewish families. In Flint Ida had worked as a teacher at the Michigan School for the Deaf, Dumb and Blind, a well-respected position (and one that her father's connections to school supervisor James Walker, also a charter director of the Genesee County Savings Bank, may have helped her procure).[10] After her marriage, a capable and energetic Ida Brown Krolik became a mainstay of Detroit civic organizations, both for Jewish and non-Jewish causes, and took particular interest in advocating for the city's growing numbers of poor young women. As we will discuss later, the Brown family connections to Flint Jewry came full circle in 1941 when Ida's son, Julian Krolik, then president of the Detroit Jewish Federation, became a consultant for a self-study of Jewish community life in Flint.[11]

When Babette Brown and her family left Flint in 1877 the lumber trade had reached its peak, with pine hewed in surrounding Genesee County forests and planed in the city's six sawmills shipped across America and beyond. Largely due to this trade, by 1880 Flint's population had grown to more than eight thousand residents, and Genesee County's to nearly forty thousand. Yet by the mid 1880s, as the county's land, once thick with towering trees, became fields of stumps, the lumber boom abruptly ended. More and more farmers arrived and put this partially cleared acreage to the plow, but the growth of agriculture did not stem the economic decline in Flint wrought by the timber trade's loss. The city's economic future depended on enlarging and diversifying its agricultural processing and especially its manufacturing base, which by the 1880s included granaries, breweries, wool mills, carriage shops, and furniture-making firms.[12] Until Flint attained prominence as an industrial center, the number of long-term Jewish residents remained small.

Of these residents Myer Ephraim was one of the most significant. Born in New York City of Dutch parents, he pioneered the making of cigars, a business that became a pillar of the city's economy from the end of the lumber era until the onset of World War I. He came to Flint in 1875 via Massachusetts and remained until his death in

1914, owning and operating the city's first cigar firm. Successful throughout these decades, in 1905 his company had more than a dozen rivals. Together these factories employed hundreds of workers, at the time Flint's most highly paid and best organized. At least some stogie-makers, including Solomon Aberdee, were Jewish, as was at least one other cigar manufacturer, Abe Davis, who founded the Blue Line Cigar Factory in 1888.[13] In terms of commitment to Jewishness, Myer Ephraim resembled Henry Brown and many other prosperous nineteenth-century Dutch and German Jewish immigrants, especially those who settled away from the major ethnic enclaves on the East Coast. Like Brown, he invested in downtown real estate, joined the Masons, was buried in Glenwood Cemetery, and made no effort to establish Jewish institutions. In contrast to Brown's family, who removed to Detroit and embraced their Jewishness following Henry's death, Myer Ephraim's sons stayed in Flint, assumed their father's manufacturing and real estate interests, and did not identify with Judaism.[14]

Most other Jewish residents of Flint in the late nineteenth century had occupations in the retail trades. Meyer Brown, for instance, who used the name "Mickey" in his business, had a tailor shop at a prime downtown location, the corner of South Saginaw and Kearsley streets. Jonathan Finkelberg, a milliner, also had a downtown store, while Nathan Epsteyn worked as a salesman in a clothiery, and David Einstein owned a grocery store, another line of business that would be important for Jewish merchants for decades to come. Only one Jewish woman seems to have been the proprietor of her own business during these years. Mary Cohen, a widow with several children, supported her family through her South Saginaw Street millinery, the "Ladies Bazaar." Jewish professionals were few, but included teacher B. Steinthal and dentist Simeon Salls.[15]

FLINT: CITY OF INDUSTRIAL PEACE
Leads the world in vehicle manufacture
Has the largest automobile plant in the world
Twenty-five church buildings
Two great railroads
Manufactures 10,000,000 cigars yearly
—*Brochure issued by the Flint Board of Commerce, 1910*

Despite the presence of these individuals and scores of others, an organized Jewish community life did not emerge in the four decades that followed Henry Brown's settlement in Flint. The traditional requirements for minyan, or quorum for public prayer, probably were met, yet in most years it seems no such services took place, either in a family parlor or a rented hall.[16] Thus while the history of Jews in Flint dates from just prior to the Civil War, the history of Jewish institutions dates only to the first decade of the twentieth century, when the city's ascent as a national manufacturing center attracted, and retained, more Jewish residents.

The growth of Flint's Jewish population in these decades also stemmed from developments taking place far from Michigan. As would be the case at other critical junctures throughout the twentieth century, virulent anti-Semitism in Europe prompted an outpouring of Jews to the United States. Many came from the Russian empire and from the Russian- and Austrian-held provinces in Poland, where pogroms, vicious and often deadly attacks against Jews, began in the 1880s. When

Sloan Museum

Harry Winegarden, owner of the New Orleans Fruit House (*second from left*). Years later Winegarden sent this postcard to a friend, recalling with humor his days as a struggling entrepreneur. The reverse reads: "Dear Johnnie: I know you remember me when I was in big business working for [$]5.00 a week from 5 in [the] morning to 9 at nite including Sundays & living on free lunches and bananas for dessert. Mr. Winegarden," n.d.

emigrants from these areas of Eastern Europe came to Flint they encountered few other Jews to help them and, before the turn of the century, no Jewish societies to join. On the other hand, neither did they need to adjust to an entrenched Jewish society dominated by German Jews, as did many who settled in larger communities.[17] To a great extent, Flint Jewish life thus would be built by and for Eastern European immigrants and their descendants. As Flint became a leader in automobile production and the city's economy expanded, these newcomers carved out institutions of their own.

THE DAWN OF THE AUTOMOBILE ERA

From an early age, Russian immigrant Harry Winegarden demonstrated a knack for advertising. Shortly after settling in Flint in 1895 the eighteen-year-old opened a small wholesale produce business, calling it the "New Orleans Fruit House." The name informed would-be customers that his store offered the delicious Caribbean fruits that were just becoming available in northeastern and midwestern markets. A turn-of-the-century advertisement for Winegarden's business underscores this point while demonstrating that the firm relied on the manufacturing activity that was resuscitating Flint's economy, carriage- and cart-making: a postcard shows Harry and two workers posing with a company wagon overflowing with bananas. In 1901 Harry's brother Hyman arrived from Russia and joined the thriving business located, like so many others, along Saginaw Street south of the Flint River. After World War I the brothers expanded their enterprise, offering meat as well as fruit. Sales acumen continued to distinguish their venture. According to Gilbert Rubenstein, who grew up in Flint in the 1920s, the Winegardens' produce store was an "exciting place to go," with brightly painted signs, bananas piled high along both sides of the aisles, and clerks yelling out prices to entice customers to try the market's wares.[18]

The entrepreneurial zeal of Harry and Hyman Winegarden exemplifies the feverish boosterism of early twentieth-century Flint. Characteristically, in 1899 the owner of a local ironworks installed a pair of steel arches across South Saginaw Street declaring Flint the nation's "Vehicle City." The vehicles referred to were the tens of thousands of carts, buggies, and wagons pouring from local carriage factories, especially the firm owned by J. Dallas Dort and William ("Billy") Durant, grandson of early Michigan governor Crapo.[19] Formed in 1886 and first located on the site of a former cotton mill, by the turn of the century the Durant-Dort Carriage Company housed paint and varnish shops, planing mills, and wheelworks in its main complex located across the river just north of downtown. Reputedly the largest of its kind in the world, the multi-million-dollar firm had branch plants in several states and in Canada. Along with other prominent carriage factories, furniture makers, foundries, and engine shops, the Durant-Dort company served as an incubator for the automobile production that began in 1905.

Billy Durant led the way. He built a giant Buick Motor Company facility upstream from his carriage company; attracted huge sums of capital (much of it from local bankers and businessmen) to finance the manufacturing of the newfangled, horseless vehicles; and persuaded important suppliers and rivals (including Charles Stewart [C. S.] Mott, head of the Weston-Mott Axle Company) not only to set up operations in Flint but to join him in launching automobile manufacturing on a vast scale and highly integrated fashion. In 1908 Durant consolidated these efforts, forming the General Motors Corporation. For decades to come, Flint's history and the fortunes of its residents would be tied to the immense company founded by this native son. The connection became obvious even before the ink dried on the incorporation papers. When the "Vehicle City" signs were hoisted at the turn of the century, Flint numbered about thirteen thousand residents, a total that represented a steady increase since the city's lumbering days. As soon as auto production began in earnest, population skyrocketed, nearly tripling after 1905, when construction on the Buick shop began, to reach close to thirty-nine thousand in 1910.[20]

Crooks Collection, Scharchburg Archives, Kettering University

Vehicle City arches on South Saginaw Street, looking south from the Flint River, ca. 1905. Streetcars, bicycles, and horse-drawn carts provide transportation in downtown Flint on the eve of the automobile boom.

Workers from all over Michigan and from states throughout the Midwest and Northeast arrived to take jobs at the car shops. Immigrants came too, numbering almost seven thousand and constituting more than one in six of Flint's inhabitants by 1910. In these first years of population influx, nearly half of the foreign-born hailed from neighboring Canada. Southern and Eastern Europeans totaled more than twelve hundred, comprising another fifth of the immigrant population. As in other rapidly expanding heavy industrial centers, the majority of all newcomers to Flint were male, and the percentage among immigrants exceeded 60 percent. The labor demands of the manufacturing sector, with its rigid gender segregation, resulted in this skewed sex ratio. In 1910 Flint's industries employed just six hundred women but more than twelve thousand men; moreover, virtually no women had jobs in any aspect of transportation, the second-largest area of employment. Thus men, not women, toiled at most factories, on the railroad and trolley lines, and along the river. Immigrant girls and women tended to find employment as domestic servants, running boarding houses, taking in laundry, keeping accounts, selling goods in stores, or teaching. Many also contributed to family businesses, their labor crucial but their names generally absent from employment rosters and their occupations seldom listed in public documents.

Jews numbered among the newcomers to Flint in the first decade of the twentieth century. These settlers included the American-born children of Jews who had immigrated to the United States in earlier years; Jews who emigrated from Europe to other American towns and cities, then came to Flint when industry began to flourish; and immigrants who came directly to the auto boomtown from Jewish communities scattered across Europe. Because population figures list only individuals' nations of birth and not their religious, cultural, or ethnic identification, it is impossible to know precisely how many Jewish men, women, and children numbered among the city's European immigrants. Yet other sources demonstrate that by 1910 Flint had attracted a small but significant Jewish population.[21]

Retail business was the mainstay of the Jewish community in these years. William Hauser and Benjamin Benison owned clothing stores on the same block of South Saginaw, and three more Jewish-owned apparel stores were located further down the street. Most probably relied on the labor of several family members. Bessie Benison, for example, worked as a clerk behind her uncle's counter. Also on Flint's main thoroughfare was a small grocery owned by her brother Frank and his partner, Carl Sumetz, who boarded at the same rooming house she did. Across the Flint River a second retail area began to develop around the car shops. By 1910 there were four Jewish-owned groceries, two confectioneries, and a shoe store in what became known as the "St. John District," referring to a short street that ran alongside the Pere Marquette railway tracks and near the Buick factory. This multi-ethnic, working-class area had two additional commercial arteries, North Saginaw Street and, fittingly, Industrial Avenue. Here Jewish and non-Jewish shopkeepers purveyed goods to customers from the densely populated neighborhood spreading outward from the auto plant. Salesman Henry Rosenbloom lived in the St. John District, but worked downtown at the large furniture store owned by fellow Jewish immigrant Morris Kobacker. Near Kobacker's store was another successful Jewish-owned business that specialized in products for homes and offices, A. Agree and Sons Plumbing, Tinning, Steam and Hot Water Heating. As the city began to establish water and sewerage facilities, Agree's products, from steam radiators to flush toilets, appealed to customers who could afford the latest in modern conveniences.

Relatively few of Flint's Jews took industrial jobs, for reasons that included anti-Semitism. Previous work experience, personal and financial contacts in other occupations and businesses, and inclination also conduced to keep most from work in the manufacturing concerns that spurred the city's transformation. In this regard they mirrored Jews elsewhere in America, especially those who settled in smaller industrial centers, as Ewa Morawska has demonstrated in her incisive study of Jewish life in western Pennsylvania's iron, steel, and mining communities.[22] Numbering among those in Flint who did find industrial employment were what appear to be three sets of

Employees of the Joseph Frumkin Meat Market, 2717½ Industrial Avenue. The Frumkin family, who lived above the store, garnered a wide clientele for their market in a highly competitive business, ca. 1915.

Proud of its modern product line, the Agree hardware store displays a bathtub and toilet in its downtown show window, 1906.

Sarah and Benjamin Hoffman and son Hymen in Cincinnati, 1907. Immigrants from the Ukraine to Cincinnati, they came to Flint in 1909 expressly for Benjamin, a blacksmith, to take a job at Buick.

Sloan Museum

brothers: Nathan, Louis, and Morris Levine, who worked at a tannery; and Max, Morris, and Nathan Gussin and Barnett, Charles, and Max Kroll, all six of whom were machinists, a skilled trade much in demand in auto manufacturing.

Some who entered industrial work left it as soon as they could, often in order to start their own businesses. Julius Hurand provides one example.[23] An immigrant from the Russian partition of Poland, he traveled alone first to London, England, and then directly to Flint. He found a job as a finisher in the Stewart Body Works, a leading supplier to General Motors and later a part of Buick. Here he did "piecework," receiving wages based on the number of automobile bodies he produced during the course of a day. Hurand worked alongside several other Jews in the shop, took pride in his proficiency and speed at his job, and each payday set aside some of his earnings. The savings allowed him to open his first store, a haberdashery near the Stewart works. Immigrant Benjamin Hoffman also worked in the car shops during these early years. After the turn of the century, Hoffman (originally Gouxman), a blacksmith, fled his native Ukraine to avoid conscription into the Russian army. He settled in the commercial hub of Cincinnati, where his wife Sarah and son Hymen joined him. Hearing of the Vehicle City's need for workers, in 1909 the Hoffman family moved to Flint, where Ben put his skills to use as a polisher, assembler, and machinist at Buick. By early 1915 the Hoffman family had squirreled away enough money for Ben to become the proprietor of the Hoffman Coal Company, a small firm that delivered fuel to the city's growing number of homes and factories. Tragically, the former blacksmith died just months after opening the business, trampled by a team of horses in his coal yard.

Philip Catsman proved more fortunate, becoming a leader in the lucrative coal business. An immigrant from Minsk who had settled first in New York, he arrived in Flint in 1908 and began peddling, taking up a line of work that many newcomers pursued to eke out a livelihood while trying to gain a commercial foothold. A loan from a non-Jewish dentist allowed Catsman to realize his dream. By 1916 the Catsman Coal Company, located on Industrial Avenue in the St. John District, had become a flourishing concern.

Benjamin Hoffman building an engine at the Buick factory, ca. 1912. Dressed in a light short-sleeved shirt and sporting a mustache, Hoffman stands at his own workstation (*second from left, fifth station back*). Following the example of Henry Ford, Buick introduced assembly-line production over the course of the next few years.

Other Jewish businessmen also did well in the coal trade, including Louis and Joseph Shapiro, brothers who operated the Michigan Coal Company.

Flint's auto industry, with its increasing demand for metal, seemed to have an insatiable appetite for fuel for its foundries and forges, and in turn produced enormous quantities of scrap metal. The economic activities of fuel delivery and scrap dealership became prominent areas of entrepreneurship for Flint Jews. Not only did these niche businesses prove highly profitable for some, both fostered close economic, if not social, ties between key Jewish newcomers and the city's auto magnates and their expanding empire. Pioneer scrap dealer Louis Lebster exemplifies this pattern.

Born in Austria, Lebster came to Flint in 1905, the same year that Durant began making cars as well as carriages. When he arrived he had already operated scrap yards in Detroit and Pontiac (thirty-five miles south of Flint), was married (to Ann Shapiro of Detroit, through whose family he maintained close business ties to the city), and was knowledgeable about the fledgling auto industry. As would so many others in the Jewish community, he opened his business in partnership with a family member, his brother Max. Louis and Max's scrap dealership occupied a prime location just west of

Sloan Museum

The Catsman Coal Company, located at 1542 Industrial Avenue near the sprawling Buick facility, supplied fuel to factories and homes, 1916. The company used Flint-made vehicles, both motorized and horse-drawn, for its deliveries.

Newlyweds Joseph Shapiro and Sarah Cohen in their wedding photograph, New York, 1913. A Russian immigrant and former wallpaper hanger, Joseph came to Flint to join his brother Louis. Together they founded the Michigan Coal Company.

Sloan Museum

downtown and along the second major rail line to serve Flint, the Grand Trunk and Western. The brothers' first client was former mechanic C. W. Nash, then general superintendent of the Durant–Dort Carriage Company (and later president of General Motors and founder of the Nash Motor Company). Even before the Lebsters' business had opened, Nash drove a wagon into their yard, helped unload the scrap, and told Louis to pay him after the weigh scales were set up. The same year Louis worked directly with Billy Durant, supervising the removal of equipment from a Buick assembly plant in Jackson, sixty–five miles away, and its subsequent installation in the new Flint facility. The Lebster brothers also established excellent business relations with C. S. Mott, who allowed them to buy his scrap on credit, a substantial financial boon to the young company's owners.[24]

The connections that successful businessmen like Louis and Max Lebster and Philip Catsman had to the auto industry enabled them to recommend other Jews for employment in the car shops and to aid new arrivals to Flint who found themselves in dire straits. Catsman helped indigent newcomer Mayer Boruchin; clothier Ben Benison did the same for Solomon and Anna Lieberman and their children. These businessmen and impoverished immigrants were introduced through a Jewish agency based in New York, the Industrial Removal Organization (IRO).[25]

Established in 1901 as a part of the Jewish Agricultural and Industrial Aid Society, the IRO aimed to disperse Jewish immigrants away from the congested quarters of New York's Lower East Side and similar neighborhoods in port cities and to resettle them in expanding smaller towns and cities throughout the nation. Its leadership consisted primarily of well–established German Jews, some with elitist views toward Eastern European newcomers, who hoped "removal" would help recent immigrants find manufacturing jobs, ease the burden on strapped East Coast Jewish charities, and defuse mounting anti–Semitism. According to historian Robert Rockaway, the founders of the IRO believed that the influx of primarily Yiddish–speaking, more religiously traditional Southern and Eastern European Jews was intensifying anti–Jewish feeling. Dispersing new arrivals, IRO leaders reasoned, would dissipate prejudice.[26] The IRO thus became a national labor broker, informing industrialists that it would help them secure workers, sending immigrants off to take distant industrial jobs, and cooperating with local chapters of Jewish organizations to welcome the new arrivals.

As early as 1906, Flint, with its burgeoning industry, came to the IRO's attention. In February David Handler, a Jewish foreman at the Western Tanning and Japanning Company, wrote to the agency requesting workers to help produce the leather goods that the business sold to auto, carriage, and furniture firms. Handler wanted two "experienced beamsters," men who knew how to stretch and scrape animal hides, and would hire "even green men," that is, new arrivals, "as long as they had experience in tanning in the old country."[27] He promised steady employment at $12.00 a week. The IRO immediately sent P. A. S. Laborman to fill one of the positions. Arriving a week later, Laborman discovered the firm had changed hands and he had no job waiting.

Disappointed and angry, he wrote to the IRO, "[I]t is unright to send a man without a return ticket here."

Laborman's displeasure with Flint and its prospects would be echoed by some of the other "removals" over the next several years, as immigrants found themselves dispatched to a city where the demand for labor swung wildly and which housed few familiar Jewish institutions. The IRO did not fully appreciate the situation, though it had sufficient information to do so. In July 1908, IRO agent Henry P. Goldstein came to Flint as one stop on his tour of possible resettlement sites, but could find no one to act as the agency's representative.[28] Tellingly, his leading prospect as local coordinator, Harry S. Weiss, treasurer of the Michigan Paint Company, had just left the city. Major employers, on the other hand, expressed interest in the plan, with Genesee Iron Works, Flint Wagon Works, Buick, and Patterson Carriage Company, if not the Durant-Dort Company, willing to participate. Yet Goldstein felt discouraged about both the types of jobs available, requiring arduous physical labor, and the dearth of Jewish services. "I really think it is useless to visit such places," he wrote to IRO general manager David Bressler, "for will the removal remain once sent here?"

Despite his doubts, Goldstein made fruitful contacts. In April 1909 the IRO received a letter introducing Frank V. V. Swan as the secretary for a new organization, the Manufacturers Association of Flint.[29] This association, representing a consolidation of leading business interests in Flint, centralized hiring through Swan's office. With high demand for its cars and its huge facility completed, Buick had upped production quotas to the unprecedented figure of eighty automobiles per day. The company asked the IRO to supply "first-class varnishers" to help meet this goal. In response the IRO sent Harry Seidler, who seems to have settled in at the plant, and Hyram Shaffer, a newlywed with little experience in woodcraft. Shaffer failed first as a varnisher, then as a painter, and finally as a general laborer, quickly becoming dissatisfied with conditions in Flint and returning to his bride in New York.[30] Anxious to end this pattern of labor turnover and recognizing that some removals were homesick, Swan went to a prominent Jewish businessman for advice and then forwarded his observations to the IRO. "There are few Jewish people in Flint," Swan informed the New York agency. "I talked with Mr. Harry Winegarden, proprietor of the New Orleans Fruit House and he told me that Jews will not live in Flint, because there are no Kosher markets. . . . Also, there are no synagogues nearer than Saginaw, Bay City and Detroit." The IRO dismissed Swan's concerns, replying that "We will warn our men before they leave just what conditions they must expect in your city," adding, "it will not be our fault if they find themselves in a non-Jewish environment." Discounting the need for kashrut, the preparation of food according to Jewish dietary laws, the IRO contended that Flint's lack of a kosher market "is not necessarily a deterrent," because "the younger generation of Jewish workingmen are prone to overlook [its] absence."[31] Harry Winegarden may have proved a wiser counselor: in 1912 several men sent by the IRO complained to the agency that no boardinghouse served kosher meals.[32]

By this time, however, relations between the Manufacturers Association and the IRO already had become strained. In 1910 the volatile auto industry had entered what would be the first of its many troughs, and two years later still felt the effects of the recession. As the auto manufacturers struggled to rationalize the production process, exert greater control over workers, and cut labor costs, the plants relied increasingly on less skilled workers. In the summer of 1912 Swan informed the IRO that he wanted only "strong husky laborers" for foundry work or unloading coke. Meanwhile removal Herman Adler, a skilled ironworker, accepted a position at Michigan Motor Castings Company only to be told to shovel sand at a laborer's wage. He quit after three hours. Several other IRO men demanded money for provisions before they started their jobs, then threatened to go to the police when their employers refused to feed them.[33] Ever the faithful steward of the manufacturers' interests, Swan immediately wrote to the IRO, declaring: "Send me no more bums nor paupers. . . . The men you have been sending are the sort who live by their wits and work only when they have to do so."[34] Two days later IRO general manager Bressler defended the men in a telegram, insisting they were "strong and capable" and protesting the "designation of them as bums as harsh and uncalled for."[35]

This correspondence reflects a climate of increased class antagonism and heightened political mobilization around labor issues in Flint and throughout the nation.[36] Between 1909 and 1913 huge strikes in the mines, steel plants, rail yards, textile mills, and garment factories rocked America, while the Industrial Workers of the World, an organization calling for the overthrow of capitalism, and the Socialist Party, campaigning for dramatic changes in the economic and social order, drew mounting attention and support. Nationally the Socialist Party numbered over one hundred thousand members in 1912, with presidential candidate Eugene V. Debs, a prominent labor leader, receiving nine hundred thousand votes, enough to demonstrate the wide appeal of Socialism and trim the margin of victory for the winner, Democrat Woodrow Wilson. Socialists did even better in municipal elections, taking the mayorships in seventy-three cities in 1911. One of these was Flint, where cigar maker John C. Menton won by nearly six hundred votes in a hotly contested three-way race. A charter member of Flint's Socialist Party and the city's Central Labor Union, Menton advocated strong measures to bring about municipal ownership of all utilities, establish free public services such as hospitals and night schools for workers, and generally reverse the growing power of the local business elite. Surprised by the ascent of a mobilized working class, Flint's capitalists reacted swiftly, if belatedly, to this threat to their power.[37]

In the previous year the local business class had believed it sufficient simply to announce that their city stood apart from national trends of labor unrest. In 1910 the Board of Commerce had issued a brochure entitled *Flint: City of Industrial Peace,* extolling the might of local manufacturing (and touting the city's twenty-five churches).[38] Their declaration repudiated by Menton's election, throughout 1911 the city's manufacturers used their power to thwart most of the reforms the Socialist tried to implement. In the next election they fought back directly, fielding one of their own as a candidate. C. S. Mott ran for mayor in 1912, acknowledging the need for improved public services and offering voters a businesslike approach to providing them. He won handily, restoring Flint to the form of "industrial peace" the employers had in mind. Although Mott only briefly held public office, this election launched what would be a lifetime of paternalist civic service to the city.[39]

Flint's major manufacturers took other steps to fend off workers' militancy, blacklisting some prominent Socialists from employment in their plants and scrutinizing jobseekers more carefully. Nationally Jews were prominent in the leadership and rank-and-file of emerging unions and class-conscious political movements during these years, a period historians have called the "golden age of Yiddish socialism." As the local Manufacturer's Association tried to stem the tide of anti-capitalist agitation, they began to question their policy of accepting Jewish "removals." In August 1912, during the final weeks of Mott's successful campaign against incumbent Menton, Swan wrote to the IRO regarding a tinner, Louis Goldberg, who had inquired about a job in the car shops. "Do not send [him] to Flint," Swan declared, "in fact, we think [it] best to not have any more of your people sent here for a time as they do not prove to be of the sort we can use." Instead Flint's bosses suspected that Jewish immigrants from the East Coast might support the growing labor movement in the heartland's auto center. "We think," Swan wrote, that "perhaps there are some Jewish agitators who are stirring up trouble among their countrymen in this city and misrepresenting us."[40]

THE BEGINNINGS OF ORGANIZED JEWISH LIFE

Whatever their feelings toward the city's business class, in the next five years most immigrants the IRO resettled in Flint bent their energies toward reuniting their families. Nathan Shkolnikoff rejoined his cousin Harry Skolniek; together they welcomed other relatives, David and Masha Skolnikov. Israel Shaenfield arrived to live with his brother Greisha in the St. John District. Other Flint Jews, including Max Bombel and Morris Schulman, also accepted responsibility for the welfare of friends and relatives the IRO sent to Flint.[41] Sometimes the chain of migration was broken and family members, often women left behind in the old country, sought in vain for their kin. In 1911 the wife of Leib Braverman asked the IRO to track down her husband, whom the agency had resettled in Flint. She and her daughter, still living in Odessa, had received no word from him in more than a year. Like so many other immigrants, Braverman had stayed only briefly in Flint, departing for Detroit and thence, his friends thought, to Chicago.[42]

The city's volatile economy during the early years of the auto age spurred high population turnover. Yet within this context of flux a Jewish community slowly began to coalesce. In 1907 minyans were held at the homes of scrap dealer Louis Lebster and of new arrival Nathan Bornkind. Three years later the community celebrated its first marriage ceremony, the wedding of machinist Max Kroll and his bride Bessie. The same year M. Rabbinowitz, Flint's first *shohet* (kosher butcher), established a stand within a Gentile-owned shop on Saginaw Street, allowing residents finally to purchase kosher meat locally. Until he left Flint in 1917, Rabbinowitz also taught Hebrew school and performed such ritual services as the bar mitzvah, a boy's coming of age ceremony, conducted first in Flint for Sarah and Ben Hoffman's son, Hymen. The year 1910 marked the organization of a chapter of B'nai B'rith, a prominent national society of Jewish men. Like other chapters, Flint Lodge No. 656 undertook a range of activities, attempting to mediate disputes among local Jews, helping needy recent immigrants, and cooperating with the IRO's resettlement efforts. Jewish women such as Ann Lebster, an immigrant from Russian Poland, were also active in that year, raising funds to bring a Sefer Torah to Flint from Detroit. The Sefer Torah is a scroll handwritten on parchment paper containing the Five Books of Moses (Genesis, Exodus, Leviticus, Numbers, and Deuteronomy) and represents the single most holy object in Judaism. Thus although Flint's small Jewish community still had no building of its own in which to worship, it at last had its own sacred scroll to use in services held in private homes and rented rooms.

By the onset of World War I in Europe, Jewish presence in Flint had expanded substantially. After 1913 the automobile industry began to demonstrate that it could promote long-term, if sometimes fitful, economic growth, and this improved climate encouraged Jews to put down roots in the city. One woman, for example, wrote to her sister in Chicago and urged her to relocate, declaring that "a factory is here" where her husband could get a job. [43] The family came to Flint days later. Similarly, Morris Gold, a Polish immigrant, arrived in 1914 and immediately found a job at Buick. The city's reputation had attracted him, for "everyone knew that Flint was a good place to go if you wanted to make money." [44] Meanwhile war increased emigration from across the continent of Europe, with Jews especially eager to leave nations that tried to force them into military service while continuing to deny them basic rights or actively persecuting them. In consequence, the number of immigrants arriving in Flint increased, so that by 1919 the city's Jewish population numbered more than one hundred families.

The first tangible sign of this growing presence was the establishment of a cemetery. After Ben Hoffman's fatal accident in his coal yard in 1915, his remains were taken to Detroit for interment. Galvanized by this sudden death, community members formed a committee to obtain land for their own burial ground. The committee included members who had lived in Flint for a decade, such as Hyman Winegarden and Max Lebster, as well as newer residents who were joining the ranks of Flint's Jewish shop owners—dry cleaner Sam Cohen, confectioner Barnett Wineman, and brothers Nathan and Louis Chimovitz, owners of a dry goods store. Notably, one woman, Esther Sorscher, rounded out the group. Sorscher was an immigrant from Minsk who had joined relatives in Flint through the aegis of the Hebrew Immigrant Aid Society (HIAS). [45] Committed to repaying such generosity through efforts in her new community, she took on the task of approaching every Jewish resident of Flint for a contribution of one dollar. Within a year the committee succeeded in raising enough money to buy four acres of land north of the city, establishing Machpelah Cemetery.[46]

The first kosher butcher shop opened in 1916 when immigrant George Dickstein established a successful business in the heart of the commercial district. Because Flint still had no local rabbi and those from Detroit or Saginaw came infrequently, Dickstein also frequently acted as a lay leader of worship services. Trained in Russia at a yeshiva (rabbinical seminary), he also conducted marriages and served as a mohel, performing circumcisions. The year 1916 also saw the foundation of two Jewish women's organizations, establishing the basis for an important philanthropic tradition in Flint. Unfortunately little is known about the early years of either institution, the Ladies Aid Society, whose charter members numbered over fifty, or the local chapter of the National Council of Jewish Women, an organization founded in New York in 1893. Both served as relief societies, dispensing aid to poor immigrants settling in the city.

Some of the new arrivals brought with them searing memories of hardship and persecution.[47] The recollections of Saul Gorne (originally Gornbein) are especially poignant.[48] Born in the small Ukrainian village of Yalduskov in 1908, as a young boy he enjoyed life in a prosperous commercial family. His father had served as clerk in the Russian army during that country's war with Japan in 1905, earning the rank of corporal. By 1907 Corporal Gornbein had returned home to continue his business, acting as a leasing agent for coal mining and lumber companies and for a large sugar beet refinery these companies supplied. When World War I broke out, Saul's father made plans for the family to immigrate to Detroit, where his eldest son had settled in 1910. But the Gornbein family found flight during the war impossible, finally leaving in 1920 and after young Saul had witnessed incredible brutality during several pogroms. Most of his non-Jewish neighbors remained friendly throughout the war and the revolution that began in 1917, with some sheltering the Gornbeins and other Jewish families from the rampaging bands of men who suddenly would appear in the town square. Despite the villagers' efforts at protection, the savage attacks sometimes claimed victims. Once Saul watched in horror as a horseman drove a spear into his young cousin, killing him. Another time while hiding in a neighbor's house he saw a rider behead the local rabbi with a single saber stroke.[49] In this climate of terror, the Gornbein family gave up all their possessions and began a circuitous journey to the United States. They paid smugglers to take them to Romania, working for months in Bucharest stacking firewood and stocking shelves in the businesses of wealthy Jewish families until HIAS helped them reach Paris. From France they made their way as steerage passengers to New York, arriving in Michigan in 1921.

Other Jewish families managed to emigrate before war erupted or to send a few of their members ahead to America prior to the wartime closing of borders. Young men were likely to be sent first, so they could avoid conscription into the army. The Linder family's experience is instructive. As soon as war began in 1914, Joseph Linder left

Sam Linder (*left*) and father, Joseph Linder, ca. 1915. They sent this formal portrait, taken shortly after arrival in the United States, to family members still in Russia. Joseph's wife and four daughters immigrated to Flint after World War I.

Sarah (Linder) Akner, Joseph and Ida Linder's eldest daughter, on her wedding day, ca. 1921. Perhaps this photograph of the young bride was sent to kin remaining in Russia.

Russia with his son, Sam, then aged about twelve. Left behind were Joseph's wife, Ida, and four daughters, Sarah, Esther, Blanche, and Betty. After 1919, all five women came to Flint, reuniting the family. By this time, Sarah, the eldest daughter, had met the man she planned to marry, David Akner, whose service in the Austrian army had brought him to Russia. At their wedding in Flint in 1921, Sarah's sister Esther was introduced to Akner's cousin, Louis Harris, whom she later wed. In this case, the turmoil of war led to the formation of new families, immigrants who would settle far from the Russian and Austrian villages of their birth and some of whose members would become mainstays of Flint's Jewish community.[50]

Among those who left during and after the war were the aging parents of daughters and sons who had been their family's immigrant pioneers. Adjustment could be especially difficult for these older emigrants. Jacob Raskin, for example, was well-educated and had been a teacher in Russia. In 1920 he came to Flint, where his daughter Esther

Jacob Raskin emigrated from Russia in 1920, bringing with him a Torah (Hebrew prayer book) and tefillin. Tefillin are leather boxes worn by ritually observant Jewish men on their arms and forehead while they recite the daily morning service. Each box contains pieces of parchment inscribed from the Torah, ca. 1920.

Sloan Museum

Sloan Museum

Esther (Raskin) Leavitt and sister-in-law Molly Leavitt (*third and fifth from left*) on an outing with friends, ca. 1920. Esther and Molly Leavitt arrived in Flint between 1910 and 1912, opening boarding houses with the aid of local Jewish women. Enjoying the greater independence for women that life in America offered, Esther learned to drive a car and sometimes set off with Molly and their friends for drives in the countryside.

(Raskin) Leavitt ran a boarding house. Fluent in several languages, including Yiddish, the common tongue of Eastern European Jews, Raskin never learned English and found few in the busy auto center with whom he could pursue his favorite pastime, discussing philosophy and religion. Miriam Lebster, mother of successful scrap dealers Louis and Max Lebster, immigrated from Austria in her late eighties and, like Raskin, found adapting to life in Flint a struggle.[51]

At least these arrivals could find some familiar aspects of Jewish life in their new home. By 1918 the community regularly held religious services in a large downtown hall and had launched a fund-raising drive to build a synagogue. Two women's organizations, the Jewish Ladies Auxiliary and Agudas Achis (United Sisters), led the effort to expand the community's institutional and social life. In February 1918, for example, the auxiliary hosted a festive ball, with proceeds to benefit the local Hebrew school and, with the United States now a combatant in World War I, to provide aid to "war sufferers."[52] A Jewish men's society, known as the "Progress Club," also met regularly, holding "activities of a social and constructive nature" at which members and, on special occasions, their wives, sisters, and sweethearts could find "refreshing diversion from the ordinary HumDrum of life."[53] By 1920 the community had hired its first full-time religious leader, and two years later the fledgling congregation founded the city's first Jewish religious institution, Congregation Beth Israel (CBI). The women's organizations that had spearheaded fund-raising for the building promptly merged to become the Congregation Beth Israel Sisterhood, becoming a mainstay of financial support for both the synagogue and the Hebrew classes held there.[54]

Key to the early success of the CBI sisterhood was Mrs. Harry Bernstein, the group's president for the first five years.[55] Born in Hungary, she changed her name from Gisele to Kate when she immigrated, wanting a more American-sounding name. Her marriage to Buick factory worker Harry had been arranged, and after more than a decade of unhappiness she divorced him. A mother of two, she supported her family by running a grocery store in the St. John District. She continued her energetic organizing for the fledgling congregation for several years, but in 1923, in part to leave behind the notoriety of her divorce, she moved to Chicago, where kin already had settled. Her energetic organizing exemplified the spirit of lay women's activism that led to the establishment of the synagogue.

A plain brick building distinguished only by six arched windows, Congregation Beth Israel reflected the modest size of Flint's Jewish community and the small incomes of most of its members. Its location on McFarlan Street in the St. John District situated the synagogue amid the growing cluster of Jewish residences and businesses on the city's industrial north side yet still fairly close to congregants who lived across the river, near the businesses lining South Saginaw Street. Such proximity was especially important to those CBI members who adhered strictly to Jewish law. Refusing to use any devices or machines on the Sabbath, they walked to services, whatever the weather. Other congregants at CBI held to looser constructions of this and other

Friends Sarah Shapiro (*left*) and Molly Dickstein in front of their synagogue, Congregation Beth Israel, 735 McFarlan Street, ca. 1930. Sarah Shapiro probably worked with her husband, Joseph, at the Michigan Coal Company. Molly Dickstein, married to kosher butcher George, worked as a supervisor at a tire company owned by a non-Jew.

traditions. On the Sabbath, just as on other days, they rode the trolley or drove the GM cars that brought their city fame.

Thus even as Flint Jews came together to found their first house of worship, the community comprehended widely divergent views about issues of religious belief and methods of practice. This diversity would shape the organizational contours and social relations within the community for decades. In this regard the experience of Flint Jewry mirrored that of other Jewish communities throughout the United States. By the time of CBI's dedication, three major movements within American Judaism had become institutionalized, each with its own schools for training rabbis, association of congregations, principles of worship, and codes of conduct for adherents.

Reform Judaism, the most liberal movement and the first to be established, had its roots in the large immigrations of the mid nineteenth century, primarily of German-, Dutch-, and English-speakers. To coordinate the Reform movement, in 1873 thirty-four congregations joined to form the Union of American Hebrew Congregations. Two years later Hebrew Union College, Reform Judaism's rabbinical seminary, opened in Cincinnati, a center of German Jewish settlement. Reform leaders instituted sweeping changes in the style and substance of Judaism, from the physical layout of synagogues to the language of service to the transformation of ritual observances, including dietary laws. Regarded as progressive, modern, and in tune with the American context by its

Sloan Museum

Inside Congregation Beth Israel, 1946. The Conservative congregation worshiped here from 1922 until 1952. Noted Jewish community member and professional photographer Sam Cossman took this award-winning photograph of men reading a Torah scroll.

proponents, Reform Judaism seemed overly accommodating and assimilationist to those who favored more traditional practices and beliefs.

A countermovement to Reform quickly coalesced. Describing their form of Judaism as Conservative, in 1886 the leaders of this second movement established a school for rabbinical training, the Jewish Theological Seminary, in New York. As Yiddish-speaking Jews from across Eastern Europe flooded into America, New York emerged as the hub of Jewish life both for older, often more assimilated Jews, and the recent immigrants. Whether they settled on the East Coast or fanned out across the United States to smaller cities, many newcomers found the style of worship at Reform congregations alien. Some also encountered a chilly reception from the more Americanized Reform Jews, many of whom had more education and financial resources. Dissatisfied but determined, Eastern Europeans swelled the ranks of Conservative congregations, bolstering this movement's attempt to retain many familiar customs and practices while updating some aspects of old world Judaism to mesh with conditions in the new homeland.

Other recent arrivals decried Conservatism's innovations, establishing Orthodox congregations that upheld traditional doctrines and codes of behavior, including

VARIETIES OF AMERICAN JUDAISM

The three major movements (or sects) of American Judaism—Orthodox, Conservative, and Reform—share a number of beliefs and practices: that God is One; that a covenant exists between God and the Jewish people; and that the Torah is the primary text defining that covenant.* The movements observe the same religious holidays, with some variation in the length of the holidays and the observance of minor festivals and fast days. All three observe the ritual of circumcision for boys at eight days of age. The observance of other life cycle events, including the coming of age for boys and girls at age thirteen (age twelve for Orthodox girls), weddings, and funerals, share common components. The greatest distinction lies in the degree to which each movement embraces traditional Jewish law, *Halacha*. This table depicts the general practices and beliefs of these movements, but within each observance and philosophy varies widely among congregations and individuals.

BELIEFS AND PRACTICES	ORTHODOX	CONSERVATIVE	REFORM
View of Torah (Five Books of Moses)	God's word revealed	Word of God; contains human component	Written by separate human sources, then redacted
Philosophy	Traditional, clear-cut faith	Balance between tradition and modernity	Based on tradition, liberal, open to new ideas
613 Mitzvot in Torah (Commandments)	Precisely observed without question	Observed with flexibility, adaptation to culture, society	Some observed; values and ethics of Judaism retained
Observance of Kashrut (Dietary Laws)	Strictly observed	Observance expected	Personal choice
Observance of Shabbat (Sabbath)	Strictly observed	Observance expected; driving, working, or cooking pemitted if necessary	Observance encouraged; spirit of law more important than letter of the law
Religious Services: Mixed Seating	Men and women sit separately	Men and women sit together	Men and women sit together
Religious Services: Hebrew/English	Service/prayer book in Hebrew	Service/prayer book primarily in Hebrew with English translation	Service/prayer book half in Hebrew, half in English
Religious Services: Participation by Women/ Counted in Minyan	No	Yes, since 1972 counted in minyan	Yes, since the 19th century
Religious Services: Women as Rabbis	No	Yes, since 1983	Yes, since 1972
Religious Services: Head Covering	Required at all times	Required in synagogue for males	Personal choice
View of Israel	Holy Land of Jewish people; must be based on traditional Jewish Laws	Spiritual-cultural center of world Jewry	Spiritual-cultural center of world Jewry
Social Action	Limited to areas of Jewish interest	Human and civil rights important	Incumbent on every Jew
Who is Jewish?	Mother must be Jewish or Orthodox conversion required	Mother must be Jewish or traditional conversion required	Child is Jewish if either mother or father is Jewish and raised as Jewish

*A fourth movement, the Reconstructionist, represents approximately one percent of American Jewry.

SOURCES: Arnold M. Eisen, *The Chosen People in America: A Study of Jewish Religious Ideology* (Bloomington: Indiana University Press, 1983); Gilbert S. Rosenthal, *The Many Faces of Judaism: Orthodox, Conservative, Reconstructionist and Reform*, ed., Seymour Rossel (New York: Behrman House, 1978); Jonathan D. Sarna, *American Judaism: A History* (New Haven: Yale University Press, 2004); Abraham Segal, *One People: A Study in Comparative Judaism*, ed. Bernard M. Zlotowitz (New York: Union of American Hebrew Congregations, 1982); R. J. Zwi Werblowski and Geoffrey Wigoder, eds., *Oxford Dictionary of the Jewish Religion* (New York: Oxford University Press, 1997); and Jack Wertheimer, "Recent Trends in American Judaism," in *American Jewish Year Book* (Philadelphia: Jewish Publication Society of America, 1989), 89: 63–162. Additional information provided by Emily Bank Alter and Rabbi Karen Companez.

strict observance of dietary laws, rigid restrictions on Sabbath activity, and physical segregation of the sexes during worship services. The Orthodox movement began with hundreds of tiny congregations, most meeting in private homes or rented quarters in the midst of thickly settled Jewish neighborhoods. Yet just as it boosted Conservatism, the accelerating immigration of Eastern European immigrants fueled the growth and consolidation of Orthodoxy. In 1898 this third strand of Judaism formed a national organization, the Union of Orthodox Congregations.

A vast literature details the complex history of the development of the Orthodox, Conservative, and Reform movements, all of which became represented among Flint Jewry. The accompanying table presents some of the key differences in belief and practice of these branches of American Judaism. Like all such schema, it necessarily oversimplifies, neglecting distinctions salient to adherents of each branch; collapsing in time developments that emerged over decades; and portraying each as internally consistent and unified. Nonetheless it offers a guide to the main areas that have distinguished these movements for more than a century and which proved important for the evolution of Jewish life in Flint.[56]

As the sole Jewish religious institution in the city, Congregation Beth Israel attempted to provide a religious home for all Flint Jewry. The synagogue's physical structure and the nature of its services embodied the effort to bridge contentions about proper doctrine and practice, trying to strike a balance by keeping much of the old and incorporating some of the new. Following Conservative custom and in line with Reform practice, both men and women worshiped in the main sanctuary. An adjacent space allowed Orthodox men and women to attend services in sex-segregated areas.[57] Similarly, while CBI conducted most of its services exclusively in Hebrew, it occasionally incorporated some English into worship. The congregation adopted a traditional form of music in its services, featuring unaccompanied vocal performances by either a rabbi or cantor, a man trained in ritual song. In contrast, by the 1920s some Conservative congregations had incorporated choirs and organs into their services, innovations pioneered by the Reform movement.

CBI prospered, but it did not long remain the exclusive house of worship for Flint Jewry. In 1927, five years after the synagogue's dedication, some of its congregants left to form a Reform temple. Meanwhile a few devoutly Orthodox families continued to meet privately. This institutional proliferation extended to the social and economic realms, with Flint's Jewish community founding an array of organizations, clubs, and businesses during the 1920s.

Thus more than six decades after Henry Brown settled in the burgeoning lumber town, a sizeable Jewish community began to come into its own in a booming manufacturing center. Yet contention sometimes roiled this more mature and established community, while outside events wrought tremendous challenges. Bracketed by two world wars, the decades of the 1920s through the 1940s marked a second period in the history of Flint Jewry.

CHAPTER TWO

Creating a Community

DOING BUSINESS IN A ROARING GM TOWN

On 28 November 1918 the city of Flint hosted a parade to celebrate the end of World War I. A throng stood in the cold rain waving flags, children wearing Red Cross caps marched behind a band, and young and old cruised through the downtown hallooing from their Flint-made Chevrolets and Buicks. Parade-goers had reason to be proud, for local factories had produced airplane engines and tractors for the army while increasing output of cars and trucks for domestic sale. They also had reason to mourn, for the county lost 162 servicemen during the devastating global conflict.

The following year, as the economy adjusted to peacetime, the nation lapsed into recession, the first of several downturns during a decade that witnessed an overall expansion of manufacturing and commerce. Flint experienced only brief bouts of contraction, punctuating an era of unprecedented growth; in the birthplace of General Motors, the 1920s roared with particular ferocity. Several verses of "Flint," a waltz composed in 1922 by local songwriter P. J. Hammond, capture the boosterish mood:

> Where the old Flint River is flowing,
> On its banks the city stands,
> If you want to fill your wallet,
> Its the proper place to land.
> On the banks of the old Flint River,
> "The Industrial City" stands.
> Like the hand of God had placed it
> To make a home for man.
> Flint's the motor making city.
> She is working night and day.
> Turning out the finest motors,
> Buick, Dort, and Chevrolet.[1]

41

Crooks Collection, Scharchburg Archives, Kettering University, Flint, Michigan

Workers pour out of the "Chevy 4" plant on Chevrolet Avenue, 1926.

In the high-flying 1920s many Flint workers did toil night and day, even if few filled their wallets as a result. Propelled by skyrocketing demand for cars and trucks, GM boosted production at existing facilities and built new ones. Native- and foreign-born newcomers poured into Flint searching for jobs, swelling the city's population from 92,000 in 1920 to 135,000 in 1925. By 1929 the city's residents numbered 165,000, more than quadruple the number in 1910.[2] Despite a wave of construction, the city simply could not absorb the rapid influx, and an acute housing shortage developed, particularly in the densely settled working-class neighborhoods.[3]

Veterans who returned to Flint, including at least eighteen Jewish men, found their hometown flush with prosperity, with homes rising in farmers' fields, new shops lining the streets, and factories running full tilt. Among them were three young men who found employment in different parts of the growing city, each in a type of business where Jewish entrepreneurs expanded their presence during the 1920s. Sam Safer worked as a salesman at his parents' firm, Liberty Coal Company, in the industrial St. John District north of the Flint River; Philip Fisher became a clerk at Lande's Grocery, located at the northern tip of the sprawling Buick plant in an area where tents served

The Vogue, 531 South Saginaw Street, 1917. Shoppers could reach the stylish women's clothing store by streetcar until 1935, when the city ended the service.

Sloan Museum

as makeshift workers' housing; and Phil Goodman opened a women's apparel shop in a prime downtown block of South Saginaw Street.[4]

To an even greater extent than Henry Brown, the pioneering dry goods merchant who had settled in Flint sixty years before, Goodman had substantial competition from other Jewish retailers. A dozen Jewish clothing stores stood along South Saginaw where parade watchers had cheered Allied victory, four of them "ladies furnishing" shops like Goodman's. The most prominent was the Vogue, just a few doors away. Opened by Max Fischgrund in 1916 and advertised as the "House of Courtesy," the Vogue catered to a wealthy clientele. By 1920 it had became the county's most fashionable women's apparel shop.[5] Ten other Jewish-owned clothing stores dotted the city's industrial wards. Most, like the "Square Deal Clothier," specialized in lower-priced goods aimed at working-class buyers.[6]

In all, Jewish businesses totaled nearly a hundred in 1920, ranging from an art studio to a tire company. Jewish shopkeepers purveyed foods, furniture, and hardware; cleaned clothing; made shoes and hats; and pawned goods. Flint even boasted a Jewish-owned car dealership, with William Hauser and Abraham Foote acting as

JEWISH BUSINESSES AND PLACES OF WORSHIP IN FLINT, CA. 1920

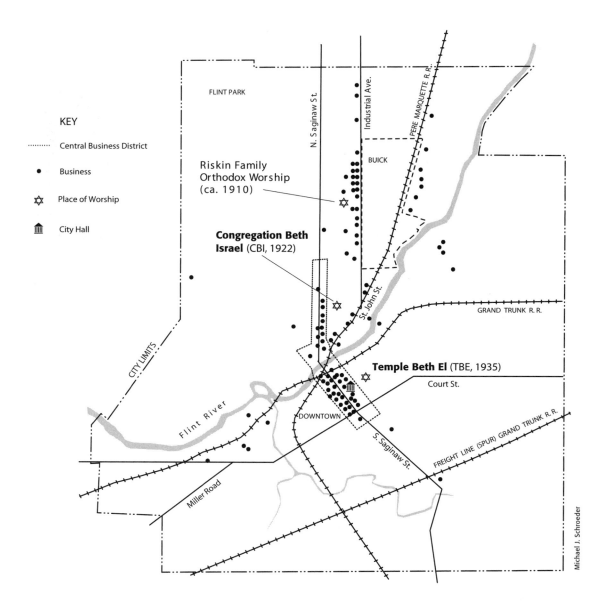

KEY

········· Central Business District

●   Business

✡   Place of Worship

🏛   City Hall

Riskin Family
Orthodox Worship
(ca. 1910)

**Congregation Beth
Israel** (CBI, 1922)

Temple Beth El (TBE, 1935)

FLINT PARK

BUICK

N. Saginaw St.

Industrial Ave.

PERE MARQUETTE R. R.

St. John St.

GRAND TRUNK R. R.

Court St.

DOWNTOWN

Flint River

CITY LIMITS

S. Saginaw St.

FREIGHT LINE (SPUR) GRAND TRUNK R. R.

Miller Road

Michael J. Schroeder

Flint Park, 820 West Stewart Street, late 1920s. The park featured a shooting gallery, thrilling rides, and shady picnic grounds. In this atmosphere of high spirits, Jews mingled with non-Jews. The Rosenberg family operated their concession near the dance hall (*at left*).

"exclusive agents" for the popular Hudson motorcar, while partners Jacob Bernstein and Meyer Vinacow quenched their patrons' thirst with "Stroh's Temperence Beer," a beverage introduced to meet the restrictions of Prohibition. In this booming factory town Jewish immigrants and their children thus carved out a niche, clustering over-whelmingly in retailing and wholesaling. Flint Jewry consequently resembled that in Detroit, the much larger automotive center only sixty miles to the southeast, constitut-ing "primarily a bourgeois community," according to historian Kenneth Waltzer, which "lacked [the] substantial working class and powerful currents of organized labor and Socialism" that characterized Jewish enclaves in some other American cities during the 1920s.[7]

As the map of Jewish businesses and places of worship circa 1920 illustrates, Flint's Jewish businesses clustered in four locations: along South Saginaw Street in the central business district; just across the river along North Saginaw Street, an extension of the main downtown area; in the industrial St. John District, mainly along St. John Street itself, which bordered the Buick facility to the east; and along Indus-trial Avenue, which formed the long western perimeter of the GM plant. Some Jew-ish merchants also sold goods door-to-door, like Samuel Hurwitz, who traveled the countryside fitting glasses and fixing watches, while others peddled wares at the factory gates.[8] Veteran Joe Schiller, an autoworker, sold "near-beer" outside the barracks-like housing GM erected next to the Buick plant, saving his proceeds to

Sloan Museum

Joseph Himelhoch's market, 3401 St. John Street, ca. 1928. Behind the counter (*center*) is Joseph Himelhoch; he is flanked by his sister-in-law and brother-in-law, Lillian and Harry Ura.

open a haberdashery.[9] Still others set up stands where workers and their families gathered for recreation after the long days in the factories. The most popular spot was Flint Park, built in the city's northwest corner on one of the few large open plots of land, where the Rosenberg family operated a concession. From early morning until late at night they sold distinctly American fare—cotton candy, ice cream cones, and hot dogs—to the crowds who came to ride the roller coaster, play bingo, go boating on the lake, or lounge on the grass.[10]

Aspiring merchants required capital to start these businesses, but before the 1940s few banks in the nation extended even small loans to immigrant entrepreneurs. To address this need, during the 1920s over five hundred Jewish free loan societies and *aktsiyes* (much like credit unions) operated across the United States.[11] In Flint, as elsewhere, would-be Jewish business owners turned to their own for help. Formed early in the decade by some dozen prosperous members of the community, the Flint Free Loan Society met at a classroom in Congregation Beth Israel. Here those seeking funds to open businesses or tide them over rough times applied for loans to a board of directors. For nearly twenty years the association not only provided crucial capital for individuals but cemented economic and social relations within the Jewish community.[12]

In 1924 several dozen Jewish grocers in the St. John District formed a smaller self-help organization, the United Grocers Association.[13] Through this cooperative the shopkeepers pooled their resources to buy canned goods in bulk, saving money on

Interior of Winegarden's furniture store, ca. 1924. Floor-to-ceiling windows, strategically placed mirrors, and shiny wood floors made the large store, filled with merchandise, appear bright and roomy.

Downtown Flint, looking south from the Flint River along South Saginaw Street, 1926, with signs for Kobacker's and Winegarden's stores (*at right*).

Crooks Collection, Scharchburg Archives, Kettering University, Flint, Michigan

The display tower for Winegarden's furniture store, late 1920s. The panels on the tower give details about the featured item, a gas range, which occupies the lowest tier. Also, a truck (*bottom right*) from the brothers' other major business, the New Orleans Fruit House.

products much in demand by their working-class customers. Like many such efforts by immigrant entrepreneurs and workers, this one proved short-lived. Chronically stretched for resources, after a few years the grocers found they could muster neither the funds nor the time to sustain the cooperative. Yet even after the demise of their organization, the bonds forged by these store owners encouraged less formal cooperation. Kinship further undergirded ties among some of the grocers. Three brothers active in the cooperative, Latvian immigrants Isadore, Aaron, and Julius Himelhoch, operated the Industrial Market on the Buick factory's west side, while their cousin Joseph Himelhoch owned a grocery on its east.[14]

Across the river in downtown Flint, brothers Harry and Hyman Winegarden continued to operate their successful meat and fruit market, plowing their profits into a second retail venture. In 1924 they opened Winegarden's Furniture, stocked with up-to-date products for the modern home. They located their new store two blocks west of a long-established Jewish-owned furniture business, Kobacker's, headed by partners Morris Kobacker and Maurice Rosenblum. Adopting common promotional techniques of the day, both furniture stores took out large advertisements in local newspapers and installed giant signs visible to shoppers throughout the downtown.[15] Yet the Winegardens, already known for their flamboyant marketing style, created a unique advertisement for their business. Next to the entrance to another commercial building they owned and just doors away from Kobacker's, they erected a wooden structure touted as the "world's smallest skyscraper." Emblazoned with their furniture store's name and topped with a revolving light, the triangular tower measured less than six feet on each side at its base but soared over a hundred feet high. Using a system of trap doors, workers lowered large placards and even pieces of furniture onto each level of the tower's six stories. For more than thirty years, Flint shoppers gazed up at the Winegardens' tower and selected chairs, tables, lamps, and stoves from the brothers' remarkable display.

ORGANIZATIONAL GROWTH

While they competed in business, Harry and Hyman Winegarden cooperated with Maurice Rosenblum in a key development in the organizational life of the city's Jewish community: the establishment of Temple Beth El (TBE), a Reform congregation. In November 1927 they numbered among the thirty-three signers of the articles of association founding the temple. Lillian Rapport, Rosenblum's daughter, was the sole woman signatory, although the drive to found the congregation had been led by Temple Beth El Sisterhood, formed earlier that year by a group at the synagogue who wanted a less traditional style of worship.[16] Thus in Flint, as in many American Jewish communities, women led the way in creating both the Conservative and Reform congregations. They would continue as backbones of these institutions, despite the decades-long monopoly by men of the official positions of authority in both.[17]

After the formation of Temple Beth El, the TBE sisterhood's first priority became raising funds to renovate and furnish the congregation's rented quarters downtown in the Paterson Building, a substantial commercial structure.[18] The site was convenient for many of the temple's founders, who needed only to walk a few blocks from their businesses on South Saginaw Street to attend Friday evening services. In addition to Rosenblum and the Winegarden brothers, TBE's initial members included lawyer S. S. Pearlstine; dentist Abe Eisman; retail clothiers Max Fischgrund, Leo Goldstein, Benjamin Weiner, and Moses Rosenthal; department store owners Nate Seitner and Sigmund Seitner; and jewelry shop owner Saul Weinberg. All were prominent businessmen. TBE founder Sam Lande's furniture and radio shop was also on South Saginaw, but his family's coal and scrap businesses were across the river near the Buick plant, their major customer. Similarly, Ellis Warren's firm, Standard Cotton, which made upholstery material for the auto shops and mattresses for furniture retailers, was located south of the downtown near several other GM plants.[19] Warren, along with large fuel and scrap dealers like Lande, was among the few Jewish businessmen with ongoing, direct economic connections to GM.

It was so separated in those days [between the synagogue and the temple]. You had your own little clique at the shul [synagogue], and we didn't even know them [at the temple].

—*Charlotte (Lewis) Kasle, recalling the 1920s and 1930s*

Those who organized TBE, then, ranked among the most influential and wealthiest men in the city's Jewish community. The formation of the temple consequently drained significant financial resources from the synagogue as well as dividing Flint Jewry along religious lines. Furthermore, the temple's establishment created a social separation in the community whose nature and dimension changed over time, sometimes bridged by affiliations in other organizations, and recalled variously by members of the congregations. Notably, adherents of both congregations agreed on the shorthand terms used for the two institutions, with the Conservative Congregation Beth Israel uniformly called "the shul" (or synagogue) and the Reform Temple Beth El simply called "the temple."

Sloan Museum

Temple Beth El, 521 Liberty Street, ca. 1937.

From its inception, services at Temple Beth El differed dramatically from those conducted at Congregation Beth Israel. Dressed soberly in dark-striped gray trousers and a black jacket, TBE's rabbi Bernard Zieger, who had trained at a Reform seminary, conducted services in English as well as Hebrew. An organist played music (on an instrument purchased and installed by the TBE sisterhood), and after the sermon a collection basket circulated among the congregants, practices unknown in Conservative congregations and deemed unseemly by the synagogue's more traditional members. The well-appointed rooms at the Paterson Building and, several years later, larger ones at another commercial building, served the temple's growing membership well, except during the holiest days of the Jewish calendar. During Rosh Hashanah (New Year's Day) and especially on Yom Kippur (The Day of Atonement)—the most solemn day in the Jewish religious year, observed in September or October—the rented quarters proved crowded. Moreover, to some TBE members the less elaborate ritual at the Reform congregation seemed unsuitable for this holy occasion. Those who sought more traditional observance consequently returned to CBI on Yom Kippur, paying fees to reserve seats at the front of the synagogue and participate in the Conservative ritual of prayer. According to one CBI congregant, after the first part of the liturgy, the Kol Nidre (prayer for absolution), the TBE members then left and "went back to the temple" to conclude the service.[20] Some maintained this practice for years, even after the Reform temple dedicated its own roomy building. In 1935 the congregation purchased a stately two-story brick structure, constructed as a private residence and then owned by the Knights of Columbus, a Roman Catholic fraternal organization, situated on a shady, quiet residential street just east of the downtown.

Meanwhile a few members of Flint's Jewish community continued to worship privately, finding the temple far too Americanized and even the synagogue too lax in doctrine and practice. These Orthodox families met in homes or the backrooms of groceries, often at that owned by the Riskin family on Trafalet Street near the north end of the Buick plant. In these modest quarters a minyan (quorum of ten adult men) gathered to recite the daily morning service and perform other rituals in the traditional manner. Observing dietary laws strictly, their wives could ride or walk the fifteen short blocks south to buy meat from kosher butcher George Dickstein, whose shop and residence were near the Conservative synagogue, many of whose congregants also kept traditional food practices.

Social organizations also developed within Flint's Jewish community during the 1920s, some bringing members of the Reform and Conservative (and less frequently

Sloan Museum

Sorority sisters, 1920s. As more young women pursued high school and college educations, many coeds joined sororities made up of those who shared their backgrounds. These daughters of turn-of-the-century Jewish immigrants to Flint sport the latest fashions in dress, jewelry, and hairstyle.

the Orthodox) congregations together, along with others who identified as Jewish but did not affiliate with any religious institution. In 1920, two years before the dedication of Congregation Beth Israel, young women in the community, most the daughters of immigrants, established a club to sponsor dances, card parties, rummage sales, and similar activities. Second-generation Jewish women founded a sorority and joined a literary club that year, testifying to their belief in education both as an end in itself and as a pathway to advancement. Together with their male counterparts, they formed the Young Judean Club, briefly issuing a weekly newspaper, the *Community Herald*, that highlighted social events.[21] A local chapter of Hadassah, a national woman's organization, proved more durable, for decades attracting a broad membership within the community.

Originally named the American Women's Zionist Organization, Hadassah was founded in 1912 by Henrietta Szold, a teacher of Russian immigrants in Baltimore.[22] A nationalist organization that sought a territorial solution to the anti-Semitism that Jews faced worldwide, Hadassah supported Jewish settlement in Palestine and the creation of a distinctly Jewish state there. In the late nineteenth and early twentieth

Sloan Museum

Independent Coat and Apron Supply, 1931. Partners and brothers Maurice Hertz and Israel Sendler established the firm in 1926. Hertz (*third from left*) and Sendler (*far right*) stand with company employees.

centuries only a small minority of American Jews embraced Zionism as an intellectual and political movement, and the establishment of Hadassah marked an important stage in the growth of this cause. By the period of the Second World War, Zionism had become a dominant movement among American Jews nationally, and Hadassah the largest organization of Jewish women in the United States. Developments in Flint reflected this national pattern.

The driving force behind Hadassah in Flint was Ann (Shapiro) Lebster, who had helped bring a Sefer Torah (a parchment scroll containing the Five Books of Moses) to the city and was also a founder of the Congregation Beth Israel sisterhood. In 1922 she gathered fifty-five women together to establish a local Hadassah chapter.[23] Immigrating in 1890, her family first had settled in Norfolk, Virginia, then moved to Detroit, where she worked as an apprentice dressmaker. At seventeen she married Louis Lebster and moved to Flint, where her family, by then well established, helped him set up a highly successful scrap business. When she organized the Hadassah chapter she was thirty-seven, the mother of three children, and already a longtime Zionist activist, having served before World War I as the first secretary of the city's small Zionist organization.[24] Arriving in Flint in 1926, Ida (Lifschitz) Sendler, fifteen years younger than Lebster, became another stalwart of the chapter.[25] Born in 1900 in Russia, she had come to the United States via Japan, settling in Detroit at the end of World War I. Shortly thereafter she married Latvian immigrant Israel Sendler, who had come to

Flint in 1906 to join his brother as a worker in the car shops. With help from the Lifschitz family, Israel Sendler became co-owner with his brother of Independent Coat and Apron Supply Company, delivering crisply laundered linen garments for workers in local shops, offices, and institutions. Like Ann Lebster, he participated in the city's earliest Zionist activism. After her marriage, Ida Sendler joined him in these efforts, organizing "Pioneer Women" to raise funds for Jewish settlement in Palestine and pursuing the Zionist cause within the Congregation Beth Israel sisterhood.

During the 1920s and 1930s Hadassah seems to have drawn most of its leadership from Temple Beth El, including Kate Rosenthal and Helen Seitner (wives of a clothier and a dry good merchant, respectively), but members of Congregation Beth Israel also participated.[26] Charlotte (Lewis) Kasle grew up in the synagogue and emphasizes the distinct social worlds that shul and temple congregants inhabited.[27] Nevertheless she recalls that her Yiddish-speaking mother, who struggled to save the ten cents a day members pledged to the chapter, went door-to-door soliciting donations for Hadassah with an affluent member of the temple. Joint fund-raising softened the resentment some CBI members had toward wealthier TBE congregants. "Whenever somebody from the shul would say to my mother that the temple members are snots," Charlotte Kasle remembers, "my mother would say, 'they're always friendly to me.'"

When [GM workers] were off of work, they did not have money . . . to buy fresh rye . . . and they would buy day-old rye for half price and not have the money for that.

—*Esther (Leitson) Fineberg, recalling the 1930s*

Hadassah met in clubrooms behind the sanctuary of the synagogue, as did most other Jewish organizations in Flint, including B'nai B'rith, the loan association, the literary society, a dramatic club, several sororities, the Zionist group, and the Hebrew school.[28] These meeting rooms also served as the site of dances and other social events for Flint Jewry and, somewhat confusingly, came to be referred to as the "Jewish Community Center," a title reserved in most other cities for separate buildings that housed an array of facilities, usually including a gymnasium and often a pool. Despite plans to do so, Flint Jewry never succeeded in erecting such a separate facility. The size of the community and the nature of relations among its members probably hampered the effort. In this community of several hundred families, ties of business, kin, and background were too dense and friendships too overlapping to permit the creation of separate Reform and Conservative institutions, but internal divisions were too substantial to sustain a joint fund-raising effort. Thus until the early 1950s, when both congregations established new quarters, many Reform members seemed willing to return to the McFarlan Street synagogue for community activities, and CBI earnestly endeavored to remain the communal center, if not the exclusive spiritual home, of Flint Jewry.[29]

External pressures, mounting after World War I and throughout the 1920s, facilitated this need for cooperation and solidified the community's sense of its Jewishness. Waves of nativism, anti-radicalism, and anti-Semitism swept the nation during these years, with southeastern Michigan the home of several of these noxious doctrines'

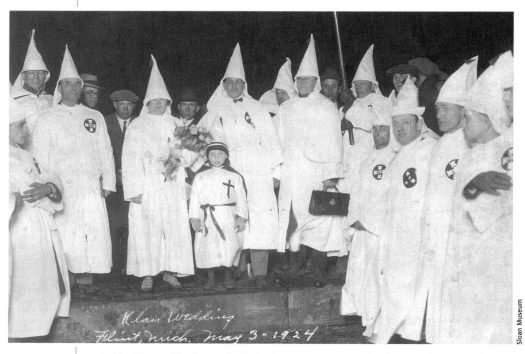

Ku Klux Klan wedding in Kearsley Park, Flint, 1924. An American flag flies from the pole (*right*) and waves over the bridal couple.

most vigorous exponents. Flint joined other cities in the nation by ringing in the new year of 1920 with "red raids" that jailed thirty-two men, including seven Russian immigrants, most of whom were guilty merely of reading literature of which the U.S. government disapproved. While only one apparently was Jewish, the national and local media repeatedly equated "Reds" with Russians and Russians with Jews, stressing the terrible consequences for Flint were radicals to gain a foothold in the GM citadel.[30]

Fifty miles to the south, Henry Ford, owner of the rival Ford Motor Company, had launched his personal campaign against the dangers Jews posed to America. His newspaper, the *Dearborn Independent,* published vile anti-Semitic articles that depicted Jews as plotting to control the vast economic resources of the nation, despoiling the country's values in the process. One of America's most renowned industrialists and public figures, Ford enjoyed tremendous credibility; by 1924 his paper had a circulation of nearly three-quarter of a million readers.[31] As early as 1920 prominent Americans spoke out against Ford, and in 1927 he issued a public apology for his series on "The International Jew," but evidence is rife demonstrating his continued anti-Semitism. Ford supported another loud voice raised against Jewish Americans, Roman Catholic priest Father Charles Coughlin. In 1926 Coughlin began broadcasting a radio show from his parish, the Shrine of the Little Flower, in Royal Oak, just north of Detroit. At the height of his popularity, the charismatic priest reached more than thirty million listeners weekly. Devoted mostly to championing a plan for broad social and economic changes in the nation, by the mid 1930s his program increasingly laid the country's woes at the feet of "Wall Street" and "international bankers," well-known anti-Semitic code phrases.[32]

The Ku Klux Klan also flourished in Michigan, attracting a large following in Flint in the early 1920s, especially among the thousands of whites migrating from the South to work in the auto shops.[33] According to a leading historian of the city, in Flint the Klan emphasized anti-Catholicism, support for Prohibition, and the need for foreigners to assimilate quickly, its parades and picnics linking adherents to the rural Protestant past familiar in their home states.[34] Yet this nostalgia had deep anti-Semitic and virulently racist qualities, aspects not lost on Flint's Jewish and nonwhite residents and known as well to the city's business elite, most of whom found the Klan's overwrought patriotism and denunciation of vice congruent with their interests. Peaking in the mid 1920s with dozens of public events at which Klansmen and their families gathered in robes on city streets, Klan activity subsided later in the decade, but lasted long enough for Flint to host the statewide convention in 1927 at a park on the city's fashionable east side.

By then Flint's leading citizens had launched a far-reaching Americanization campaign, with the members of the "Cosmopolitan Club" recruiting hundreds of the foreign-born to take English classes, study American history, and become naturalized citizens. In 1924 enrollment in the five-year program exceeded two thousand.[35] Though the program was voluntary in theory, in practice most immigrants no doubt felt pressure from their bosses, landlords, and coworkers to enroll, finding ways to make the program suit their own purposes. Some Flint immigrants joined in efforts to assimilate newer arrivals. In 1922 the local YWCA began an "International Institute," founded as part of the national organization's effort to offer English-language and citizenship courses in an atmosphere they believed more respectful to the foreign-born. Joseph Laro, the son of a flour merchant, emigrated from Shedlische, Poland, in 1914 and joined the institute when he settled in Flint in 1929.[36] Establishing a successful coal and iron company and becoming a member of Congregation Beth Israel, he helped teach the institute's citizenship classes. Others adopted more informal methods of teaching skills to newcomers. At a silent-movie house on Leith Street, one Jewish immigrant woman taught English to her Yiddish-speaking neighbor, translating the film captions as the friends watched the action unfold. Both worked at their families' nearby groceries, taking in matinees during slow afternoons at the stores.[37]

The formal assimilation campaigns reached full swing just as the flow of immigrants to Flint and across the nation slowed to a trickle, for in 1924 nativist sentiment had succeeded in fueling the passage of a draconian immigration restriction act.[38] Hence most Jewish immigrants who settled in Flint in the late 1920s and early 1930s had, like Joseph Laro, left their homelands before the enactment of the law, the "Industrial City" becoming their home only after having lived elsewhere. Yisroel Ring provides another example. In 1917 he fled war-torn Russia, making his way with another young man, probably a cousin, to relatives in Warsaw, Poland. Five years later he immigrated to Detroit and in 1932 came to Flint, where he opened a grocery and continued his vain effort to bring his father and two sisters from Russia to join him. Brothers Henry and David Schafer (who changed their last name from "Schoichets" after immigration in 1921) were more successful, but had to bide their time before being reunited with their brother, Meyer Schoichets, who arrived in Flint in 1928. Meyer demonstrated equal patience. He brought his wife Ida and children to Flint in 1935, only after they had lived several years in Brazil and thus could enter the United States as residents of another Western Hemisphere nation, one of the circuitous routes emigrants used in order to exploit a loophole in American immigration law. In the meantime Henry had returned to the brothers' native village of Lutsk to marry his childhood sweetheart, Rae Kleiner, a sister of Meyer's wife Ida, and escort her to Flint. Active in the synagogue, for the next several years the extended Schafer family lived in the house next to their grocery store.[39]

HARD TIMES AND LABOR TRIUMPHS

Friday was payday at GM factories, and shops and stores did their briskest trade when the thousands of autoworker families had money in their pockets and purses. This caused a dilemma for some Jewish merchants, since Shabbat (the Jewish Sabbath) begins on Friday at sunset and continues until sunset on Saturday, a period that traditional doctrine decrees be free from labor and devoted to prayer and ceremonial observance. Most Jewish storeowners accommodated the payroll schedule, adapting their observance to the reality of the marketplace. For many the situation in Flint represented only a heightened version of circumstances to which they previously had adjusted in their European homelands or in other American cities, as members of a minority religion within an overwhelmingly Christian population and an assertively Christian civic culture. As historian Hasia Diner notes, "American conditions made full compliance [with Sabbath dictates] difficult," so most American Jews rejected observance as "an all-or-nothing proposition" and "probably picked and chose from among the restrictions and rituals."[40]

Jewish grocery store owners in Flint often ran "payday specials" on Fridays and Saturdays to attract customers to their shops, but many also joined their families in lighting the Sabbath candles on Friday evenings and attended Jewish community social functions on occasional Friday nights. Dancing or playing cards at a B'nai B'rith party marked a clear departure from traditional religious observance, yet represented a way to bring members of the Jewish community together at the shul. Within families, children often became less observant than their parents; even husbands and wives sometimes adopted different practices. Each Sabbath Nathan Silver had to operate his grocery store with the help of only his non-Jewish employee because his wife, a

Yisroel Ring, after his arrival in Michigan, ca. 1922. Yisroel Ring sent this photograph of himself, wearing a Jewish Star of David, to his father and sisters in Russia. Writing in Yiddish, on the reverse he promised to send money and a companion to escort them to America. Sadly, this family never reunited; the sisters perished during World War II.

Sloan Museum

mainstay of the business, reserved the day for practicing traditional customs at home or walked the many blocks to the synagogue from their house on the city's far north side.[41]

Most Jewish merchants, large and small, extended credit to their customers.[42] During the 1920s credit-buying tided autoworker families over from day to day and through the layoffs that occurred during the weeks of "annual model change," when GM factories routinely shut down most operations to retool for production of new cars. Working-class customers expected and relied on credit-buying, and storekeepers promoted the policy; Max Maher, for instance, named his store "C & C Sanitary Market" to highlight that his neighborhood grocery accepted both "cash and credit."[43] With the onset of the Depression, GM's payroll, the lifeblood of the city, dried up. Seasonal layoffs gave way to massive unemployment, whatever small savings most working-class families had squirreled away rapidly became exhausted, and for increasing numbers of Flint residents buying goods on credit became an ongoing necessity.

Flint ranked among the American cities hardest hit by the Depression.[44] Soon after the stock market crash in October 1929, anxious consumers stopped buying cars, and soon banks, caught up in the panic, began calling in the loans they had made for vehicle purchases. As the automobile bubble of the 1920s burst, the bottom quickly fell out of the economy of the city, where 80 percent of the workers toiled at GM. By 1932, sales at Chevrolet and Buick, the two GM divisions with huge manufacturing facilities in Flint, had plummeted by 75 percent from their peak years of the mid 1920s.[45] Emerging from that decade of flourishing profits as the world's largest industrial corporation, GM responded rapidly to the sudden economic downturn, instituting severe retrenchment. The company cut costs by closing facilities, dismissing employees, slashing the pay of its remaining blue-collar workers and low-level managers, and simultaneously speeding up, mechanizing, and further rationalizing production at the assembly lines it kept running. In the heart of its empire, GM demanded that the men and women it still employed work faster and harder for less money and do so under increasingly taxing, dangerous, and demeaning conditions, some days for twelve hours, other days for two, and often for none. The alternative was clear for those who complained, resisted, or tried to organize for better conditions: join the throngs of the jobless that milled outside the car shop gates.[46]

Analyzing an array of economic and social data, historian Ronald Edsforth concludes that during the Depression "virtually all of Flint's industrial workers endured periods of prolonged unemployment," with thousands of families losing their homes and some facing hunger because they could not afford to buy food, despite a general decline in prices.[47] Many of the unemployed were recent arrivals with few kin on whom to rely, migrants who had flocked to Flint during the 1920s from Eastern Europe, the state's rural areas and Upper Peninsula, or the South, including both many whites and smaller numbers of African Americans.

Largely absent from the ranks of autoworkers even before the Depression began, on the whole Flint Jewry did not suffer during these hard years to the extent common among working-class families. Yet like their counterparts in other cities, if many Jewish families were in less dire circumstances than their neighbors, some experienced severe economic distress and all witnessed the devastating effect of growing joblessness on their city.[48] Moreover, as the purchasing power of the majority of Flint residents evaporated, a downward spiral set in, dragging some in the middle class down along with the unemployed and underemployed factory workers, forcing the closure of businesses. Their savings sunk into their commercial establishments and with few alternative means of support, many members of the Jewish community struggled to hang on to their livelihoods. William Lewis, for example, had arrived in Flint in 1922 and during the 1920s owned three successive small businesses, a jewelry shop, a tire store, and a pool hall. Less than a year after the stock market crash, his wife Rebecca began taking in boarders to help pay their mortgage and he was reduced to repairing shoes, an activity in greater demand as people sought to make do with what they had.[49] Ukrainian immigrant Hyman Podolsky, a founder of Temple Beth El, lost his job when the Seitner family, also early temple members, closed the department store where he worked as a floor manager. For two years Podolsky could not find work, then he took occasional jobs; he was underemployed until 1936.[50] Trained as a furrier, William Hauser had moved up when times were good, running two businesses, but he slid back down the ladder during the Depression, lucky to be able to become a furrier once again.[51]

Building ties with others helped some in their efforts to make a living. Former autoworker, haberdasher, and grocer Julius Hurand became a deliveryman for the Jewish-owned Leitson Bakery and developed good relations with Jewish storeowners as well as the growing number of non-Jewish Poles who had opened groceries near Industrial Avenue. Nevertheless, when the rent came due the Hurand family often had to move to different quarters in the neighborhood.[52] Others adopted new strategies to attract business. When Prohibition ended, one storekeeper divided his building, with half remaining a grocery and the other half becoming a bar. Members of the Flint Free

> I thought the name Rubenstein might look good on an Army roster.
>
> —*Gilbert Rubenstein, recalling the 1940s*

Taystee Bread promotion, ca. 1933. Storeowners Sarah and Isaac Levenson and the "Taystee Bread Girls" in front of the store at 434 East Pasadena Street, near the northern edge of the Buick plant.

Loan Society helped underwrite the venture.[53] At their small grocery, Sarah and Isaac Levenson set out special displays to make their wares attractive and featured items their working-class customers needed to stretch their budgets, such as vinegar for pickling. To drum up more business they made use of a special sales team, the "Taystee Bread Girls." While one young woman played the accordion three others sang commercial jingles, encouraging passers-by to come into the Levensons' store and buy loaves of the soft, white bread. A low-priced national brand heavily advertised on the radio, Taystee bread was marketed as modern, unlike the rye and whole wheat breads baked in immigrant kitchens or lining the shelves of bakeries like the Leitsons'.

No matter what their business or what tactics they used to promote sales, Jewish retailers faced a shrinking customer base. During the first four devastating years of the Depression, Flint's population declined by more than twenty thousand. For many of the unemployed, the complete shutdown of the Buick plant in August 1932 ended any lingering hopes that the economy soon would recover on its own and under the current political leadership. Grass-roots protests against GM had failed. In the summer of 1930 fifteen thousand people had turned out to support a strike by workers in the metal finishing and paint departments at a huge Fisher Body plant, the supplier of car bodies to Buick. The strike had ended dismally, as corporate managers and city officials had branded the strike leaders as dangerous radicals and mounted police had been dispatched to crush the work stoppage.[54] Little wonder thousands believed they might have better luck elsewhere.

GM long had nourished cozy relations with city hall and relied on the machinery of the state to back up its control of labor. Flint's political culture thus represented a particularly clear-cut instance of the strong ties between corporations and government that characterized Michigan and the nation, especially during the Republican-dominated 1920s.[55] The severity of the Great Depression shattered this politics of "normalcy." The election of 1932 ended Republican hold on the highest public office, as the aristocratic and urbane New York Democrat Franklin Delano Roosevelt swept into the White House with promises to address the economic crisis that the defeated incumbent, Herbert Hoover, had done so little to stem. Having witnessed the shuttering of the Buick plant three months before, most average citizens in Flint enthusiastically cast their ballots for Roosevelt, and the city's voter turnout was double that of the previous presidential-election year.[56]

This political realignment and mobilization sparked a new sense of possibility among many in Flint's working class. As Roosevelt's New Deal started to pay off in housing reform, increased welfare support, and jobs at federally funded projects—including airport improvement, sewer system expansion, and park construction—the city's labor movement began to revive.[57] Sales of automobiles slowly inched upward as well, and GM called back some of the unemployed. While some labor advocates felt the Democrats moved too slowly and cautiously, leaders of the newly formed Congress of Industrial Organizations (CIO), committed to forming unions of workers throughout entire industries, took heart after passage of the 1935 Wagner Act, which guaranteed the right of employees to collective bargaining. Like other major corporations, GM vehemently opposed the act, deeming it an unlawful infringement on its powers to treat workers as it wished. Later in 1935 the weak economic recovery stalled, just as Roosevelt began his reelection bid. Yet when he and wife Eleanor, whom many regarded as a symbol of compassion and tolerance, came to Flint a month before the 1936 election, they were greeted by the largest crowd in the city's history.[58] In November Flint's voters helped return him to the presidency and to elect another New Deal Democrat, former Detroit mayor Frank Murphy, as Michigan's governor. Six weeks later the Great Flint Sit-Down strike began.

The dramatic story of the strike is well known.[59] On 30 December 1936 workers at a Fisher Body plant seized control of the building. They shut down the assembly lines and refused to leave until GM agreed to recognize their union, the United Automobile Workers (UAW), and bargain with them over wages, hours, and the degrading and hazardous conditions under which they toiled. Thousands of other GM workers soon sat down and occupied their plants, including a massive facility that manufactured engines for Chevrolets made nationwide. GM resisted strenuously by various private stratagems and public means. Following the company's bidding, city police tried to oust the strikers, provoking a nightlong standoff with ten thousand UAW supporters.

Partners in the Industrial Market, these brothers also purchased identical new Buick sedans in 1936. As the car salesman (*left*) gestures, standing (*left to right*) are Aaron, Isadore, and Julius Himelhoch.

GM then requested that the National Guard be dispatched to Flint break the strike. Governor Murphy sent in troops, ordering them to maintain the peace and not remove the workers. Its power thwarted in this new political climate and its production of automobiles virtually halted, after forty-four days GM finally caved in.

When the UAW began negotiating with the corporation and got a glimpse of its finances, the union discovered how profitable the company had become after 1932. Edsforth estimates that "between 1930 and 1936, General Motors eliminated at least nine thousand blue-collar jobs in Flint without any loss of productive capacity."[60] Disastrous for those it put out of work, increasingly intolerable for those still on the job, and devastating to the city's economy, GM's retrenchment and speed-up had paid off handsomely in corporate profits. Since 1934 the Buick division, reorganized under notably hard-driving manager Harlow H. Curtice, had proven especially lucrative. Once GM recognized the autoworkers' union, production resumed and money once again flowed into its capacious coffers.

Led by a tiny group of workers and political radicals, conducted by a minority of autoworkers, and supported by thousands of ordinary men and women, the 1936–37 strike also was highly divisive, generating fierce opposition and bitter feelings among Flint's business class and among the thousands of other residents who sided with GM outright, opposed the union and its tactics, or feared the strike's threat to public order. The high-profile dispute, shown throughout the world's movie houses in newsreel footage, rent the social fabric of a city that in many ways and for many years had oper-ated like a company town. Unsurprisingly, Flint Jewry comprehended an array of views on this polarizing event.

Few members of the Jewish community seem to have participated in the strike itself, though most storeowners long had recognized that higher, more predictable incomes for autoworkers would translate into a more secure living for themselves. Several Jewish retailers who actively supported the strike had family members in the shops or knew firsthand what grueling conditions obtained there; they proudly extended credit to the sit-downers.[61] The Leitson family stands out for its strong com-mitment to the UAW cause, their bakery supplying breads and doughnuts to strikers and pickets at the giant Chevrolet engine plant. Twenty-three years old at the time of the sit-down and in her second year as a teacher of typing and shorthand at Flint's large Northern High School, Esther (Leitson) Fineberg recalled how she and her par-ents, Israel and Ann Leitson, felt about the bakery's customers and their cause:

> These people were fine hard working people and they worked like dogs in the fac-tory before the strike. They had nothing to say before the union started and GM drove them, drove them to speed up on the line and if they couldn't keep up they were fired.[62]

At work she kept such sentiments to herself. She knew other teachers shared her views, but while on the school grounds, "We didn't dare open our mouths out loud" in favor of the strike.

Immigrant Saul Gorne, one of Flint's first Jewish physicians, also strongly sup-ported the UAW, despite most local doctors backing GM. Gorne recalls that when the sit-down began, another doctor urged him to go to the plants and tell his patients to leave because, "There won't be any heat in there, and they'll get pneumonia and die." Perhaps remembering his own flight from persecution in Russia or his brother's injury while working at a Packard plant, the newly minted physician replied, "I'll never do that. I'll tell them to stay there because they have every right to stay there." He later joined another colleague in treating strikers injured in a clash with police. For the next five years influential doctors shunned him, refusing even to acknowledge him at medical society meetings. This treatment ended only after he enlisted in the army medical corps.[63]

But Fay (Laro) Alfred, just a year younger than Esther Leitson, recalls that her family not only opposed the strike but fought off unionization at their scrap and fuel company.[64] Like many Jewish women, she and her mother participated in the family business. Her mother kept books at the makeshift office at the yard, in winter dressed in a "babushka and boots" and a "gray squirrel coat." Fay Laro drove a truck through-out the county, picking up dead batteries, bringing them to the scrap and coal yard in Flint where her father, Joseph, fixed them, and then delivering the repaired batteries to waiting customers. Joseph Laro, immigrant teacher of citizenship classes at the International Institute, believed his employees did not want or need a union. His daughter claims that when a UAW organizer, flush with the success of the sit-down, "tried to get the people in the [junk]yard to strike, too," the angry and determined business owner "hit" the union man, then drove him off the property.

The Laro Coal and Iron Company was located several blocks south of the Flint River and west of South Saginaw Street, in a manufacturing district that included the Standard Cotton Products Company, owned by Ellis Warren and his non-Jewish partner, Oscar Banfield. By 1937 the firm made goods exclusively for the auto industry, selling upholstery and floor cushions to GM plants in Flint and throughout Michigan.[65] When workers at Standard Cotton sat down on the same day as those at Fisher Body, the smaller company opposed the unionization effort just as vociferously as did the giant automaker to which it had such intimate ties—and with the same result. The majority of Standard Cotton's approximately one hundred and twenty workers were young Southern white men, many of them migrants from a tiny area in northeast Arkansas and southeastern Missouri, a region where GM had sent recruiters during the 1920s.[66] Conditions at Standard Cotton resembled those at Flint's auto plants, with the addition of choking dust and even lower pay, but without the grueling speed-up of the assembly lines. The UAW victory there came five days after that at the large car shops, Warren and his partner signing an agreement with their workers only after it became clear that the unionization of GM had changed the labor market for all industrial workers in Flint.

The sit-down strike thus had different consequences for particular members of the city's Jewish community, its effects mainly relating to class position.[67] For Jews and non-Jews alike, whatever their position in society and their political views, it altered the local landscape of economic and civic relations. Yet the establishment of mass industrial unionism did not usher in a sustained period of economic recovery; by 1938 the Depression had returned, with unemployment once again soaring. In Flint and elsewhere in the United States, economic expansion awaited national mobilization for global war.

The Depression years did provide openings for Jewish Americans to enter the professions, as many universities and graduate schools cast aside formal or informal quotas limiting Jewish enrollment in their efforts to attract students. Taking advantage of this circumstance, a cohort of young men from Flint's Jewish community scraped together the cash, often by working part-time, to attend law, medical, or dental school, some at Detroit institutions, such as Wayne (State) University, and others at the University of Michigan. Located only fifty miles south in Ann Arbor, this highly prestigious institution seemed a long cultural distance away to some aspiring second-generation students.[68]

Those who completed their training during the Depression sometimes found Flint a hard place in which to start a practice. In the mid 1930s several young men

Bessie (Shapiro) Feldman, ca. 1937. After her mother's death in the mid-1930s, Bessie Shapiro returned from college to help her family, driving a truck for the Crapo Coal Company. She later graduated and had a successful career as a teacher.

Sloan Museum

changed their names to conceal their Jewishness from potential patients: Clem Zipperstein, for instance, whose parents ran a resort on Lake Michigan that catered to a Jewish clientele, became Clem Alfred when he launched his dental clinic.[69] After the establishment of the UAW, as autoworkers' pay increased and they began to receive medical benefits, Flint held many more opportunities for professionals, growing numbers of whom were Jewish. In 1930 the city had fewer than ten Jewish dentists, physicians, and lawyers; by 1940 there were more than fifty. Only two, lawyer Ruth Winegarden and lawyer Evelyn V. Cohen, were women.[70] The daughters of Flint's Jewish immigrants were more likely to become teachers, as did Bessie Shapiro.[71] Working on and off as a truck driver for a coal business, in 1939 Bessie graduated from college, fulfilling her parents' dream that she receive an education. She returned to Flint and began teaching at a school next to the large AC Spark Plug plant in a working-class neighborhood known as "Thrift City."

The coming of age of a second generation constitutes an important aspect of the story of Jewish life in Flint during the 1930s and 1940s. So too are the internal dynamics and organizational efforts of a community faced with economic upheaval, then global war and the reemergence of their city as a vibrant manufacturing center. And, tragically, fundamental to the narrative of these years is the nightmare of the Holocaust, a horror whose dimensions would be acknowledged only at the end of World War II.

STRAINED RELATIONS AND DARKENING SHADOWS

Until his death in 1934, Russian immigrant Philip Rubenstein held unofficial mediation sessions in the back room of his clothing store, trying to resolve disagreements within the ranks of Flint Jewry through persuasion and appeals to the larger good of the community. Rubenstein's good sense, judiciousness, and integrity often brought the disputing parties to a compromise; when necessary, lawyer S. S. Pearlstine furnished free advice to formalize the settlement. Similarly, Clara Bell Pearlstine, the attorney's

Sloan Museum

Congregation Beth Israel annual "Donor Dinner," 1934. Held in the elegant ballroom of the Durant Hotel, the highly successful fund-raising event attracted wide attendance from Flint's Jewish community. At the head table (*center*), wearing a necktie and wire-rimmed glasses, is Congregation Beth Israel's rabbi, S. Z. Fineberg.

wife, regularly went door-to-door with a friend offering volunteer counseling and social services to needy or troubled Jewish families. Those in the most distress, impoverished Orthodox itinerants from Detroit who sometimes passed through Flint, also received help from the network of aid that knit together the Jewish community throughout the Depression years. Organizations, notably B'nai B'rith, also aided Jewish families with economic or personal problems and sought to bolster communal ties.[72] Despite these formal and informal mechanisms, sustaining a stable, strong, and unified Jewish community proved difficult.

The lean and uncertain times, the emergence of contentious events such as the strike, and the eruption of ideological disputes strained relations and sometimes provoked conflict. Both Congregation Beth Israel and Temple Beth El faced financial crises during the early 1930s. Payments of membership dues at the synagogue plunged, and the rabbi at the temple saw his annual salary slashed by nearly two-thirds. Repeated calls by the synagogue's rabbi to collect money for improved recreational activities for young people went unheeded, while the fund-raising effort to purchase quarters for the temple launched in 1927 dragged on for seven years.[73] By 1934 economic conditions had improved somewhat, allowing the temple to buy a building, increasing organizational proceeds raised through personal solicitations, and boosting attendance at such community events as the synagogue's annual dinner and athletic contests put on by B'nai B'rith. Enrollment at the Hebrew School, sponsored by CBI, also began to grow, as immigrant parents placed new emphasis on the importance of a formal Jewish education for their American-born children. As elsewhere in the nation, greater numbers of daughters as well as sons attended, more families acknowledging that girls needed to receive more than domestic religious training. These students, still probably a minority among Flint's Jewish young people, walked or boarded a bus to the Leith Street classroom every day after public school ended.[74]

As attendance expanded, a broader group within the community became concerned about the Hebrew school's curriculum, raising a fundamental question: What should Jewish children be taught—religion, culture, or some mixture of the sacred and the secular? Should the school focus solely on Hebrew, the language of the holy texts, and the texts themselves? What of Yiddish, which many parents spoke at home, or English, the language children used on their way to and from their religious lessons? Which customs should be emphasized, which interpretations of tradition stressed, which values conveyed, and which teachers employed? Like Jewish communities throughout the United States, in debating the content of the curriculum and purpose of the school, Flint Jewry confronted issues about what constitutes Judaism, how to maintain its key religious and cultural features in America, what boundaries to draw around the Jewish community, and how to reconcile differences within it.[75]

No agreement emerged, and during these and subsequent years Flint Jewry struggled to define what it meant to be Jewish and Jewish American. In this small community, personal relations often crosscut lines of discord and fostered a sense of internal cohesion despite differences of religious style, secular orientation, class position, and political perspective. Yet the size of the community also rendered it vulnerable to cleavage, magnifying the impact of particularly divisive issues or individuals. In this period one such subject was Zionism.

By the 1930s, the cause of Zionism had moved from a marginal position to a central though contested theme in American Jewish life. In Flint the leading Zionist organization remained Hadassah. The local chapter claimed nearly a hundred members by the middle of the decade and held annual fund-raising dinners attracting 250 guests. Moreover, the group had attained significant social standing within and beyond the Jewish community, the city newspaper reporting the organization's meetings in its society pages, alongside stories on notable non-Jewish women's groups such as the Junior League, the American Association of University Women, and the Girl Scouts.[76] Like the national organization, Flint Hadassah donated funds to support health care and social services to Jewish settlers in Palestine, and in 1937 worked for the newly founded "Youth Aliyah" project, an effort to "bring to [Palestine] . . . underprivileged Jewish children from unfriendly European countries."[77] Throughout the decade, longtime Zionist Ann Lebster served as a leader of the group, which continued

Rabbi Elmer Berger, ca. 1937. Berger (1908–96) became the rabbi at Temple Beth El at the age of twenty-eight, remaining there until 1943. Charismatic and controversial, he was a national leader of the small American anti-Zionist movement. From 1942 until 1967 Berger held executive positions in the American Council for Judaism and thereafter in American Jewish Alternatives to Zionism.

to draw members from both Congregation Beth Israel and Temple Beth El. The chapter met regularly at the community rooms at the shul, but occasionally also conducted gatherings at the temple.

Beginning in 1936, the temple's rabbi was Elmer Berger, ordained just four years before. Tall, handsome, and charismatic, TBE's young leader soon earned a reputation for his eloquent lectures on Judaism, delivered to audiences comprised of both non-Jews and Jews. His speeches also addressed the need to combat anti-Semitism in the fascist states of Europe, a matter of deepening concern within American Jewry and a point on which he and Hadassah members agreed. Berger, however, took a starkly different position than that of Hadassah on how to combat anti-Semitism, both nationally and abroad, and particularly regarding the morality as well as the expediency of the Zionist cause. Proudly opposing Zionism, he declared that Judaism was a religion of universal values and individual conscience, rejected as "corrosive" the nationalist thought undergirding Zionism, and asserted that Jewish Americans had only one homeland, the United States, not Palestine.[78]

By the late 1930s, as the anti-Semitic campaigns escalated in Europe, such views became decidedly less common and much more unpopular among American Jews, some seeing condemnations of Zionism not only as impolitic but as irresponsible and even disreputable. Still Berger persisted, claiming that Zionism did not offer an answer to the plight of European Jews and reiterating his belief that to meet the international emergency Jewish Americans should look to their own government and demonstrate unilateral loyalty to the United States. In 1942 he published a widely circulated, and much vilified, essay *Why I Am a Non-Zionist,* as well as a short pamphlet, memorably titled *The Flint Plan: A Program of Action for American Jews,* outlining methods for combating Zionist activism based on his own experiences.[79] The next year he left Temple Beth El to become the executive director of the American Council for Judaism, a tiny anti-Zionist organization founded on 7 December 1942, the first anniversary of the Japanese attack on Pearl Harbor, the date chosen by the group to highlight its patriotism.[80]

While Berger was still at the temple, leading members of Flint's Jewish community publicly condemned his views. In one telling incident, a heated exchange between

Berger and the synagogue's "fire-and-brimstone" rabbi, S. Z. Fineberg, escalated into a shouting match, and ended with Fineberg's forced eviction from the temple.[81] The open rift between the rabbis compounded a larger controversy within the community over how best to combat anti-Semitism while attending to the needs of local Jewry. This discord then spilled over into other arenas of community life.

In this contentious atmosphere, for example, some shul and temple members tried to consolidate local and foreign relief efforts under a single umbrella, forming the Flint Federation of Jewish Charities, a nonprofit organization modeled on those in other cities. They met with only partial success, the community unable to agree on a list of priorities and some members unwilling to give up favored causes, including Zionism, to pursue a common agenda. The limited support for the Flint Federation demonstrated the depth of the community's division and the inability of prominent lay members to broker a compromise.[82] After several years of frustration, in May 1941 the Flint Federation decided to address this disunity head-on by surveying its causes and its extent. With the concurrence of some other Jewish organizations in Flint, the federation commissioned a self-study to conduct a census of the city's Jewish population and survey its members' views on a broad range of topics, from the proper content of religious education to the most important charitable endeavors. In October one of the authors of the report, Julian Krolik of Detroit, came to Flint and presided over a meeting in the Durant Hotel on "Local Community Problems—The Flint Self-Study," his presence evoking the community's history. The son of Flint's own Ida Gertrude Brown Krolik and the grandson of pioneering settler Henry Brown, he presented findings that pointed to wide variations in how community members conceived of Judaism, lack of cooperation among community organizations, and a need for greater coordination of activities.

That Flint Jewry required more integrated organizational efforts was an unsurprising and self-validating conclusion, affirming the premise of the institution that had authorized the study; in future it provided a rhetorical platform for the federation's actions and expansion. Less clear is the impact that its more substantive findings, on the demography and attitudes of members of Flint's Jewish community, had on the evolution of organizational life.[83] The rush of international events seems to have overwhelmed any attention the report otherwise might have received. Only two months after the meeting at the Durant Hotel, the United States joined the twentieth century's second world war, and Flint Jewry's attention became riveted on the war effort.

Even before American entry into the war, the community had witnessed a trickle of refugees fleeing the tide of fascism and anti-Semitism washing across the face of Europe. Like Jews elsewhere in America, beginning in the mid 1930s those in Flint increasingly had looked across the ocean, wondering about the fate of families left behind, such profound worries perhaps fueling their controversies with each other. In the debate over how to help European Jewry the stakes were incalculably high. The story of one such refugee, who came to Flint in 1943, provides a telling example.

Hermine Gruner, always called "Mimi," was born in Vienna during the last year of World War I.[84] She recalls growing up in a large family who lived modestly, her father owning two small stores in Austria's cosmopolitan capital city. The German annexation of Austria in 1938 brought their tranquil life to an end, as the anti-Semitic laws of the Third Reich went into effect, banning Jews from employment, elections, schooling, and accommodations while requiring them to carry identification papers. Vienna's Jews faced harassment and violence daily. On 9 November came the rampage known as Kristallnacht, "Night of Broken Glass," as mobs throughout Germany, Austria, and other German-held territories smashed windows, looted stores, burned synagogues, and attacked Jews on the street and in their homes, murdering nearly a hundred, injuring thousands more. In the following days, ruffians forced Jewish women, including two of Mimi's sisters, to scrub city streets on their hands and knees. Arrests followed, not of the perpetrators of violence but of their victims, with many shipped to the Dachau or Buchenwald concentration camps. Mimi's father was imprisoned and released, "his hair [turned] gray" and his mind made up to hide his family and escape to the United States.

The Gruner family stayed several nights in a nearby building, the housekeeper lying to the police that no Jews were there. Mimi's betrothed, Joseph Hanflik, wanted her to leave Vienna immediately with him, but her mother insisted that the couple first be married by a rabbi. After the risky and clandestine ceremony, Mimi and Joseph Hanflik traveled five hundred miles by train to Aachen, a city in northwestern Germany on the border with Belgium. They managed to walk across the border, Joseph's command of French helping them arrange a ride to Paris. Thereafter they relied mostly on kin. One of Joseph's cousins found them a small apartment in Paris. After six weeks, one of Mimi's sisters brought them to Antwerp, Belgium, where she lived. Soon others in the Gruner family arrived in Antwerp, where Mimi stayed for fifteen months with her parents, a brother, and his wife and child. Since as Jews and foreign nationals they could not obtain regular employment and because they had to pay dearly for their living expenses, their reserves of cash, jewels, and other valuables dwindled rapidly.

Meanwhile, like thousands of others, they waited anxiously for approval of their applications for immigration, receiving financial help from the Hebrew Immigrant Aid Society (HIAS) and assistance in obtaining visas from an American patron of the family. Joseph, who had an aunt in New Jersey, gained the proper papers late in 1939, but Mimi and other family members had to "wait for our quota to come." Remarkably, all managed to emigrate in the next several months, before the German advance trapped so many other would-be refugees. Mimi left Belgium on 8 April 1940; the German army launched a surprise attack on Denmark and Norway the following day, invaded the Netherlands and Belgium a month later, and marched into Paris in June. Joining her husband and brother Max in Chicago, three years later she and Joseph moved to Flint, where her parents as well as her sisters Stella Koenig and Fay Parnes and their husbands had settled. Adding to the Gruner family reunion, another sister and her

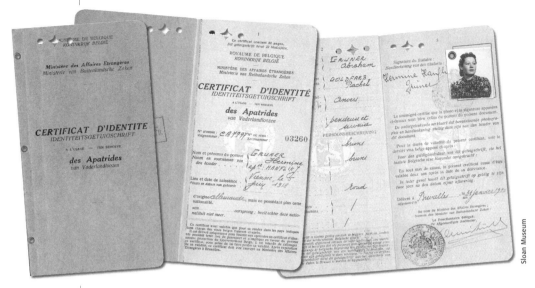

Belgian identity papers issued to Hermine (Gruner) Hanflik, 31 January 1940. The twenty-one-year-old had escaped from Vienna the year before. She left Belgium on 8 April 1940 to join her refugee husband in New York.

Koenig's Market, 1405 North Street, ca. 1946. Stella (Gruner) Koenig and her husband Herbert fled Vienna in November 1938 as the campaign against Jews escalated into mass arrests. Settling in Flint, they opened this grocery store, stocking it with name-brand American foods, including dairy products, soft drinks, and sliced white bread.

husband, Anna and Alan Berg, also came to Flint. All three couples set up grocery stores, Mimi and Joseph receiving a loan from a member of the local Jewish community to buy a small building, where they sold goods on the first floor and lived in an apartment upstairs.

Such reunions were rare and extraordinarily precious. A more common story is that of family members on separate sides of the Atlantic, millions of those in Europe killed in the genocide. One example provides a glimpse into the unfathomable pain and destruction of these years. In 1934, after nearly two decades of separation, Mala Vosczyna wrote from Poland to her son Morris Weinstein (his name changed upon immigration), asking that he consult with his father about plans to bring her and their other two sons, both now married, to Flint.[85] Instead her husband had decided to return to Poland, reconstituting the family in his native village and bringing them his savings from America. Married and with three sons, Morris stayed in Flint, where he was co-owner of a beverage bottling company. Later all but one of the Vosczyna family members in Poland perished in the Holocaust; only Morris's brother Sam, a prisoner of war in a labor camp, survived.

WARTIME IN THE INDUSTRIAL CITY

Early in 1942, just months after the United States entered World War II, Jewish war veterans unveiled a plaque at Temple Beth El listing the names of all in the Flint Jewish community who previously had served in the American military. By late 1945, 174 more names had been added to the list, including those of five men killed during the war.[86] For many in the city's Jewish community, as for thousands of other Flint men and women in uniform during World War II, patriotism motivated military service. Grateful for the freedom and opportunity he had found in America, Saul Gorne enlisted in 1942 because, "I owe[d] this country a lot." Yet for Jewish Americans love of country often commingled with the desire to demonstrate specifically Jewish commitment to the war effort, thereby blunting domestic anti-Semitism, and even more with desperation at the plight of Jews abroad, particularly as reports of the genocide became more widely known. Gilbert Rubenstein, who served as a master sergeant, recalled, "I had a very, very strong feeling that Jews were being killed and that we can't afford or permit or allow Hitler to win . . . and not because I was going to help win [the conflict], but I thought the name Rubenstein might look good on an army roster."[87]

Feelings of patriotism mixed with a determination to fight for the survival of the Jewish people also animated those on the home front. Under the determined leadership of Dora Gold, for example, the Congregation Beth Israel sisterhood turned to fundraising for the war effort, selling over a million dollars worth of bonds and receiving national recognition for the accomplishment.[88] Given the rationing of some consumer goods such as gasoline, meat, coffee, and sugar, and the overall shortage of many others, including clothing, shoes, and construction materials, many Flint residents had

Sloan Museum

Charles Weinstein, ca. 1943. Weinstein served as Radarman Second Class in the Navy. Son of Polish immigrant Morris Weinstein, who died in 1939, after his military service Charles returned to Flint and resumed management of his late father's beverage bottling business. His grandparents, uncles, aunts, and cousins perished in Poland.

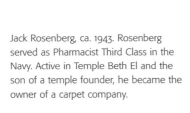

Jack Rosenberg, ca. 1943. Rosenberg served as Pharmacist Third Class in the Navy. Active in Temple Beth El and the son of a temple founder, he became the owner of a carpet company.

Sloan Museum

few outlets for spending; consequently war bonds represented both a ready investment and a gesture of loyalty. That so many had money to save reflected the rapid turnaround in Flint's economy.

Conversion to military production began in earnest during 1942, the city once more becoming a major center of industrial production. Employees at AC Spark Plug turned out machine guns; those at Buick built aircraft engines, tanks, and tank destroyers; and workers at Chevrolet assembled army vehicles. In the small suburban town of Grand Blanc, just south of Flint, the government erected a modern facility to produce tanks. By the fall of 1942 local factories already had achieved an impressive record of military production. In recognition of the city's contribution to the war effort, on the first anniversary of the attack on Pearl Harbor the government sponsored an "Army Salute to Flint." The same day that Elmer Berger became a founder of the American Council for Judaism, city residents watched with pride as a cavalcade of Flint–built troop trucks and tanks rolled down South Saginaw Street.

Sloan Museum

Beecher Department Store, 5322 North Saginaw Street, ca. 1943. By selling a broad range of goods that appealed to factory workers and staying open seven days a week, proprietors Isadore and Morris Goldenberg tried to stave off competition from chain stores, which began cropping up during the early 1940s. The store was located just north of the city limits.

As in the 1920s, the city, and now its suburban fringe, became a magnet for those seeking work. Wartime production resulted in the creation of twenty-five thousand production jobs in Flint factories, and even more workers were needed to replace the twenty-eight thousand Genesee County men and women who enlisted or were drafted into military service between 1941 and 1945.[89] Many of the newcomers to the factories were women and African Americans, including migrants from the South. By the middle of the decade Flint's population approached its pre-Depression peak of 165,000, and by war's end tents again housed those unable to find other lodgings. Reflecting the city's shifting demography, the ill-housed workers of the 1940s tended to be native-born and black.[90]

For Jewish storekeepers the city's recovery meant better times. The city's reputation as a good place to do business encouraged the extended Gruner family to gather here, reestablishing themselves in the grocery trade. Longtime resident Julius Hurand, his son serving in the army in Europe, started a new business in 1942, the "Buttercup Pastry Shop," in a neighborhood a mile north of the central business district. The bakery became popular with workers from the nearby Buick plant and with middle-class families, many of them Jewish, who occupied substantial houses built during the

Sloan Museum

Display window at the Vogue, ca. 1944. The patriotic display, complete with a cardboard tank, features work clothes designed for women with factory jobs. Across the river, women and men at the Buick plant produced the M18 "Hellcat" tank destroyer.

1920s. This tree-lined residential area, with its pockets of commercial shops, flourished during and after the war, as did the even newer "Beecher-Ballenger" section of the city, which took its name from the intersection of two major streets on the city's northwest side. Located a mile west of the Chevy engine plant, the area housed residents whose incomes climbed as distance from the GM plant increased. Near the working-class end of North Saginaw Street, just beyond the city limits, Isadore and Morris Goldenberg opened a one-story department store that stocked both foodstuffs and hardware and was open seven days a week. The brothers optimistically declared their business the "North End's Foremost Working-Man's Store."

Meanwhile established businesses tried to keep up with the changing times, including the crippling shortage of customary wares. Its regular stock of upscale women's clothing in short supply, for example, the Vogue turned to selling apparel designed for women in industrial jobs. On its racks stylish silk dresses gave way to utilitarian cotton snap-fronted work suits. In patriotic window displays the store advised potential customers that since "Every Second Counts" in fighting the war on the home front, they should be sure to purchase the "quick-to-get-into" fashions. Appeals to buy war bonds completed the store's transformation of its image during the war years.

With so many community members in the service and so many on the home front

Sloan Museum

Members of the Chimovitz family and their friends gather for Rosh Hashanah dinner, September 1944. They appear ready to begin the first course of the meal to celebrate the Jewish New Year. Nate Chimovitz, Ann Chimovitz, Geraldine Voight, Louis Chimovitz, Helen Chimovitz, Mark Voight, Julia Gross, Bob Chimovitz, Margie Chimovitz, Henry Gross, Bridgee White, Sara Klein, David Klein (*left to right*). Two family members are absent because serving in the military: Irving R. Chimovitz and Charles White.

working long hours in family businesses, Jewish organizational life declined. Both Congregation Beth Israel and Temple Beth El postponed plans for new facilities. As the war raged, religious observance took on special meaning for some, while family and community gatherings offered occasions to share worries about the safety of loved ones in combat and about the plight of European Jewry. Concerned by evidence that suggested the persistence of anti-Semitism in the United States, the temple's new rabbi, Canadian-born Morton M. Applebaum, sought to foster better relations with the local Christian churches.[91] His efforts to spur interfaith activities culminated in September 1945 when Temple Beth El hosted a highly successful "Children's Harvest Festival," where Christian children joined in the celebration of Sukkot, a holiday commemorating the wandering of the Jewish people in the wilderness.[92]

Thus four months after the defeat of Germany and only weeks after the surrender of Japan, Jewish and non-Jewish young people sat together in a temple to hear a story of deliverance from evil and unite in a prayer of thanksgiving. The war that had cost fifty million lives, including the systematic extermination of six million Jews, was

Sloan Museum

Temple Beth El, 1945. The sanctuary on Liberty Street filled with Jewish and Christian children at an interfaith "Children's Harvest Festival" held weeks after the end of World War II.

over. The unthinkable had occurred. How could Flint's Jewish community face a world so dreadfully altered? Confronted with the horrors of the past and the uncertainties of the future, how should its members proceed? In the years ahead, as the United States became the center of world Jewry and the establishment of a Jewish homeland became a major global issue, no single answer would emerge. Yet in the first few months after the end of the war, a few actions seemed clear. The first duty was sorrowful: to begin mourning the dead. The second was joyous: to welcome back those who had served their country and their community.

On an evening in September 1945, Congregation Beth Israel held a reception for all of the city's returning Jewish veterans. Gilbert Rubenstein's mother urged him to attend, but the decorated soldier was reluctant, telling her, "Ma, I'm not going to go. I haven't got any clothes." He recalls that she insisted, "You can go in your uniform," adding, "I'm so proud of you." He went to the community celebration with other servicemen, and when they entered the synagogue "everybody got up and applauded." For Rubenstein, "[i]t was a very exciting night in my life." He later married one of the young women he met that night, Florence Bayliss.[93]

The homecoming was an important occasion for Flint Jewry as a whole. Gathering to acknowledge the service and sacrifice of its young people, the community strengthened ties across generations and symbolically bound its diverse members together in the wake of their era's great conflict. The ex–GIs, like the cohort of veterans a quarter century before, returned to a vibrant, prosperous Flint. In 1945 their nation stood at the pinnacle of global economic and political power in a drastically transformed world. For three decades after the Second World War, Flint partook in the tremendous expansion of the U.S. economy, the automobile town representing the manufacturing might of this abbreviated "American Century." The evolution of Flint Jewry reflected the ebullience of this postwar boom time, but simultaneously displayed a current of despair mixed with anxiety that stemmed from the legacy of war, the persistence of discrimination, and the reemergence of internal divisions.

CHAPTER THREE

A Golden Age?

POSTWAR PROSPECTS

Americans greeted the end of World War II, first the victory in Europe in May 1945 and then the victory over Japan in August, with relief and joy, leavened by sorrow for the unprecedented toll in death and destruction the conflict had wrought. In the midst of celebration, many remembered the hard years of the 1930s and worried about the future. Would the peace they had yearned for bring with it a swift cooling off of their red-hot economy, the nation plunging from its unprecedented height of wartime production into another lengthy and severe depression? Returning veterans wondered whether they would find jobs and housing. Consumers were concerned that prices on goods would spike once government controls on inflation were lifted. Organized labor feared that a slow conversion to peacetime manufacturing would result in massive lay-offs. At the same time industrial workers were resolved to rid themselves of the many restrictions under which they had toiled during the war, including a controversial "no-strike" pledge that the United Automobile Workers (UAW) and other unions had signed shortly after Pearl Harbor. In Flint, where factories had mobilized rapidly and thoroughly for military production, the prospect of converting to a vibrant peacetime economy appeared especially daunting: housing was in critically short supply; prices on automobiles were poised to jump; and rank-and-file UAW members strongly supported the idea of a company-wide strike against General Motors (GM) in order to gain higher wages, obtain a voice in corporate decisions, and keep costs for vehicles at prewar levels, thereby curbing inflation.

In this restive climate, early in 1945 the Buick Division of General Motors launched a public relations campaign on and about its home turf. Buick hired author Carl Crow, known for a 1939 book on how to market American goods to China's "four hundred million customers," to write a history of the "interesting and dynamic city of Flint." Crow's breezy and selective chronicle lauded GM (the "Child of Flint"); omitted mention of the sit-down strike and the UAW; and proclaimed that city residents "fac[ed] the future with a confidence that the period of transition may be difficult, but that peacetime years will bring employment and prosperity."[1] Indeed, Crow concluded, "If every industrial community in America could look toward the future with the confidence enjoyed by the people of Flint, the country would have no cause for concern over the possibility of a postwar depression."[2] According to Crow, the city owed its rosy prospects, as its happy past, mainly to the enlightened and decisive leadership of the auto company's executives.

In many respects, Crow's *The City of Flint Grows Up: The Success Story of an American Community* constitutes merely another installment in a long line of boosterish literature. Yet two qualities of the 1945 book mark a development in the genre and have portent beyond it. "Buick is Flint," Crow proudly declared, "and Flint is Buick," and by "Buick" he clearly meant the company's managers, not its workers.[3] Thus he equated—and conflated—not the industry, but its leadership, with the city as a whole. Moreover Crow did so at the behest of that leadership and,

Flint and transportation have come a long way together. Their mutual future is limitless. From Flint's first days to now, and into Flint's future: Flint equals transportation; transportation equals Flint.

—Flint Board of Education, "The Background Story of Flint and Transportation," 1965

by extension, the executives of the largest manufacturing corporation in the world. At this dawning of the "American Century," giant firms no longer needed putative civic organizations, such as the Chamber of Commerce, to serve as the authors of pro-business texts. GM boldly and openly pronounced its claims itself: the corporation *was* the city; its interests were those of the public.

In the postwar era this creed, so candidly expressed in Buick's authorized version of Flint's past, became a major theme in American life. It was only ten years after Crow's book appeared that his story's greatest hero, Harlow Curtice, then the head of GM, became *Time* magazine's "Man of the Year." By 1955 the equivalence of corporate and public interest had become national. As Charles Wilson, Curtice's predecessor, explained, "What is good for our country is good for General Motors, and vice versa."[4] Yet looking back on these years, a member of Flint's Jewish community offered his own version of this 1950s dictum. "GM was good without me," Lou Kasle quipped, "but I wasn't good without GM."[5] The wealthy scrap dealer deftly captured the corporation's true relationship to the residents of its hometown: rather than having some fictive identity with the public welfare of the city (much less the nation), GM wielded overwhelming economic power over Flint, defining the context in which local residents earned their livelihoods.

Among Flint Jewry, Kasle was unusual because his business relied largely on contracts with GM. After World War II, as they had since the mid nineteenth century, most members of the city's Jewish community made their living in retail trade or, increasingly, in the professions. Yet whatever their occupation, the vast majority of Flint's residents, Jews and non-Jews alike, depended directly or indirectly for their financial well-being on the prosperity of the firm some wryly dubbed "Generous Motors." In these salad days of the nation's manufacturing might, Flint represented not a micro-cosm of America but a distillation of its key economic feature. As Crow admiringly, but accurately, observed, "What makes the story of Flint significant is the fact that the integration of the American people with industry is perhaps more closely illustrated here than in any other American city."[6]

Just months after *The City of Flint Grows Up* appeared, the UAW made good on its threat of a nationwide strike against GM. The strike began in late November 1945 and lasted sixteen weeks, its results setting the tone for labor-management relations in Flint throughout the postwar years. GM refused to allow union inspection of company finances and maintained strict control over managerial decisions, including the price it set on vehicles; the union achieved increased wages and expanded benefits for its members, including vacation pay and overtime premiums. As a consequence, over the next three decades UAW members became among the highest-paid industrial work-ers in the nation and their union one of the country's most prominent. In Flint and elsewhere rank-and-file activism declined within the UAW, some longtime militants silenced by the virulent anti-Communism of the cold war.[7] Thus at the level of leader-ship, if not on the shop floor, the company and the union reached a rapprochement, a broad framework of labor-management relations that relied on GM's continued dom-inance in auto production and America's supremacy in manufacturing.[8] For a quarter century this deal between capital and labor, epitomized in the economic dynamics of Flint, largely stayed intact.[9]

BOOMING PRODUCTION AND CONSUMPTION

With the signing of the GM-UAW contract in March 1946, nearly a year after the nation's victory over Germany, the postwar boom in Flint and Genesee County began in earnest. The city's auto plants churned out cars and trucks, while for several years the factory in nearby Grand Blanc continued to produce tanks and other military equipment for America's peacetime army as well as manufacturing vehicles for the domestic market. The area's plants sustained a staggering scale of production, the nation's huge pent-up demand pushing output to record levels. Buick, for example, manufactured—and sold—more than half a million automobiles in 1950 alone, the bulk of them built in Flint.[10] GM as a whole had produced twenty-five million cars between its founding in 1908 and 1940, yet even taking into account the wartime con-version to military production, the corporation needed only fourteen years to build its next twenty-five million passenger vehicles. When GM produced its fifty-millionth car in 1954, it chose Flint as the site for celebration, the corporation's birthplace still the center of its far-flung empire.[11] Fittingly, the next year Flint Division Chevrolet plants set another production milestone, workers on three shifts smashing corporate output records by turning out more than ten thousand vehicles in a single twenty-four

**NEIGHBORHOODS, FACTORIES, AND JEWISH HOUSES OF WORSHIP,
FLINT AREA, CA. 1962**

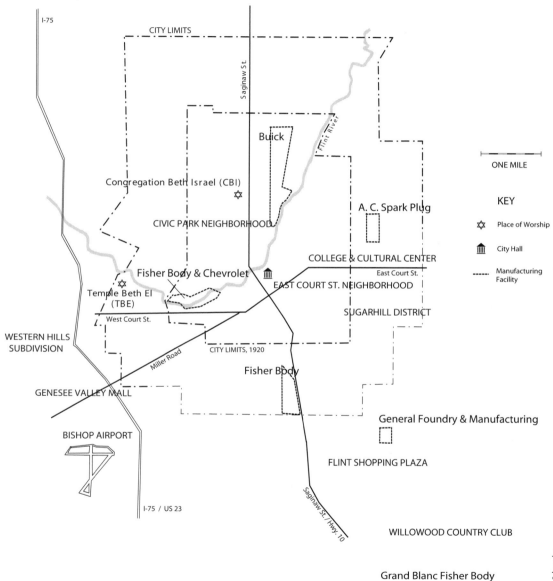

I-75

CITY LIMITS

Saginaw St.

Flint River

Buick

Congregation Beth Israel (CBI)

CIVIC PARK NEIGHBORHOOD

A. C. Spark Plug

ONE MILE

KEY

Place of Worship

City Hall

Manufacturing
Facility

COLLEGE & CULTURAL CENTER

Fisher Body & Chevrolet

East Court St.

Temple Beth El
(TBE)

EAST COURT ST. NEIGHBORHOOD

West Court St.

SUGARHILL DISTRICT

WESTERN HILLS
SUBDIVISION

CITY LIMITS, 1920

Miller Road

Fisher Body

GENESEE VALLEY MALL

General Foundry & Manufacturing

BISHOP AIRPORT

FLINT SHOPPING PLAZA

Saginaw St. / Hwy. 10

I-75 / US 23

WILLOWOOD COUNTRY CLUB

Grand Blanc Fisher Body

GRAND BLANC

Michael J. Schroeder

A crowd in front of the Vogue, 531 South Saginaw Street, 1945. Would-be bargain hunters and window shoppers mingle in front of this upscale women's clothing shop. Several African American men stand on the edges of the crowd, their marginality on the downtown sidewalk reflective of the racial segregation that characterized postwar Flint.

Sloan Museum

hour period. GM's level of investment matched these workers' output, the company greatly expanding its productive capacity in Genesee County. In the decade following the war the company enlarged and refitted older plants within Flint and, significantly, built even more massive new ones just outside the municipal boundaries, a huge complex rising on the city's southwestern border.[12] Together, the plants' workforce totaled more than eighty thousand men and women.[13]

These were heady days for Flint. By 1960 the city's population numbered close to 197,000, an increase of 20 percent within a decade; the county nearly matched this pace. More tellingly, between 1948 and 1958 the number of dwellings in the city rose by 34 percent.[14] By the mid 1950s more than three out of four Flint residents owned their homes, many getting loans through the GI bill and making payments through GM's financial arm, the General Motors Acceptance Corporation.[15] Jammed factory parking lots testified to full employment and to the growing ranks of autoworkers who consumed the product they made. As GM employees, they purchased vehicles at a substantial discount, usually financing them through the company's installment plan.

Consumption of retail goods soared as well, with shoppers crowding city stores. The rising wages and salaries of GM employees and of blue- and white-collar workers at affiliated companies throughout the area spurred sales across a wide range of businesses, many Jewish-owned. A postwar surge in credit-buying further buoyed retail trade. On downtown's South Saginaw Street, for example, customers flocked to women's apparel stores for fashions unavailable during wartime, some using the popular "lay-away" plan to purchase the latest styles. The Vogue once more showcased high-end women's dresses, and Maas Brothers, remodeled after a fire, offered an

Sloan Museum

Customers await the grand re-opening of the refurbished Maas Bros. clothing store, 538 South Saginaw Street, 1946. Across the street is Goodman's, another Jewish-owned women's apparel store.

Sloan Museum

Sign for B. F. Krasner Company, a leading jewelry store, 108 East Kearsley Street, ca. 1948. Jewish-owned stores such as Krasner's crafted advertising directed at the overwhelmingly non-Jewish population of Flint and Genesee County, such as this sign touting jewelry as the perfect Christmas gift.

Flint Journal

Exterior of a newly opened "Yankee Stores" at 3750 South Saginaw Street, near the Fisher Body plant in south Flint, 1961. The store's large parking lot had particular appeal for shoppers in this autoworkers' city. In the mid-1960s the store added a gas station.

Flint Journal

Interior of "Yankees Stores" at 3750 South Saginaw Street, 1961. Proud proprietor Joe Megdell stands on flooring that advertises the name of the business.

array of clothing and accessories aimed at a broad clientele. In 1949 these major downtown stores quietly joined forces, as Sid Melet became a partner in both. Melet proved a strong advocate for downtown retailers and Flint civic affairs while assuming a major part in Jewish organizations, this dual role presaging the budding, if limited, interaction between some Jewish businessmen and professionals and their non-Jewish counterparts.[16] Further along South Saginaw, Krasner's Jewelers found customers for its wares among both the established middle class and the increasing numbers of autoworkers hungry for the visible fruits of the "good life" that American victory had promised and that union contracts had secured.

Meanwhile entrepreneur Joe Megdell, along with his silent partner Wilbert Roberts, opened a tiny store across the river on Detroit Street, where rents were cheaper. Here they sold army surplus goods to customers who sought sturdy products at low prices, many probably having had firsthand experience with such merchandise during wartime.[17] Megdell, who also became prominent in both Jewish community affairs and Flint civic life, shared the dramatic flair for advertising that continued to make the Winegarden brothers' produce and furniture stores successful. Naming the business "Yankee Stores," Megdell blended patriotic and sports motifs into a paean to America, adopting a red, white, and blue color scheme and decorating the interior with Uncle Sam hats, copying the emblem of the era's most powerful baseball team. Like the New York Yankees, Megdell's business prospered through the 1950s and mid 1960s, the retailer pioneering the development of discount chain stores in Genesee County. When he retired in 1967, "Yankee Stores" consisted of nineteen outlets, most in Flint's growing suburban fringe.[18]

A popular downtown restaurant and delicatessen also featured a New York City theme. Opening in 1947, Uncle Bob's Diner emphasized Jewish fare, serving cheesecake advertised as "Better than Lindy's" in Times Square and offering an array of kosher and non-kosher foods from dill pickles to pastrami. Several years later partners Robert Newblatt and John Kish, a Gentile, added the more formal "Miami Room" to the diner, furnishing it in the style of the Florida vacation spot increasingly associated with East Coast Jewry. The dining room with the oceanfront atmosphere quickly became a prime spot for business meetings and shoppers' luncheons in this landlocked midwestern autotown.[19]

The expansion of M & S Beverage Company further illustrates the success of Flint's many Jewish-owned businesses during the postwar years. Founded in 1918 by Morris Weinstein and Sam Buckler, the small firm took its name from the initials of its co-owners; after Morris's death in 1939, his son Charles ran the company. By the late 1950s M & S distributed nationally known soft drinks and its own brand throughout a three-county area. Adopting a modern version of peddling, employees, including the owner and his family, drove Flint-made vehicles from store to store and door to door, picking up empty bottles and delivering cases of soda pop to groceries, restaurants, bars, social clubs, and homes. Like many members of Flint's Jewish community,

Sloan Museum

Morry Weinstein, age eleven, son of M & S Beverage owner Charles Weinstein, during a delivery in Flint's "East Court" area, a tree-lined middle- and upper-middle-class subdivision developed on the city's east side after the war, 1952.

Charles Weinstein's peacetime commercial success mixed with wartime family tragedy; as discussed in chapter two, his grandparents, uncles, and aunts had perished in Poland during the Holocaust.

EXPANDING COMMUNITY LIFE

In the postwar years the legacy of the genocide reverberated throughout American Jewry. In Flint, as elsewhere, the resettlement of refugees and survivors embodied the tie between Europe, whose Jewish population had been decimated in the previous decade, and the United States, which consequently had become home to more Jews than any other nation. While some refugees had arrived in the city before the end of the war, most came under the provisions of either the "Displaced Persons Act" of 1948 or the "Refugee Relief Act" of 1953. Nationally many received help from the Hebrew Immigrant Aid Society (HIAS) and locally from the Flint Jewish Community Council (FJCC), established in 1943 as the successor to the Flint Federation of Jewish Charities.[20] The FJCC's Resettlement Committee, chaired by Russian immigrant Rae (Kleiner) Schafer, coordinated local fund-raising and aid efforts for some forty families, providing temporary quarters for the refugees in a local hotel, then finding them

Solomon Saltiel, while serving in the Greek army, ca. 1939. Resettled in Flint as a refugee in 1955, he joined the labor force at GM's AC Spark Plug plant.

Sloan Museum

apartments, stocking kitchen shelves with groceries and closets with clothes, and referring those needing jobs to willing employers.[21] The wartime circumstances of the survivors had been harrowing and their experiences before emigration often desperate, as illustrated by the sagas of three refugees who rebuilt their lives in Flint.

Born just before World War I in Thessaloniki (Salonica) in northeastern Greece, an ethnically diverse port city with a substantial Jewish settlement, Solomon Saltiel joined the Greek army as a young man and fought against Mussolini's Italy.[22] Captured, he became a prisoner of war in Italy. Saltiel escaped but was captured again, this time by the German army. Transferred to a German prisoner of war camp, he disguised his background, relying on his ability to speak French and Italian to deceive his captors about his birthplace and his Jewishness. British prisoners aided him, sharing food and medicine and protecting his secret. Following the camp's liberation in 1945, Saltiel returned to Thessaloniki, only to discover that his mother and all his other relatives had been killed, victims of the massive deportations to Auschwitz, Buchenwald, and Dachau that had reduced the city's Jewish population from more than forty thousand to fewer than two thousand.[23] With civil war raging in Greece, he resolved to emigrate. It was not until 1955, after he had married and had two children, that HIAS managed to bring him to the United States, sending the family directly to Flint. Eager to learn English, Solomon and his wife Dora immediately enrolled in classes at the International Institute, which had moved from the working-class St. John neighborhood to a location closer to downtown. The Lebster family, whose earliest members in the city had helped resettle Jewish immigrants sent by the Industrial Removal Organization half a century before, hired Solomon to work at their scrap company. After his English improved, he took a job at GM's AC Spark Plug factory, working on the assembly line until his retirement nearly three decades later.

Sarah Feldman, who grew up near Warsaw, Poland, was also in her early twenties when fascism overtook her country.[24] She lived through the war by hiding in bushes, being sheltered by Christian friends, obtaining forged identification papers, laboring in a restaurant kitchen in Germany under her false name, and bribing or defying those who questioned her background. Having lost her husband and all but one of her relatives, at the end of the war she decided to join her brother Max Frankel in the United

States. Striking up a conversation with an American GI on the streets of Stuttgart about how she might reach Flint, Michigan, she found the soldier happy to tell her—and shortly thereafter to ask her to marry him. In 1947 the war bride and her husband joined her brother in Flint.

The story of Pepia Ruth (Naczycz) Rosenthal, known as Peppy, shares many aspects of the traumatic and heroic tales of Saltiel, Feldman, and so many other survivors.[25] Born in the Ukraine in 1935, she was a small child when the campaign against Jews began. Catholic farmers sheltered the family, but German soldiers found and killed her mother. Her father left her with the farm family and joined the underground resistance movement. Following the war father and daughter spent five years in an Italian refugee camp, and in 1950 came to Flint. Of settling in the United States, Rosenthal recalls, "I was 15. There was stability after 10 years of having no home. America was the freest nation in the world and, to a young immigrant, I took that literally."[26] Her experience of oppression as a Jew in Europe would translate into a lifelong commitment to social justice.

[T]he flight to the suburbs, the whites leaving the blacks to the center cities really started hurting retail in the mid to late sixties. . . . [T]he forties, the fifties were the peak, the pinnacle, the ultimate time of Flint's retail in downtown.

—*Michael Melet, owner of the Vogue*

Unlike Solomon Saltiel, Sarah Feldman, and Peppy Rosenthal, who put down roots in Flint, some of the refugees resettled to the "Industrial City" moved on, preferring places with larger Jewish populations, more urban amenities, and greater professional opportunities. Austrian exiles Alan and Anna (Gruner) Berg, for instance, moved to Boston.[27] To at least a few of those active in the local Jewish community, this lack of commitment to their city smacked of ingratitude, a pattern of resentment that would resurface in the late twentieth century with the arrival in Flint of refugees fleeing the Soviet Union and Eastern European nations. As one community member put it, some of the postwar newcomers helped by the FJCC "became very, very successful in a very short period," and after they "made their money, [they] took off."[28]

Despite evidence of disgruntlement among some who helped the refugees and of disappointment among some of those who received aid, on the whole the resettlement effort represented a very positive experience for the city's Jewish community. By making a new home for a few survivors, Flint Jewry united in a cause both critical to Jews around the world and expressive of the American ethos that the downtrodden could find refuge in the "nation of immigrants." Most community members recognized the importance of this opportunity, for themselves as well as for those resettled, and also realized the serious challenges of adjustment that the newcomers, witnesses to horror and usually bereft of family, had to face. For their part, those refugees who stayed in Flint seem to have adapted well, most joining the widening ranks of the city's middle class and many becoming active in Jewish communal life.

The refugees arrived when the Conservative synagogue, Congregation Beth Israel (CBI), and the Reform congregation, Temple Beth El (TBE), were in transition, both

Sloan Museum

Henry Hanflik, age four, perched on the fender of his family's shiny new car, 1948. His parents, Mimi and Joseph Hanflik, were Austrian refugees who opened a grocery store in Flint in 1943.

having outgrown their quarters and eager to construct new facilities to accommodate an increasing population. In early 1948 CBI reactivated the building committee it had established during the financially strapped 1930s; after a hard fund-raising effort, the congregation dedicated a new synagogue four years later. By then the congregation numbered nearly five hundred families. The new shul, the term commonly used for the synagogue, boasted a beautiful sanctuary, four classrooms, a large social hall that doubled as a gymnasium, and, on the lower level, a "youth canteen" equipped with a dance floor, jukebox, and tables for pool and Ping-Pong. The synagogue's architecture reflected the congregation's belief that its main goal was to raise a new generation for Conservative Judaism, both by sponsoring social activities designed for children and young people and by emphasizing formal training in language, culture, history, and traditional observances.[29] This focus on youth and an accompanying greater attention to festive family celebrations of Passover and Hanukkah, holidays occurring at about the same time as the Christian holy days of Easter and Christmas respectively, put CBI squarely in line with national trends in Judaism.[30]

Construction of this new facility had been delayed because CBI had difficulty finding an appropriate site. The congregation wanted its new building to be within walking distance of the homes of most of its members, who in the years immediately following the war remained clustered in two adjacent areas, the industrial St. John neighborhood west of the Buick plant and nearby more middle-class Civic Park. Yet a sufficiently large plot proved difficult to locate proximate to these sections of the city. The lot finally selected stood at the corner of Hamilton and Oren avenues, on the edge of both neighborhoods and just a mile northwest of the location of the former shul.

Even before the new CBI opened in 1952, however, it faced problems in location and adequacy of facilities. The movement of Jewish families out of the St. John and Civic Park neighborhoods had gotten underway, a trickle of relocation to new subdivisions within the city and to outlying suburban areas that became a flood fifteen years

Look, Nov. 29, 1955

Eager students in a Hebrew School class at Congregation Beth Israel, Hamilton and Oren Avenues, 1955. This photograph was included in William Attwood's article, "The Position of the Jews in America Today."

Four cousins dress up as Queen Esther to celebrate Purim at the newly opened Congregation Beth Israel, ca. 1953. A holiday celebrated in February or March, Purim commemorates the deliverance of the Jewish community in Persia from massacre during the time of Queen Esther. Their immigrant grandmother made their dresses and paper crowns. Eileen Parnes, Linda Hanflik, Diana Berg, and Florence Koenig (*left to right*).

Sloan Museum

Sloan Museum

A bat mitzvah party for daughters of Congregation Beth Israel members, Durant Hotel, 1961. Debbie Lovitky, Andrea Wolin, Lee Bernstein, Julie Colish, and Nancy Leavitt (*left to right*).

later. Moreover, a 1950 ruling by the Rabbinical Assembly, Conservative Judaism's association of rabbis, had sanctioned the use of automobiles for transportation to Sabbath services. At a stroke, the close proximity of the soon-to-be dedicated synagogue to its congregants' current residences became nonessential. The next year another Rabbinical Assembly pronouncement emphasized boosting children's attendance at Hebrew School and Sunday school, rendering the four classrooms in CBI's new building inadequate to accommodate its large crop of baby boom youngsters.[31] To cope, the new synagogue was forced to use its choir loft, the existence of which signaled another innovation in Conservative practice, as an additional classroom. Compounding pressure on the shul's facilities was the growing trend within Conservatism to provide girls as well as boys with a religious education, a movement most CBI congregants thoroughly endorsed. By 1956 the synagogue proudly began the practice of celebrating the bat mitzvah, a coming-of-age ceremony for girls that parallels the bar mitzvah, a traditional rite for boys held at age thirteen.[32]

The smaller Reform congregation, totaling about two hundred families, acted more quickly after the war to build a new home.[33] At the insistence of their rabbi, Morton M. Applebaum, as early as 1943 TBE began conducting surveys to plan for a new facility, and by 1950 constructed a new building on a six-acre lot in the rapidly growing "Beecher-Ballenger" neighborhood. Located just within the municipal limits on

Flint's western edge, the new TBE was more than three miles from its former down-town site but very close to several developing subdivisions on the city's outskirts and to a major highway, making it readily accessible by car to congregants in Grand Blanc and other growing suburban communities to the south and north. The spacious building featured a combined sanctuary and social hall seating nearly a thousand, a modern kitchen, dressing rooms, and a gymnasium with a large stage. Its facilities easily accommodated athletic events, "Temple Teen" dances, fund-raising dinners, and productions by the "Temple Players," a group of sixty young adults who staged theatri-cal fare ranging from dramas to musical comedies.[34] Moreover, its classroom wing offered enough space to conduct religious school for more than a hundred children and host meetings for temple organizations and civic groups, including its own Girl Scout troop, a chapter of the well-known national organization, the vast majority of whose members were Christian. Moored firmly in the Jewish community and exempli-fying the boom in temple and synagogue building and religious education sweeping postwar Judaism, as a Reform congregation TBE downplayed traditional observances, revamped long-standing rites, and self-consciously stressed its ties to the American mainstream.[35]

Significantly, the dedication of TBE prompted congratulatory letters from the top officials of the state and the nation, with Governor G. Mennen ("Soapy") Williams and President Harry Truman sending personal greetings to Rabbi Applebaum. Democrats, the governor and the president recognized the increasing importance of Jewish voters to the party coalition forged during the 1930s by Williams's hero and Truman's pred-ecessor, Franklin Roosevelt.[36] To a great extent, Flint's postwar Jewish community embraced their part in the Democratic coalition, an allegiance expressed by both tem-ple and synagogue members. One of the most successful events hosted by CBI's men's club, for instance, was a 1954 address by Eleanor Roosevelt, widow of the New Deal leader and wartime commander-in-chief, and in her own right an important figure in party politics and national and international affairs. Long admired in Flint, her repu-tation as a civil rights advocate made her a particular favorite among American Jewry.[37] She thrilled a packed auditorium of nine hundred listeners, relating her recent travels in the young nation of Israel and calling for peace in the Mideast. Her subject as well her person drew the rapt crowd. As we discuss throughout this chapter, even more than the plight of the displaced persons, support for Israel came increasingly to unite a broad cross-section of Flint Jewry in the postwar decades, as it did Jewish commu-nities throughout America.

Meanwhile, the establishment of the synagogue and temple in different areas of Flint symbolized the continued social distance between them, and the extent of this gap was an enduring matter of contention among those active in Jewish community life during Flint's heyday. Lawyer Clifford Hart, a TBE stalwart and son of an influential early member, downplayed the institutions' separation. Born in 1935 and recalling his youth and young adult years, Hart maintained: "There was a myth going around here

Sloan Museum

Aerial view of recently constructed Temple Beth El (*center*) at the intersection of Beecher Road and Ballenger Highway, on Flint's rapidly expanding far west side, 1950. The temple is flanked by two medical facilities: the county's tuberculosis sanitarium (*left*) and a private hospital.

Sloan Museum

Members of the "Temple Players" following a 1948 performance of *Good News*, a hit 1930s musical comedy of college life set in the 1920s and revived in a popular 1947 film. Amateur theatrical groups were prevalent in postwar America, and the enthusiasm for this activity at Temple Beth El influenced the design of the building dedicated in 1950. In the new temple the players could mount more lavish productions.

STRENGTH AND BEAUTY ARE IN HIS SANCTUARY

Sloan Museum

Temple Beth El religious school, 1952. The rows of girls and boys attending classes in the temple's modern school wing testify to the postwar baby boom that expanded the ranks of Flint's Jewish community.

that there was antagonism between the temple and the shul. I grew up in the temple and never saw any antagonism."[38] Yet physician Saul Gorne, a longtime temple member and contemporary of Hart's father, disagreed: "We've had two completely separate establishments, two independent places, as if [we] didn't know each other."[39] Similarly, Caroline (Wise) Panzer, a young teacher who came to Flint in 1950 with her dentist husband, remembered being surprised at the poor relations that existed between CBI and TBE. She and husband Milt, both raised in the Reform tradition, she in Baltimore and he in Philadelphia, joined the temple just after construction of its new facility, but a half century later she remained disturbed and puzzled by the "animosity" that existed for decades between the two religious pillars of Flint Jewry.[40] Natalie Pelavin, also a newcomer to Flint, saw the same dynamic at work. She settled in the city a decade later than Panzer, after she "married a Flint guy," lawyer Michael Pelavin, whom she had met while an undergraduate at the University of Michigan. A member of the Reform congregation, she recalled several "funny experiences" that occurred when women in TBE and CBI undertook joint projects. "One time cooking for a carnival," she explained, "we had to go buy pots to cook kosher hot dogs in and [one of the TBE women] just went berserk. [She didn't see] how she could be expected to know [how to keep kosher]." Pelavin told her, "you're [just] boiling hot dogs"—an adroit admonition to stick to the job at hand and stop insulting Conservative observance of dietary laws, foodways that Reform Judaism had abandoned in the previous century.[41]

Trivial on its surface, the incident exposed a persistent disagreement within Flint Jewry about the nature of religious practice, a division woven into

Sloan Museum

Jewish Girl Scout troop meeting at Temple Beth El, 1952. As younger "Brownie" scouts look on, Jewish Girl Scouts pledge allegiance to the American flag. In the 1950s the Flint Board of Education led a movement to organize Girl Scout and Boy Scout chapters throughout the city, with troops meeting in schools, social halls, and religious institutions.

both congregational practice and domestic life, and with substantial meaning for many in the community. That the temple was widely perceived to have a wealthier and more highly educated membership than the synagogue only deepened the affront some shul congregants felt at what seemed to them the patronizing behavior of some TBE congregants.[42] This division along Reform and Conservative lines was common in American Judaism, but had a more personal dimension in Flint's small community than it did in cities with larger Jewish populations. As their new facilities attested, in the postwar years of expansion CBI and TBE could each afford to host a range of events focused exclusively on its own membership and did so, with programs sponsored by youth organizations, men's clubs, and, especially, the sisterhoods, which remained at the center of social life at each congregation.[43] The women's groups spearheaded some joint activities between the synagogue and temple, only a few marred by unfortunate episodes such as that recalled by Natalie Pelavin. In 1957, for example, the CBI sisterhood initiated a successful luncheon series to which they invited their TBE counterparts. Just a year after completion of the new synagogue, the sisterhoods supported the first of what became an annual tradition, a party for students at both religious schools to celebrate the beginning of Hanukkah, an eight-day holiday marked by the lighting of candles.[44] Yet each congregation also continued to host its own separate Hanukkah party for children, each serving latkes (potato pancakes) to its students, but only CBI observing kosher practices at its party. Other cooperative activities in these years displayed the same tentative and limited quality. Consequently, within Flint's Jewish community Reform and Conservative members were unlikely to meet each other through their congregations.

Young people who belonged to CBI and TBE more often met in their neighborhoods; through the public schools, where they constituted a tiny minority of students; at programs hosted by local Zionist organizations (such as Junior Hadassah); at the speeches and debates held by the Jewish Young People's League; or, most often, through the highly popular recreational activities and dances sponsored by B'nai B'rith

The children of CBI members Bess and Art Hurand light the Hanukkah lamp at their home, 1955. Lynne (*standing*), and Robbie, David, and Gary (*left to right*). This photograph was included in Attwood's article, with a caption that described the lamp as "a symbol of religious freedom," underscoring the author's view of this family, and by extension Jews throughout the United States, as distinct in religion but thoroughly American in basic values.

Look, Nov. 29, 1955

and its youth auxiliaries. B'nai B'rith's high school boy's club, Aleph Zadik Aleph or AZA, was especially lively.[45] Established during the Depression but fairly inactive through the war years, Flint's AZA quickly revived, holding Ping–Pong matches, basketball games, and other athletic events at both the shul and temple and hosting tournaments at a gymnasium in downtown's cavernous Industrial Mutual Association.[46] Flint also had an active B'nai B'rith Girls Club, which, along with Junior Hadassah, supported some recreational activities for young women. Yet even during these peak years, athletic opportunities for Jewish youth were constrained by the lack of a community center or its analogues, a Young Men's or Women's Hebrew Association.[47] In part to fill this gap for their daughters and sons but also to complement the religious schools' education, in 1954 Flint Jewry established a summer day–camp program, where children from kindergarten to high school could study Jewish culture amidst a program of music, handicrafts, and sports. Named Camp Maccabee, after the general whose victory Hanukkah commemorates, the camp had no permanent site, and was instead held at various locations in the nearby countryside.

For many adults, social life within the Jewish community in the postwar period similarly revolved mainly around events sponsored by the shul or the temple, with the calendar filled with dinners, card parties, lectures, picnics, and dances, including the black–tie "Pink Ball" that the CBI sisterhood hosted annually. B'nai B'rith's bowling league had a large and loyal following, too. Yet especially after the completion of the new temple and synagogue, much of the community's attention and its fund–raising were directed to the work of the Flint Jewish Community Council, both its local efforts, including the resettlement program, and its aid to Israel.

One of the most significant geopolitical outcomes of World War II, the creation of the state of Israel, endorsed by the United Nations (UN) in 1948 despite the outrage and resistance of Arabs throughout the Mideast, unleashed an outpouring of elation, hope, and material support from most Jewish communities throughout the world, but especially from those in the United States. Zionism—at the turn of the twentieth century a cause backed by a small minority of American Jews and by the 1930s a more consequential but still contested movement—gained increasing support in the wake of the

Holocaust. The wartime refusal by the United States and other countries to open their borders and accept those attempting to escape the genocide demonstrated to many American Jews that it fell to them, rather than to supposedly sympathetic pluralist nations, to insure that Jews "never again" would be without refuge in the face of potentially deadly outbursts of anti-Semitism. Thus at the end of the war many American Jews rushed to embrace the establishment, protection, and development of a Jewish homeland in Palestine. By 1968, Israel's twentieth anniversary of nationhood, the Zionist cause had become a cornerstone of American Judaism, with an overwhelming majority of American Jews supporting the state of Israel.

There were no Jews on the boards of the Institute of Music or the Art Institute, with maybe one or two exceptions. United Way or Red Cross rarely had a Jewish board member. Of course there never used to be women, forget Jewish women.

—*Natalie Pelavin, community volunteer, recalling the 1960s*

Flint Jewry followed the national pattern. Activists of long-standing, such as members of the local chapters of the Zionist Organization of America and Hadassah, stepped up their efforts to promote Jewish settlement in Palestine during World War II, and thereafter to help Israel economically, politically, diplomatically, and, in some cases, militarily. Many community members who before the war had taken little interest in the topic of a Jewish homeland became convinced of its critical importance. The case of Art Hurand, who saw the death camps while serving as a U.S. army captain, was perhaps the most dramatic, but most of Flint's Jewish residents felt some personal, often intimate and deep, tie to those lost, and saw support for Israel as a way to express their sorrow at the past and hope for the future.[48] Lou Kasle, a Zionist even before the Holocaust, retained his membership in CBI but in 1943 became an associate member of TBE to show his approval at the departure of the temple's nationally prominent anti-Zionist rabbi Elmer Berger.[49] As discussed previously, at the time of its appearance Berger's *Flint Plan*, outlining ways to thwart the spread of Zionism in the United States, had made many area Jews both angry and ashamed; after the war, most regarded the rabbi's anti-Zionist position as disreputable and even self-hating, and subsequently his career became effaced from community memory (and when mentioned, often deplored).[50]

In the postwar years the FJCC became the foremost local vehicle for fund-raising for Israel. The council funneled its donations through the United Jewish Appeal (UJA), an international organization founded following Kristallnacht (Night of Broken Glass), the 1938 Nazi rampage against Jews in Germany and Austria. From the outset the UJA pursued a dual mission: assisting those who sought refuge from anti-Semitism and building a Jewish state in Palestine. Flint's donations to the UJA were modest during the war, amounting to less than $20,000 annually, but by 1946 this

The "Campaign Cabinet" of the Flint Jewish Community Council at a luncheon in the Durant Hotel, 1950. By joining the cabinet, these fifty prominent business and professional men agreed to make sizeable personal donations and raise monies from others in Flint's Jewish community to help local causes, resettle refugees, and provide support for Israel. Absent from this picture because excluded from this inner circle, Jewish women were nonetheless important donors and fund-raisers for the council.

total jumped to more than $172,000 and after the announcement of the UN's recognition of Israel to more than $236,000, an increase exceeding the average for U.S. Jewish communities by 60 percent. Recognizing the local Jewish community's willingness to finance an expanded FJCC as well as bolster its support for the UJA, in 1948 the council hired its first executive director; two years later it began issuing a newsletter, the *Flint Jewish Reporter*, which remains the primary vehicle for news about the area's Jewish community.[51]

Participation in FJCC cut across congregational lines and drew in some of the few Flint Jews who chose not to affiliate with either the synagogue or the temple. To highlight the council's broad base of support and its growing Zionist commitment, the *Reporter*'s second issue featured an article on the travel to Israel of two prominent community leaders, Ellis Warren of TBE and Joseph Block of CBI. The same issue ran a story entitled "Where Your Money Goes," demonstrating that two-thirds of all contributions went directly to the UJA.[52] Like its counterparts elsewhere, Flint's council developed sophisticated fund-raising campaigns, organizing trade divisions to target

Sloan Museum

The head table at a 1953 dinner sponsored by the Flint Jewish Community Council for the United Jewish Appeal (UJA). The banner reads in full, "Give—because lives depend on us," and refers to the UJA's campaign to resettle European Jews both to the United States and to Israel. The dinner marked the fifteenth anniversary of the UJA. Pictured here (*left to right*) are Abe Schreiber, unidentified, Bernice Mittelman, Louis Lebster, unidentified, Art Hurand, Lou Rudner, Lou Kasle, unidentified, Saul Gorne, Ellis Warren, Betty Pelavin, B. Morris Pelavin, and Marty Gordon.

members by occupation, youth divisions to develop a lifetime habit of giving and cultivate future leaders, and a women's division that adopted "plus giving," a system whereby a wife's contribution was listed separately from that of her husband, the latter routinely designated by the council as the household head.[53]

Even though the FJCC then excluded women from its "campaign cabinet" and highest leadership positions, it realized that their participation was critical for its success. The organization thus welcomed women to its board of directors, and early on tapped two former Hadassah leaders to serve as board vice-presidents: TBE's Ann Lebster in 1949 and CBI's Ida Sendler the following year. By choosing these well-known women for a key post, the FJCC simultaneously reached out to those who had championed Zionism before the war and extended an invitation to both the Reform and Conservative sisterhoods, mainstays of their congregations, to exert their fundraising prowess on the council's behalf.[54] Women proved increasingly active within the FJCC, often leading efforts to bring Jews from behind the "Iron Curtain" to settle in Israel as well as participating in overall council programs.[55]

Flint's Jewish community also supported the Zionist cause by buying bonds issued by the Israeli government, a program established in 1951 to generate investment

Sloan Museum

Dressed in the style of First Lady Mamie Eisenhower, members of the Flint Jewish Community Council (FJCC) participate in a 1959 rally to allow Romanian Jews to resettle in Israel. Pictured (*left to right*) are Bess Hurand, unidentified, Leah Wolin, and Florence Epstein. Throughout the cold war American Jewry campaigned for Jews in all the Soviet satellite states to be granted their freedom to immigrate. By the late 1950s the FJCC saw Israel, rather than the United States, as the more appropriate destination for emigré resettlement, the shift signaling a recognition that American popular opinion opposed further immigration.

capital for the ambitious projects to build houses, construct infrastructure, develop education and health care facilities, install irrigation, and expand control over land. A local resident, Max Linder, apparently was Michigan's first-ever purchaser, buying a bond while Israel's inaugural prime minister David Ben-Gurion made a state visit to the United States that May. The excitement generated by Ben-Gurion's official reception and the heightened legitimacy it conferred on the state of Israel spurred Flint residents to purchase more than $125,000 worth of bonds during a single month, a significant outlay for a small Jewish community.[56] Flint Jewry would continue to distinguish itself in this material sign of faith in Israel's future, Lou Kasle perhaps the most visible in his efforts: each year during the High Holidays at the synagogue he urged congregants to purchase bonds, amassing a lifetime total sales of $35 million, much of it raised in Flint.[57]

Kasle's appeal symbolized the intertwining of support for Israel with the celebration of Jewish religious observance that became prevalent in postwar Flint, especially among Conservative Jews. Ten years after the end of World War II, memories of the Holocaust, yearning for the maintenance of a vibrant Judaism in the United States, dedication to an expanding and prosperous organizational life, and commitment to a Jewish state in the Mideast had, for many in Flint's Jewish community, become inextricably bound up with each other. This freighted combination of sentiments, aspirations, and political priorities had far-reaching and largely unforeseen consequences within and beyond Flint Jewry in the decades to come.

THE POSITION OF THE JEWS IN AMERICA TODAY

Temple Beth El had planned to host a farewell banquet for Rabbi Applebaum, departing in June 1953 to serve a congregation in Akron, Ohio. However, the day before the scheduled dinner a deadly tornado roared through Genesee County, wreaking its greatest destruction just a mile north of Flint. With Applebaum's hearty endorsement, the banquet organizers canceled the dinner and donated the funds they had collected to the tornado relief fund.[58] The temple's actions constituted only one instance of how Jewish organizations, like other local groups, pitched in to help neighbors devastated by the storm.

As discussed in the introduction to this book, the generosity demonstrated by its citizens in this emergency helped Flint earn the designation as the 1954 "All-American City of the Year," jointly awarded by the National Municipal League and *Look* magazine.[59] This reputation for civic-mindedness, along with a booming economy, prompted the magazine's national affairs editor (and future ambassador) William Attwood to visit Flint the next year for his feature on "The Position of the Jews in America Today."[60] Focusing on the family of Art Hurand, Attwood's account mentioned the bakery owner's donation of foodstuffs to tornado victims but ignored the steps taken by the temple and other Jewish organizations to aid the needy, not only during this emergency but on an ongoing basis.[61] The journalist's determination to paint the Hurands as just another all-American family, albeit with a particular (and to most of his readers, peculiar) style of worship, and to demonstrate the thoroughgoing "Americanization of Jewish cultural life" led him to ignore the web of Jewish associations in which the Hurands and so many other Flint families were enmeshed.[62]

> "The Six Day War [in 1967] galvanized the Jewish community."
>
> —*Lou Kasle, prominent supporter of State of Israel Bonds*

Attwood acknowledged that Jews in Flint, like those elsewhere in the United States, were barred from most clubs and kept at a distance by many of their non-Jewish neighbors. As documented in a series of sociological investigations, including an influential study conducted in Detroit, in the 1950s social relations between Jews and Gentiles still typically hovered on the "edge of friendliness," with most confining their interactions to business matters or polite socializing during working hours but few spending leisure time in each others' company.[63] This "five o'clock shadow," as it was known, continued as a routine practice throughout America well into the 1960s.

Soaking up the sun at the Sea Isle Hotel in Miami Beach, Florida, 1951; pictured here (*left to right*) are Bob and Thelma Kerner (owners of the Sports Bar in downtown Flint) and Sid and Suds Melet (owners of the Vogue, a women's apparel store). Barred from some exclusive vacation spots, many well-to-do members of Flint Jewry sought respite from Michigan winters at resort communities such as Miami Beach.

Sloan Museum

To counter this discrimination, Jews founded parallel social institutions, a pattern absent from Attwood's discussion. In Flint, one such organization was founded just before the journalist's visit, and by the time he filed his story had become an important fixture in the Jewish community.

The Phoenix Club had its roots in the discrimination experienced by several of the wealthiest Jewish men in Flint, business leaders who had ongoing economic and civic relationships with those at the very top of city society, many of whom were at the apex of GM as well. With the blessing of GM's redoubtable C. S. Mott, the backing of the Mott Foundation he had richly endowed, and the hands-on coordination of Michael Gorman, editor of the *Flint Journal,* in 1955 the city's powerbrokers were embarked on the bold and costly project to build a "College and Cultural Center."[64] While the project's planning board eventually agreed to accept small donations from groups and individuals, the great majority of the funding for the complex was raised through large contributions, with local manufacturers and substantial business owners urged to become project "sponsors" by donating a minimum of $125,000. The top-down and, some believed, high-pressure strategy proved very successful.[65] In the next several years, the planners raised the remarkable sum of thirty million dollars, erected a complex of nearly a dozen buildings, and thereby realized their vision of institutionalizing high culture in the "Industrial City." In a single sweep, the "men [who] built industrial might" thus brought the GM-approved brand of "beauty, and culture, and friendship" to the autotown, helping transform it into what the Chamber of Commerce that year proudly termed "Fabulous Flint."[66]

Factory owner Ellis Warren served on the College and Cultural Center planning board, the only member of Flint's Jewish community on the body.[67] After a meeting of the planning board with project sponsors, Warren asked Sam Catsman, owner of a coal and fuel company and a longtime Jewish community leader, why he did not participate in more Flint civic groups. According to an observer, Catsman answered, "Ellis, let me ask you a question. Can you go up to [the Flint] City Club in the Durant Hotel and become a member?" When Warren admitted that he could not, Catsman continued, "Well, you've got a hell of a lot of nerve wanting me to be more charitable when we are both barred from the City Club because we are Jewish." Catsman and Warren decided on the spot to ask others to join them in opening their own exclusive businessman's club in the Durant Hotel.[68] With eight others they established the Phoenix Club on the hotel's eighth floor and, pointedly, hosted a cultural center sponsors' meeting there. Professionals also became members, for anti-Semitism worked against them as well. The club's founders included Michael Winegarden, scion of the wealthy retailers, who served as the lawyer for prominent Citizen's Bank but was banned from the City Club; dentists Max Hart and Clem Alfred; and physician Isidore Gutow.[69] The club soon became a lively center for prosperous Jewish families, the site of formal balls, business lunches, and informal card games.[70]

Retailer Sid Melet, who participated with non-Jews in the Chamber of Commerce and other civic associations, also wearied of the social exclusion. His son, Michael, recalled that Flint "blue bloods" would compliment his father on his energy and his ideas. Yet "the bottom line was . . . at five o'clock when they all walked out of these meetings it was, 'We'll see you tomorrow, Sid.' And they went to the Flint Country Club or the Flint City Club . . . and my dad was never, ever invited."[71] Like his father, Michael Melet experienced discrimination, in his case from the Flint Golf Club. Sponsored for membership by a Gentile friend, the club reportedly refused even to consider his application because he was Jewish.[72]

By 1958 both father and son could join Willowood, a country club established by the local Jewish community in the countryside ten miles southeast of downtown Flint, near the growing suburb of Grand Blanc.[73] Along with a nine-hole golf course, Willowood boasted a clubhouse with a dance floor, an Olympic-sized swimming pool, a children's wading pool, and a shady picnic area. Affordable for many members of Flint's Jewish community, the country club became a favorite spot for both Reform and Conservative members to socialize. However, in the late 1960s, a decade after its founding, membership at Willowood began to drop off as a nearby country club began admitting Jews. The Atlas Country Club, located even further to the southeast and with a larger golf course, proved especially attractive to the avid golfers who had constituted the core of Willowood's membership.

By 1970 Willowood had closed, its demise reflecting the changed climate in the United States, as the "five o'clock shadow" began to fade. A pattern of more widespread informal socializing between Jews and non-Jews preceded the dropping of restrictions by private clubs, but after the mid 1960s most such organizations, as well as prominent civic groups, began to accept Jewish members. In particular, increased socializing at country clubs, especially on the golf course, fostered relationships

Clubhouse at Willowood Country Club, ca. 1958. Established in 1958 at the corner of Maple and Vassar roads southeast of Flint, Willowood offered middle-class and prosperous Jewish families, excluded from other country clubs, a retreat where they could golf and swim in summertime and socialize year-round.

Bea Cossman and son Marshall lounging beside the pool at Willowood, ca. 1958.

between Jewish and non-Jewish women of the same social class who otherwise would have had few occasions to meet. Yet the barriers to acceptance in leadership positions fell more slowly. Several Flint women with extensive experience in Jewish organizations recalled that local chapters of charities such as the United Way and Red Cross as well as the array of institutions in the College and Cultural Center began to welcome them as volunteers but seemed reluctant to have them assume positions of authority.[74] In contrast, beginning in the 1940s, local civil rights organizations, notably the Urban League and the National Association for the Advancement of Colored People (NAACP), had proved eager to have Jewish men and women participate at all levels, and throughout the postwar years many did so.

The ascent of the civil rights movement in the postwar decades constitutes the crucial context in which Jewish Americans witnessed the decline of bigotry and discrimination and the widening of opportunities for themselves and for others. African Americans comprised a growing proportion of Flint's population after the war, and the campaign to dismantle segregation, end second-class citizenship, and broaden political participation to include them and other racial minorities revealed one of the crucial fault lines in the city. It was a volatile era in GM's land of plenty, the economic good times both muting discord and raising expectations that the promise of the putative model city held true for all.

ALL-AMERICAN CITY AND TOUGH TOWN

In 1956, a year after William Attwood filed his sunny report on Jewish life in *Look*'s "All-American City," *Coronet,* another highly popular national magazine, pronounced Flint the "Happiest Town in Michigan."[75] The same year Steve Lee, contributor to a less illustrious publication, *Stag,* offered his readers a very different picture of GM's birthplace. Rather than a harmonious, well-ordered model city, the pulp-magazine reporter claimed to have uncovered a "wide-open town" of violence and vice where he spent the "roughest weekend" of his life.[76] Lee found murder, robbery, fighting, and "boozy sordidness" in this "tough town": narcotics trafficking, gambling, and after-hours clubs flourished; "caterwauling" music blared from "hillbilly joints"; and prostitutes in smoky dives "[threw] themselves into the arms of their prospective customers and [broke] down sales resistance by sheer force." Flint not only turned out millions of cars, Lee declared, but mounds of obscene literature, producing "almost as many 'feelthy' postcards as Buicks."[77]

The *Stag* exposé is quintessential 1950s sensationalism, both its punchy prose and accompanying grainy black-and-white photographs reflecting the prurient fascination with police investigations of the seamier aspects of life that made the television show *Dragnet* such a hit during the decade. The sleazy account nonetheless offers a telling contemporary counterpoint to the dominant narrative of Flint-as-model-city, for conflicts swirled beneath the surface of consensus, consumption, and corporate control. Both stories capture important aspects of life in Flint, each focusing on, exaggerating, and distorting aspects of a 1950s boomtown where corporate paternalism, union-management deals, and economic plenty masked underlying tensions, notably of gender, class, religion, and especially race, that sometimes broke through the carapace of celebratory civic culture.

In the auto plants, for example, the shop floor often bristled with conflict, despite the generally smooth relations between the leaders of GM and those of the UAW. Largely insulated from arbitrary firing by their union contract, men in car shops sometimes displayed features of the "rougher side of masculine culture," according to historian Stephen Meyer, "drinking, fighting, gambling," harassing female co-workers, taunting foremen, and loudly and belligerently confronting supervisors.[78] Although other male workers fostered more familial relations with co-workers and even bosses, the rough aspects of shop floor culture often spilled outside the factory gates and shaped life in places where workers gathered after their shifts ended—on city streets, in parks, and, especially, at local watering holes.

While Lee exaggerated in depicting Flint as chock-full of "big, crowded saloons" and "beered-up lushes," the city did have bars of all descriptions, many jammed with rowdy autoworkers—most men, but some women, too. Unnoticed by the *Stag* reporter, who focused exclusively on heterosexual activity in the city's nightspots, Flint had a thriving gay scene. Scholar Tim Retzloff has identified half a dozen "gay and mixed meeting places" downtown during the mid 1950s, tucked amid "storefront businesses, all-night coney island restaurants, a Buick dealership, and a Sears department store."[79] All were within three blocks of the Durant Hotel, whose "Purple Cow" bar was a center for gay dating—the same elegant hotel, named for GM's founder, whose uppermost floor housed the elite Flint City Club and, just a floor below, the Phoenix Club, its Jewish counterpart.[80] Throughout postwar Flint, then, as at the fashionable Durant, discrete social groups often existed in proximity to each other, with the elite occupying the loftiest positions and those on descending tiers seeking to carve out spaces of their own. Increasingly, the ability of blacks to do so beyond rigidly defined boundaries—they were excluded from the Durant until the mid 1950s—became a matter of dispute.[81]

Though derogatory, Steve Lee's references both to "hillbilly" music and to jazz "entertainment" likewise pointed to key demographic aspects of the city. Many residents, including shop workers, had shallow roots in Flint, the city continuing its long pattern of rapid population flux. A 1948 study demonstrated that only one of six city residents was born in the Flint area, another one in ten moving to the city while still a child.[82] Only 10 percent were foreign-born. Hence at midcentury nearly two-thirds of Flint's population were migrants from elsewhere in the United States, newcomers drawn from rural areas, small towns, and cities across Michigan and the nation. Many came from the South, both whites, including many from Appalachia and the Ozarks— presumably responsible for the "steel guitar and washboard stuff" Lee had heard played in bars—and blacks, whose places of birth stretched from Louisiana to Kentucky to the Carolinas and in whose clubs he heard jazz, a musical form he also disparaged.[83]

Those newcomers who had arrived in Flint during the war years endured an intense shortage of housing and a lack of urban infrastructure that may have reminded many of conditions on the farms they had left behind. More than half of the homes hastily constructed near the auto plants on the city's fringe, for example, had no running water and three-fourths also lacked flush toilets.[84] Despite a postwar frenzy of new construction and home improvement, adequate housing for workers and their families remained a problem throughout the boom years of the 1950s, heightening competition for desirable property and access to municipal services, and thereby producing flashpoints for race relations. The demand for social services, schools, and medical facilities similarly expanded as the population grew, the number of school-aged children increased even more rapidly, and union contracts secured more health care benefits for autoworkers.

On a magnitude and with a thoroughness that helped Flint gain its model-city image, the Mott Foundation, in concert with other elite-dominated area charitable institutions, civic groups, and the public schools, established an array of projects to meet some of these needs. Pioneering the idea of the "lighted schoolhouse," or, less evocatively, the "Community School Program," the Mott Foundation poured money into activities to keep schools open in the evenings and throughout the year, the buildings serving as neighborhood hubs to promote learning, health, and citizenship throughout Flint. Projects held in conjunction with the schools and other civic organizations ranged from athletics to safety education, homemaking classes to night school courses, summer camps to a children's health clinic.[85] In 1955 the program's architect, Frank J. Manley, hosted a statewide conference in Flint to spread the concept throughout Michigan; four years later, with the personal support of C. S. Mott, he sponsored a national conference.[86] Thus by the time the College and Cultural Center institutions opened, Flint had emerged as a showcase for how corporate capital, channeled through private foundations, could transform the civic life of an industrial center.[87]

The philosophy behind the Community School Program was progressive in the historical sense of the term, embodying the spirit of turn-of-the-century educational leader John Dewey: "to give the individual an opportunity to become a better person, thus a better citizen, by helping him develop a sense of dignity and worth."[88] In line with this spirit of universal uplift, the activities sponsored by the program were open to Flint residents regardless of race or creed. Despite the commitment to access for all, because most activities took place in neighborhood schools and community centers they tended to draw participants from surrounding city blocks, consequently replicating the class and racial profile of each neighborhood. The program's noble aim of inclusion, propounded by those at the top of Flint society and shared by many ordinary white and black city residents, thus was often contradicted by the reality of increasing de facto racial segregation.

"What makes Flint so tough?" *Stag*'s Steve Lee asked rhetorically after he prowled the streets and "cased the joints" in the autotown.[89] The answer for the city's overwhelmingly working-class residents was not "boozy sordidness," but the daily grind of factory labor. By the time Lee made his whirlwind tour (and Attwood his brief visit), the benefits of twenty years of industrial unionism, ushered in by Flint's own strike, had done much to ameliorate the worst conditions in the plants. Still, life on the line remained hard on the body, mind, and soul, the major counterweight to its burdens the hefty paychecks that afforded UAW members entry into in an expanding world of consumption. The array of GM-backed, paternalist civic programs further buoyed autoworkers' standard of living, helping make Flint, at least in these respects, the "happiest city" in the state for many of its citizens. Yet for blacks, by far the city's largest racial minority during the postwar years, what made Flint "so tough" was routine and blatant discrimination on and off the job. It would take the emergence of the civil rights movement to address this inequality. The changing social relations that ensued, in tandem with altered demographic patterns and economic conditions, transformed Flint, and this transformation had multifaceted ramifications for members of the city's Jewish community.

CIVIC LIFE IN FABULOUS FLINT

Many Americans, including some themselves immune from discrimination, learned a powerful lesson during World War II about the potentially lethal consequences of socially sanctioned and state-sponsored religious bigotry, ethnic chauvinism, and racism. In the wake of the war the U.S. armed forces led the way in breaking down the policies and practices that had assigned many blacks and other racial minorities to segregated units, confined them to menial tasks, and denied them the possibilities of command. Jewish Americans, although discriminated against by prejudiced individuals and often subjected to harassment, were not the objects of systematic, legitimated ill-treatment within the wartime armed services. Instead, for many, including those from Flint, military service during and after World War II brought them into close daily contact with those of other religions and ethnic backgrounds in an atmosphere that officially advocated tolerance, often furthered understanding, and sometimes nurtured abiding friendship. Interfaith fellowship among Protestants, Catholics, and Jews was supported from the highest ranks; rabbis served as chaplains in all branches of the military; and, when feasible, Jewish personnel were encouraged to uphold their traditional observances.

In the postwar period, this climate led to a widespread imagining of the United States as a "Judeo-Christian nation," a polity whose moral underpinnings and intellectual roots stretched from the very earliest books of the Bible's Old Testament—the Books of Moses—through the preachings of Jesus Christ and his many latter-day disciples.[90] The concept of America as a "triple melting pot" of three major religions was

Veterans from Flint gather in Japan in 1946, a year after that nation's defeat. War service created an opportunity for close bonds to be forged across ethnic and religious lines, as seen in this group of friends, two of whom, Richard Heitzner and Norman Schafer, were Jewish. Pictured here are (*front, left to right*) Bob Mainprize, Larry Soldas, and Tom Milne; and (*back, left to right*) Duane Tillinghast, Heitzner, Schafer, and Joe Spielmaker.

popularized in 1955 by Jewish intellectual Will Herberg in his widely selling *Protestant, Catholic, Jew,* which further consolidated the view that these faiths constituted "three diverse representations of the same spiritual values [of] American democracy." For many Americans this idea became part of a "new national creed."[91]

As early as 1947, Flint Jewry had adopted this iconographic mantle to campaign for tolerance, participating in efforts to make their city and nation "forever free" from both "religious and racial hate." In that year, B. Morris Pelavin, in his role as president of the local B'nai B'rith, joined an interfaith coalition to promote social justice in Flint; the next year he became president of the FJCC, serving until 1951 and stamping the organization with an abiding commitment to a broad-based civil rights movement. Pelavin embodied the postwar tie between activism within the Jewish community and participation in broader struggles for equality. Born in Belarus, he came to Flint in 1932, studied law with a local attorney during the Depression, passed the bar examination in 1939, and became active in both the synagogue and the temple. Pelavin participated in efforts to expose and end discrimination in such areas as housing, employment, and even recreation. Many B'nai B'rith members, for example, enjoyed

Passover in Korea, 1954. On duty in South Korea following the end of the Korean War (1950–53), Dr. Arnold Schaffer of Flint (*left*) and an unidentified friend receive matzah (unleavened bread), a traditional food eaten as part of the celebration of Pesach (Passover). This "holiday of freedom" commemorates the Jewish exodus from Egypt following more than two centuries of slavery. The U.S. armed forces supported such religious observance; in turn Jewish Americans were proud to demonstrate that their religious identity went hand in hand with patriotism.

competitive bowling and took their contests with other teams seriously; nonetheless Pelavin convinced both the local chapter and the statewide organization to withdraw from the American Bowling Conference until it ended its exclusion of blacks from participation.[92] Similarly, while he headed the FJCC, the organization's board of directors unanimously supported the establishment of a Mayor's Commission on Human Relations, an important early step in institutionalizing the local civil rights effort.[93] Over the course of his career, the self-taught attorney served as a longtime board member of the NAACP; three-term president of the Flint Urban League; chairman of the Flint Council for the Fair Employment Commission; and treasurer for the Michigan Commission on Civil Rights.[94] In all of these organizations he stressed the common interests of Jews and African Americans in confronting prejudice and eradicating discrimination, a moral high ground that proved easier to occupy in the immediate postwar decades than it would be in later years.

In the early 1950s the sisterhoods at the synagogue and temple likewise sponsored programs that shared this discourse of an all-encompassing movement for civil

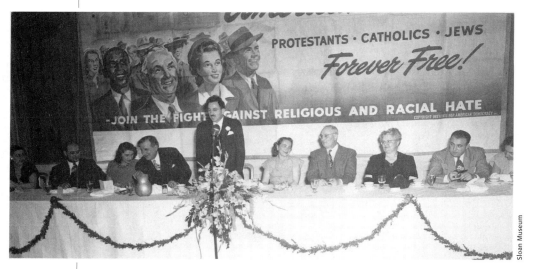

PROTESTANTS · CATHOLICS · JEWS

Forever Free!

—JOIN THE FIGHT AGAINST RELIGIOUS AND RACIAL HATE

Sloan Museum

Attorney B. Morris Pelavin, representing Flint B'nai B'rith, addresses a rally against bigotry, 1947. As American public discourse embraced interfaith tolerance in the postwar years, Flint's organized Jewish community joined other civic groups campaigning to accord respect and extend rights across racial and religious lines.

rights. At a 1951 meeting held by the CBI sisterhood, for example, a member of the Flint Urban League sketched a graphic picture of racial segregation in city housing and jobs. In response the sisterhood set up a vigorous "social action" committee, taking to heart their rabbi's counsel, delivered at the meeting, that "Judaic principles require Jews to help right [such] wrongs."[95] TBE's sisterhood also regularly held meetings with representatives from area churches, civil rights organizations, and sometimes the UAW in order to forge a coalition for social justice.[96]

Flint Jewry's initial forays into civil rights activism coincided with the heating up of the cold war, the war in Korea intensifying and the search for "reds" launched by Senator Joseph McCarthy becoming a nationwide fury. In this highly charged political context, most Jewish organizations in Flint and elsewhere emphasized their patriotism and underscored that their social activism stemmed from a commitment to the American democratic tradition, not allegiance to the Kremlin. Efforts to reiterate Jewish loyalty to the United States seemed prudent given the vicious anti–Semitism that undergirded the anti–Communist crusade, most evident in the public discussion of the Rosenberg espionage case. Arrested in 1950 for providing the Soviet Union with nuclear secrets, Julius and Ethel Rosenberg were convicted of treason and, despite an international outcry, executed in 1953. Anti–Semitism also percolated throughout the hearings conducted by the House Un–American Activities Committee (HUAC). The publicity-hungry committee conducted scurrilous investigations of putative Communist infiltration of the nation's institutions and organizations, especially the movie industry, universities, labor unions, and anti-racist groups, insinuating that Jews were overrepresented among the dangerous Soviet agents and dupes that it sought to ferret out.

In 1954 a HUAC subcommittee held hearings in Michigan, with several sessions held in Flint and all chaired by Michigan Congressman Kit Clardy, a McCarthy lieutenant and rabid anti-Communist. Vicious in tone and divisive in effect, the hearings led to purges of alleged Communists within the UAW and prompted firings at GM auto plants, with some of the so-called red colonizers taunted with anti-Semitic as well as anti-radical epithets.[97] Among Flint Jewry, the subcommittee turned its scrutinizing gaze most fixedly on attorney Morton Leitson, member of the left-leaning National Lawyers Guild and son of the bakery owners who had aided the sit-down strikers. Unlike dozens of other local residents, Leitson emerged from the hearings without being charged; ideals firmly intact, two years later he successfully represented a GM employee fired on a technicality after her brother-in-law was called as a HUAC witness.[98] In the recently proclaimed "All-American City," the anti-Communist "housecleaning" was especially thorough, corporate managers, businessmen, and conservative union leaders as well as right-wing ideologues joining the government's hunt to uncover and oust suspected agitators.

To some extent, the anti-Communist campaign discouraged participation in civil rights activism, a welcome result for those who cynically had hopped on the McCarthy bandwagon in part to forestall social progress. Yet just weeks after Congressman Clardy completed his statewide quest for Soviet stooges, the cause of civil rights took another step forward in Flint when a "Committee of One Hundred," comprised of prominent citizens of varied backgrounds, pushed for an end to racial discrimination in employment. Among the Jewish community members speaking in support of the plan at an open hearing were Morris Pelavin, FJCC director Irving Antell, CBI rabbi Philip Kieval, Yankee Stores proprietor Joe Megdell, and attorney Stewart Newblatt, son of the co-owner of Uncle Bob's diner.[99] Members of Flint's Jewish community understood employment and allied discrimination from their own experience, attenuated forms existing against them well into the 1960s: Jewish doctors clustered in a single hospital, an unspoken quota seemingly in operation at other city medical facilities; GM continued to have few Jewish employees on its payroll, including in its legal and financial offices, a pattern some believed resulted from an anti-Semitic climate pervading Flint's corporate giant; and teachers in the public schools had their pay docked if they observed Jewish holidays.[100] Jewish students likewise paid penalties for institutional policies that failed to consider the tenets of their religion. Decades after professional baseball star Hank Greenberg drew national attention to the issue in 1934 by refusing to play on Yom Kippur, Jewish young people in Flint who observed traditional practices routinely had to forgo participation in activities held on their Sabbath, events that ranged from school dances to lectures to cultural programs to athletic championship games.

Sloan Museum

This Flint team, comprised of both Conservative and Reform members, excelled in the highly competitive local Young Men's Christian Association (YMCA) basketball league. Team members declined to participate in the 1967–68 YMCA state championships because the game was scheduled for a Friday evening, the Jewish Sabbath, 1968.

Wanting to bring these matters to the attention of the overwhelmingly Christian population of the city, the FJCC and other organizations raised them at local coalition meetings, at the same time pushing for issues that affected Jews worldwide. In the mid 1950s these efforts began to pay off in the realms of foreign affairs and public policy. In 1957, for example, the Flint Council of Churches condemned the persecution of Egyptian Jews, denouncing the government of Gamal Abdul Nasser for its "violent practices . . . strongly reminiscent of the Hitler era." The backdrop to this announcement was the "Suez Crisis": Nasser's nationalization of the Suez Canal, the subsequent military attack on Egypt by combined British–French–Israeli forces, a United Nations–brokered ceasefire, and ensuing increased tensions between Israel and its Arab neighbors. Notably, George D. Stevenson, head of the Flint Urban League, joined the condemnation, requesting that President Dwight Eisenhower "take the strongest possible action toward Egypt to express our country's protest of the inhuman conduct toward a decent people."[101] Within weeks Flint Jewry obtained endorsement for another international cause. The Flint Citizens Committee on Immigration, chaired by a local pastor, spearheaded a letter–writing campaign asking Congress to increase the numbers of refugees to be admitted from Poland and the Soviet Union. Most potential newcomers, the committee stressed, would be Jews, victims of discrimination if not outright persecution in their homelands.[102]

Organized Jewry's political clout was also in evidence during these years, with leaders of both parties eyeing potential contributions as they endorsed a pro–Israeli stance. In 1956 Flint mayor George M. Algoe, a Republican with a small undertaking business, proclaimed a citywide "Israel Independence Week" in honor of Israel's eighth anniversary and urged "all friends of freedom" to contribute to the local UJA.[103] In part, local developments reflected the greater role that support for Israel played in national foreign policy in the two decades following World War II. As the cold war dragged on, the United States increasingly claimed Israel as its staunch ally and regarded other Mideast governments as within the orbit of the Soviet Union. Concomitantly, both the Republican and Democratic parties came to vie for electoral and financial backing from Jewish Americans by stressing strong commitment to the state of Israel.

These multiple connections were energized swiftly and dramatically in 1967, as Jewish American support for Israel burst forth with unprecedented fervor and Zionism became an enduring hegemonic force, thereafter constituting the "common denominator of Jewish American life," according to historian Edward S. Shapiro.[104] The cause was the Six Day War, begun after the UN complied with an Egyptian demand to withdraw peacekeeping forces from a key position on that nation's border with Israel. Regarding Egypt's actions as tantamount to a declaration of war and fearing a massive invasion, Israel struck decisively: its air force launched devastating raids against Egyptian airfields and its army then repelled ground forces. Instead of reclaiming land they believed Israel had stolen from them, Egypt, Syria, and Jordan suffered a complete rout, and Israel gained control of territory that included the Gaza Strip, the Golan Heights, the Sinai Peninsula, and the West Bank. During the course of one week in June the small state of Israel scored an overwhelming military, geopolitical, and psychological victory, changing the course of international affairs for years to come.

This watershed event prompted American Jewry to donate unprecedented sums to Israel to help defray the costs of the war and subsidize the building of Jewish settlements in newly acquired territory. Flint mirrored the national pattern, support for the FJCC increasing from less than $300,000 in 1966 to more than $710,000 in 1967, the bulk of the contributions earmarked for Israel.[105] In addition, more members of Flint's Jewish community began to visit there. Some ventured on their own while others joined tours sponsored by the FJCC, Hadassah, the synagogue and temple, or other associations. In keeping with the intent to widen Gentile backing for Israeli domestic initiatives and foreign policy, local Jewish organizations also encouraged area political leaders and members of civic, business, and labor groups to travel to Israel under their auspices.

Throughout the 1960s the FJCC, other Jewish groups, and individual members of the Jewish community also continued their collaborative work for social justice, as race relations reached a crisis across the nation and in their city. Joe Megdell, for example, became chair of the Flint Humans Relations Commission in 1960, appointed to the position after demonstrating his commitment to equal rights in his business.[106] He employed blacks throughout his Yankee Stores chain, placing African Americans in sales positions at a time when few white proprietors, including other Jews, did so. After the killing of three voting rights workers in rural Mississippi in 1964, Megdell started a boycott of Mississippi-made goods to protest the state's lack of protection for those working for desegregation. When the right-wing John Birch Society attacked him as a subversive, he fired back with an appeal to patriotism in line with his firm's logo, the Uncle Sam hat: The John Birch Society, Megdell declared, was "anti-labor, anti-Negro, anti-Jewish, and it all adds up to being anti-American."[107] Like Megdell, downtown clothier and Jewish community leader Sid Melet fostered positive race relations in both business and civic life. He became the first chairman of the Urban Coalition, a group of blacks and whites organized in hopes of preventing in Flint the violent uprisings that rocked much of urban America from the mid-1960s onward.[108]

Flint residents had particular reasons for concern. In July 1967 nearby Detroit was the site of an especially brutal and massive riot that left forty-three dead and resulted in property losses that exceeded thirty-six million dollars.[109] An underlying cause of violence in the larger "Motor City" was racial segregation in housing, a pattern that also intensified in Flint as the numbers of black residents increased. In 1950 the population of African Americans in Flint was 14,000, double that of 1940, but still constituting less than 10 percent of the population. At midcentury the vast majority of blacks lived in only two neighborhoods, the St. John District near the Buick plant, which they shared with working-class whites, and smaller, more segregated, but more middle-class "Sugar Hill," on the city's far east side.[110] Soaring production in Flint-area auto factories spurred black settlement in the boom years, the number of African Americans in the city tripling in 1960 to 45,000 and growing to more than 54,000 a decade later. By 1970 blacks comprised more than a quarter of Flint residents.

This increase in proportion reflected both black in-migration and simultaneous white out-migration. At a pace that magnified the national pattern of "white flight" and replicated the very rapid rate in Detroit, beginning in the mid 1950s whites by the thousands—from the prosperous to the working-class, and including many members of the Jewish community—moved out of Flint. Some bought houses in the new subdivisions cropping up on the city's fringe and others settled in nearby hamlets and towns that were becoming satellite communities. Blacks, meanwhile, remained clustered in the St. John and Sugar Hill neighborhoods. Their major area of expansion lay north and west of the Buick plant, in a deteriorating section of the city whose early twentieth-century frame housing stock showed the effects of age and shoddy construction.[111]

Consequently by the 1960s nearly all African Americans, whether poor or well-paid, newly settled or Flint-born, were confined to areas with cramped, inadequate housing. Those who tried to resettle in other neighborhoods or outside the city frequently were met with harassment: some were jeered, others pelted by rocks, and, in a notable 1962 incident, one family found a dummy impaled with a knife left on the front porch of their new home.[112] Even more effective in keeping African Americans residentially segregated were the insidious methods of restrictive covenants, racial "steering" by realtors, and "redlining" by banks, a policy of systematic racial discrimination in lending.[113]

Significantly, in the postwar years jobs had begun to leave Flint in advance of the substantial out-migration of white residents, as GM built and expanded facilities just outside the municipal limits, then even further beyond in the flat countryside of Genesee County. Hence for many white autoworkers relocating to the city's fringe or suburbs meant living closer, not farther away, from the factory gates.[114] Whatever mix of motives—a shorter drive to work, newer housing, a larger lot, lower taxes, as well as racial prejudice—prompted such individuals to move outside Flint, the effect was the creation of a more segregated city. Alarmingly for Flint residents of all races and property owners of all manner, the combined transfer of white population from the city and corporate growth outside its borders resulted in a substantially shrinking city tax base.[115]

The loss of tax income was compounded by "capital flight" of another ilk: the movement of retail establishments and, secondarily, the tenants of office and professional buildings, to outlying areas. Some businesses merely followed the workers whose paychecks fueled their trade, but others, including large commercial interests, helped spur population removal from the city, developers buying up farmland and planting shopping plazas in fields that soon sprouted single-family homes and apartment complexes as well.[116] This centrifugal movement of people and jobs, customers and commerce, hit Flint retailers hard. Between 1958 and 1963 the number of downtown retail stores declined by a hundred, a drop of nearly 25 percent, with stores in the central business district accounting for less than 20 percent of the metropolitan area's retail trade by the mid 1960s.[117] Sales in neighborhood stores, particularly those near the factories, also slumped.

For the many members of the Jewish community still engaged in retail trade the spreading malaise in the city's commercial sector proved devastating. Older members of the group often suffered the most, both immigrants, who had spent their whole lives as storekeepers, and their adult children, men and women who had grown up in their parents' shops and had hoped to carry on their families' businesses, perhaps passing them on to their children. Some, like Lithuanian immigrant Herman Teitelbaum, got out as the commercial downturn began. He detected signs of trouble even in the midst of GM's 1958 celebration of its fiftieth anniversary; that year he closed the landmark "Home Store," just east of the St. John District, ending a trade in hardware and workingmen's apparel that had flourished almost as long as had the giant automaker.[118] Other Jewish merchants relocated to the suburban plazas in the mid 1960s while still others hung on, trusting that loyal customers would drive back from outlying subdivisions to do their shopping downtown. Instead the trend to the suburbs—for residence, work, shopping, and recreation—accelerated. Consequently, more and more Jewish retailers either lost their businesses or joined the rush to the sprawling suburbs.

Beginning in the 1950s, Flint's political leaders and social elite, so closely intertwined, tried various measures to breathe new life into the flagging downtown and faltering neighborhoods, instituting planning boards, launching redevelopment efforts, and seeking to attract new commercial investment. The efforts had few lasting positive outcomes, the attempts not merely too little and too late but undercut by the systemic economic forces in operation, the deep racial divide cleaving the city, and key political decisions that exacerbated urban decay.[119]

Ironically, in a city that area boosters equated with transportation and while auto production at local plants remained feverish, the most glaring public policy blow to Flint may have come from the construction of two new highways during the 1960s. One expressway ran north and south and the other east and west, forming a crisscross pattern that sliced through working-class and black neighborhoods while dodging GM plants, golf courses, the College and Cultural Center, and enclaves of the middle-class and wealthy.[120] As early as 1963, when the planning documents for the highway construction were released, many city residents had grasped the potential impact of the new roads. Black civic leaders, joined by some concerned whites, including Jewish store owners, had tried in vain to alter the proposed routes, arguing that African American residents would suffer disproportionately and city businesses would be further undercut.[121] The opponents of the plan were prescient: the highways encouraged even greater suburban development, and nearly 60 percent of those displaced by the freeway construction were black.[122]

It was in this political context that the city of Flint finally took a clear step toward addressing the issue of residential segregation. In the summer of 1967, having seen the graphic television and newspaper reports of the Detroit riot, black and white residents of Flint came together, taking action that not only helped to avert similar violence in their city but led to the passage of a historic measure: the nation's first fair housing ordinance adopted by a referendum. The leader of the drive for the ordinance was Floyd McCree, Flint's first black mayor and the first African American to be elected mayor of a large urban center. Early in August 1967 McCree pushed the city council to pass a law in favor of open housing, but lost on a close vote. In support of the mayor's plan to re-open the issue, later that month three lawyers petitioned the city for permission to hold a demonstration: A. Glenn Epps, an African American; Paul Gadola, a Gentile, and Michael Pelavin, like his father, Morris, active both in the Jewish community and in the civil rights movement. Their petition granted, a unique protest began: hundreds of Flint residents, most of them young, staged a "sleep-in" on the front lawn of city hall, camping there for ten days, prompting even larger demonstrations at the municipal complex and drawing national news coverage. The fair housing ordinance subsequently passed the city council and was upheld in a February 1968 referendum. The vote revealed a bitterly divided citizenry, the measure winning by a mere thirty-eight ballots out of a total of more than forty thousand cast.[123]

The Jewish community comprehended a range of positions on the ordinance, just as it had on the momentous sit-down strike thirty years before. On the whole, however, the organized community stood behind the measure, and many individuals stepped forward to lend their support. One temple member, for example, recalls "heated meetings" regarding the ordinance, some members in the realty business opposing it and even the rabbi, a Southerner, expressing misgivings. Yet in the end TBE passed a strong resolution in favor of open housing and presented it to the city council.[124]

Flint Jewry could look with pride on actions such as these, which served to bolster

African American–Jewish relations during a tense period in the life of their city and nation. There were other notable instances, including two important court cases that contributed to righting egregious civil wrongs. The first involved the powerful arguments in favor of voting rights put forward by a Jewish attorney; the second, a memorable ruling by one of Flint's earliest Jewish judges. Both occurred in 1966, two years before the passage of the fair housing ordinance.

The attorney in the elections case was Robert L. Segar, who, with his non–Jewish partner Max Dean, challenged the constitutionality of a Virginia poll tax on behalf of Evelyn Butts, an African American woman. Donating his time and pursuing the matter through appeal, Segar ultimately argued the case successfully before the U.S. Supreme Court. The high court's ruling overturned a practice that states had used for a century to discriminate against black voters.[125] A few months later, the Michigan Court of Appeals upheld a ruling on a racial segregation case heard by Genesee County Judge Stewart A. Newblatt. The case concerned a black undertaker who had been denied permission to bury an African American man in a local cemetery, Flint Memorial Park, because of its restrictive covenant. Newblatt ruled in favor of the undertaker, requiring the cemetery to grant the burial. Impressed by his judgment, the state appeals court completely endorsed it and quoted it in full. Son of a delicatessen owner, Newblatt was raised in Flint during the Depression and the Second World War, and in his ruling invoked the lessons of that terrible war. The Memorial Park Association had claimed that in order to inter his African American client the undertaker "could seek burial among 'his own kind,'" that is, bury him at one of the cemeteries local blacks had established because of their exclusion from whites–only sites. Yet Newblatt rejected this argument, stating firmly: "When the law recognizes the philosophy represented by 'his own kind,' we are only a step away from adopting the racist philosophy which World War II was fought to eliminate."[126]

The same sentiments, grounded in an understanding of the horrors to which bigotry had led in the past and unless confronted in all its forms could lead once again, animated those members of Flint's Jewish community who made common cause with African American civil rights advocates in the postwar years. Their city would need these allies' optimism, commitment, and willingness sometimes to tolerate disagreement, for race relations became even more troubled in ensuing decades. For a few, like displaced person Peppy Rosenthal, pursuing social justice in both Jewish and African American organizations would become a life's work. Ten years after arriving in Flint as a refugee, for example, she started a sit-in at a Charlotte, North Carolina, restaurant, unable to bear the thought that her beloved America sanctioned racial segregation. Over the next four decades she remained active in the TBE sisterhood and Hadassah, the Urban League and the NAACP, working closely with pioneering local and state civil rights leader Edgar Holt.[127] In times when dialogue between the African American and Jewish communities broke down, the work and spirit of individuals like Rosenthal helped sustain ties between the groups.

LIKE OTHER JEWISH COMMUNITIES—ONLY MORE SO

In the midst of World War II, Flint Jewry had paused to look inward, conducting a self-study whose significance to the community had paled in the face of the era's dramatic events. A quarter century later, in a time of domestic turmoil and growing concern about affairs in the Mideast, the community launched a second self-study, convinced that planning for the future required a thorough taking of stock. The resulting report, *Flint Jewish Population Study 1967,* written by sociologist Albert J. Mayer and issued in 1969, presented a raft of substantive information, as well a prediction for the community's growth that testifies to the perils of forecasting.[128] Supported by the FJCC, coordinated by Natalie Pelavin, and relying on a team of volunteers to collect data from virtually every Jewish household in the city, the study culled information from more than seven hundred interviews. Making the report particularly useful, Mayer compared Flint data with those from nineteen other Jewish communities, all larger, that had conducted similar studies in the previous eight years.[129] The study stressed the many similarities between Flint Jewry and the Jewish populations in other urban areas while underscoring that in the autotown the overall trends characterizing American Jewish life stood in starker relief: "Flint," Mayer concluded, "is like other Jewish communities—only more so."[130]

This pattern was notable in occupation, income, and place of birth. Mayer found six of seven Flint Jewish family heads employed in the professions and business ownership, a profile that constituted both a "highly exaggerated version of the characteristics of the total American Jewish community," and a direct "reverse of the total Flint population," the bulk of whom were employed in manufacturing.[131] The single most common job for an adult Jewish man in Flint was medical doctor or dentist, with one in five holding this lucrative and prestigious profession. Another one in six were lawyers, judges, social workers, or teachers. Among those in business, the greatest number were in retail trade, a livelihood that for some was threatened by the changing commercial patterns discussed previously. Somewhat surprisingly, of all the Jewish communities for which he had comparable data, Mayer found that Flint's had the highest median income. Moreover, Jewish households in Flint, to a greater extent than in most other cities, achieved this income level solely through the employment of the male household head or, in the case of business ownership, through the contributions of wives who worked part-time in the family's retail store.[132] Whatever their occupation, most had migrated to Flint. Only one in six Jewish men hailed from the city, with a third foreign-born and over half resettling from elsewhere in the United States. In this regard Flint Jewry mirrored the city's population as a whole but diverged from the profile of other Jewish communities, which commonly had two of five family heads native to the city where they resided.[133]

Looking at these data together reveals that Flint's Jewish community was in transition during the 1960s, the community consisting of two overlapping populations.

One was comprised mainly of older, often aging, immigrants and their children, many of whom were concentrated in retail trades, especially family businesses; most had settled in Flint before the Depression. A second, younger group included business owners but increasingly was comprised of highly educated professionals, typically in families where wives did not work outside the home. Some were the children of those in the first group, but even more were newcomers, drawn to the booming autotown during the postwar years, eagerly setting up medical and law practices in a city where workers had good benefit plans and where a brisk housing market resulted in many property transactions. Just as in the pre-Depression era, these newly arrived entered a small Jewish community with few barriers to their participation, many quickly rising to leadership in associational life.

Religious affiliation partially crosscut these groups, although the Conservative synagogue had a higher percentage of business owners than did the Reform temple, substantiating the long-held view that the temple included adherents whose wealth and status were, on average, higher than that of those belonging to the synagogue.[134] At the same time, the self-study confirmed the community's belief that it had an especially vibrant religious life. Mayer's data demonstrated that 56 percent of Flint Jewry claimed membership in Conservative CBI, 37 percent in Reform TBE, with another 5 percent describing themselves as Orthodox, though having no specific house of worship. This overall rate of affiliation was higher than in other cities, as was the average attendance rate at religious services held at the shul and temple. Furthermore Flint had a comparatively high percentage of families who observed such practices as kashrut, the lighting of Sabbath candles, and observance of Passover rituals.[135]

Religious education, however, was another matter—or at least adherents' perception of the quality of that education. In this community where religious organizations and the activities they sponsored seemed so central to Jewish life, most adult members of both congregations expressed dissatisfaction with their knowledge of that religion. While many of the surveys' respondents, as newcomers to Flint, had not been raised in either CBI's or TBE's religious school, some had—and seemed to find their years there wanting. To address this need for the coming generation, Mayer suggested that the Flint community develop better and more extensive religious education for its young people. Yet he also noted that the number of youngsters born in Flint who would be the beneficiaries of this renewed educational effort was declining, as the baby boom receded. By the mid 1960s the birth rate in Flint's Jewish community hovered at about 2.3, comparable to that of other communities.[136] Meanwhile Mayer stressed the peculiar absence of a Jewish community center in Flint, indicating that many survey respondents suggested that such a facility, with its array of programs, would provide the missing focal point for an expansive Jewish communal life.

Grounded in the fine work of the volunteers who sought out and interviewed their own community members and informed by judicious comparisons with other Jewish populations, Mayer's study offered a detailed portrait of Flint Jewry in 1967. Yet the

Sloan Museum

A branch of the Vogue, one of the area's foremost ladies' clothing stores, opens at newly built suburban Genesee Valley Mall. Pictured are *(left to right)* Sidney Melet, owner of the Vogue; Bob Fischgrund, nephew of store founder Max Fischgrund; Michael Melet, Sid's son; and Bob Fischgrund's son.

sociologist's careful delineation and keen analysis broke down when the self-study turned to projection. Mayer forecast that Flint's Jewish population would grow by between 40 and 60 percent in the next quarter century, increasing from roughly 2,700 to between 3,300 and 4,000 persons. This very high rate of growth, he believed, would come from an accelerating in-migration of Jews from other U.S. cities, most of them professionals widening the ranks of Flint doctors and lawyers.

Tellingly, Mayer based this forecast on an accurate premise: the "economic base of [Flint's Jewish] community is dependent on the general community." Believing that the city's economy would flourish, Mayer therefore foresaw a "larger Flint" with "a larger Jewish community."[137] However this belief rested largely on city boosters' woefully inaccurate—some might say, hopelessly utopian—conviction that automotive production would continue to expand and that such expansion would redound to Flint's benefit. "The ultimate vitality of the [Jewish] community depends on the job situations which will exist in the future," Mayer maintained.[138] The self-study's author would be proved correct, but in a manner contrary to his expectations and to the severe detriment of Flint Jewry.

DECELERATION

Just a year after Mayer's report appeared, census figures revealed that the population of Flint had declined in the 1960s, from 197,000 to 193,000, the city's rank among U.S.

Flint Journal

Elders of Congregation Beth Israel carrying the Torah from the synagogue on Hamilton and Oren avenues to temporary quarters at Temple Beth El, 1971. Traditional observance requires that men wearing prayer caps and shawls carry the Torah, sheltered by a canopy, to a new place of worship. The next year the elders once again carried the Torah, leading a procession to the newly constructed synagogue on Calkins Road, to the west of Flint.

urban places thereby dropping from sixty-second-largest to sixty-seventh. The number of Flint workers employed in manufacturing also decreased during the decade, from 73,000 to 70,000. While these figures clearly run counter to the view that Flint's economy was still growing and thriving, they might indicate only a short-term downturn, a slump in the overall rising trajectory of GM's hometown. Instead, these signs of a deceleration presaged a catastrophic collapse in the ensuing decade, jobs and population plummeting and social tensions escalating. When GM's patriarch, C. S. Mott, died in 1973, many in Flint saw it as the end of an era. In many ways, they were right.

The initial effects of the city's sagging manufacturing sector were muted for many members of Flint's Jewish community because so few had direct ties to the auto industry. Professionals were cushioned most, since the newly unemployed at first continued to receive small paychecks and retained diminished benefits. For those in the commercial sector, the decline in manufacturing reinforced a decade of bad news, and some, especially those with businesses downtown, despaired that the economy would not turn around. Thus, in the face of the continued suburban flight of his customers, in 1969 Sid Melet, one of the most resolute champions of once-proud South Saginaw Street, decided to retain his downtown shop but open a large new branch of the Vogue at the just-opened Genesee Valley Mall. At ten thousand square feet the new Vogue dwarfed the downtown store, representing the family's recognition that its investment needed to follow its clientele—away from troubled Flint.[139]

The movement of longtime businesses to the suburbs made an important statement about the Jewish community's changing relationship to the city. More emblematic was the decision of the Conservative synagogue to leave its location on Flint's north side, west of the St. John District, after less than two decades. By 1970 few CBI congregants still lived in the north side neighborhood; most residences near the shul were occupied by blacks, some of whom did not have the economic resources to keep the deteriorating housing stock from further decay. Rather than continue urging congregants to drive back to the old inner-city structure, CBI's leadership resolved to build a new synagogue closer to suburban members and easily accessible by car for those in Flint's several prosperous subdivisions. The congregation chose a site five miles west of their current location and two miles west of the city limits, near the north-south expressway completed a few years before.

Hence in 1972 the new synagogue, the religious home of a majority of the area's Jewish community, was dedicated on a newly platted suburban lot. It was the fiftieth anniversary year of the founding of the congregation, a half-century in which Flint Jewry had grown and prospered with the autotown. The next decades would bring tremendous challenges to Flint and its Jewish community. During these very tough times, CBI's removal to the outskirts of the city would prove a harbinger of further institutional relocations as well the durability, resilience, and adaptability of area Jewish institutions and their members.

CHAPTER FOUR

Hard Times

GM LEAVES HOME

In 1970 General Motors manufactured its seventy-millionth Chevrolet, and once again the auto giant designated a vehicle built in the Flint area to symbolize attainment of a production milestone. The model was the Monte Carlo, a "muscle car" boasting a turbocharged engine, extensive chrome grillwork, a sleek dashboard, and an array of customer-pleasing options, from bucket seats and enhanced suspension to power brakes, power steering, and air conditioning. The Monte Carlo was fast, powerful, heavy and—even by the standards of this gas-guzzling age—a monster of fuel consumption. It was also the last Chevrolet model built in GM's hometown, or more accurately, just on its outskirts. After producing more than 5.7 million Chevrolet passenger cars, the giant assembly facility was converted to truck production, while a Fisher Body plant within the city, a major battleground during the 1936–37 sit-down strike, was shuttered.

The closure of the historic plant stunned the city's autoworkers. They knew that the nation was struggling economically, burdened by the high costs of the war in Vietnam and increased spending on domestic programs, but they also knew that GM profits were robust. The largest of the "Big Three" automakers, in 1970 GM controlled half the North American vehicle market. Some area union members found the timing of the plant closure suspicious, coming in the wake of the longest UAW strike against GM since 1946, a ten-week work stoppage that Flint union locals solidly supported. The successful strike had led to a contract granting UAW members safer working conditions and enhanced "cost of living" pay increases, further securing their position among the nation's highest-paid workers. Yet these short-term contractual gains soon paled in the face of the long-run disaster for the union's membership: devastating job losses in the U.S. auto industry and especially in Flint. Indeed, the closing of the Fisher Body plant was only the tip of a much bigger iceberg. In the thirty years after 1970, UAW national membership declined by seven hundred thousand, nearly 10 percent of whom were autoworkers in Genesee County. The absolute decline is staggering: some sixty-five thousand GM jobs in the Flint area over the course of just three decades.[1] The birthplace of General Motors has become a graveyard for the American automobile industry, the end of the line for Flint's once-vaunted working class.

Just as the roots of deindustrialization reached far beyond Flint, so too Flint's Jewish community was rocked by events originating far beyond the city's borders. A key world-historical moment linking Flint's subsequent economic decline to transformations in Flint's Jewish community was the brief Yom Kippur War of October 1973. The war precipitated an oil embargo against the United States and its Western European allies by the Arab members of the Organization of Petroleum Exporting Countries (OPEC), a slashing of oil supplies that carried far-reaching consequences. The conflict further galvanized support for Israel among Flint Jewry, while its economic aftershocks hastened Flint's decline.

DEINDUSTRIALIZATION AND MALAISE

Symbolically and practically, the oil crisis of 1973–74 marked the divide between Flint as a growing, thriving community and as a classic deindustrializing rustbelt city. Beginning in the late 1960s, high inflation, soaring federal government debt resulting from spendthrift "guns and butter" fiscal policies, growing competition from Europe and Asia, the movement of U.S. capital overseas, and rising wage pressures combined to initiate a long-term process of deindustrialization that undermined the economies of major urban manufacturing centers across a broad swath of the Northeast and Midwest. Trenton, Pittsburgh, Youngstown, Cleveland, Detroit, Flint, and scores of other industrial cities in the United States and Canada saw the beginnings of what soon became a dramatic and irreversible decline in manufacturing jobs.[2]

Flint's economic calamities thus were imbedded in broader regional, national, and international trends. In the fifteen years after the 1973–74 oil embargo, government, corporate, and personal debt soared, while the U.S. trade balance changed from slight surplus to deep deficit.[3] Between the mid-1970s and the mid-1990s, inequalities in wealth and income increased substantially; by 1990, the percentage of wealth held by the top 1 percent of the population comprised nearly one-third of all U.S. assets, approximating the percentage owned by the wealthiest 1 percent before the stock market crash of 1929.[4]

Hence the oil embargo, which helped plunge the U.S. economy into recession in the mid-1970s, only exacerbated a long-term trend.[5] Yet if it mainly exposed existing underlying weaknesses, it did so with a terrific jolt. Gasoline prices quadrupled, the federal government instituted gas rationing, and prices of heating oil and many petroleum-based consumer goods soared. The industry most drastically affected was automobile manufacturing, and GM, with its fleet of fuel-inefficient vehicles, was hit hardest, rapidly dropping market share. In retrospect, American automobile manufacturers need not have been surprised when the oil shock led to massive consumer flight to smaller, more fuel-efficient, and sometimes safer imports. In the 1960s the German-made Volkswagen had become popular with young drivers and city residents who liked the ease of parking the "Bug," and with other Americans who, for economic or environmental reasons, wanted to limit gasoline consumption. The sturdy Swedish-made Volvo had developed a small but stalwart following among safety-conscious Americans of means, while Japanese-made Hondas gradually widened their sliver of market share, appearing first on the West Coast. Still, U.S. automakers, confident of their continued dominance over the American auto market, regarded the imports as minor nuisances.

General Motors had made a memorable foray into the compact car market in the 1960s with its ill-fated Chevrolet Corvair, a rear-engine car that became the focus of consumer advocate Ralph Nader's 1965 influential exposé, *Unsafe at Any Speed.*[6] The book took U.S. automakers to task for resisting such safety features as seat belts, targeting the Corvair in particular for its tendency to roll over. GM responded by improving the Corvair's suspension, but not before the corporation had been forced to admit to a Senate subcommittee that it had spied on and tried to intimidate the ascetic and acerbic Nader. The episode became a symbol of GM's arrogance, reinforcing in the public mind that the nation's largest corporation would brook no criticism, and helping lay the groundwork for later consumer disaffection with its products, vehicles an even earlier critic had dubbed "insolent chariots."[7]

In the last decade the problems of America's auto industry have devastated the economy of Flint. . . . The economic situation of the community and its accompanying social malaise has motivated and continues to impel the area's Jewish residents to look elsewhere.

—*Daniel Steinmetz,* 1990 and Beyond: Needs and Possibilities Facing the Greater Flint Area Jewish Communities, *1990*

In the wake of the oil embargo, as the full impact of the flight from their products took hold, GM took extreme measures to remain competitive in the United States even as it accelerated its disinvestments in Flint and its movements of capital southward and overseas. Nationwide the company laid off thousands of workers, with Flint at the top of the layoff list. Later in the 1970s the company temporarily pumped up consumer demand, employment in Flint's auto industry rebounding to nearly 77,000.[8] The respite proved brief, however, as GM's market share again plunged. By 1980 a severe decline had set in, GM employment in the Flint area plummeting to 62,000, and by the end of the decade to 50,000.[9]

Responding to the crisis, in August 1979 U.S. Senate Budget Committee member Donald Riegle held hearings at the federal courthouse in Flint "to try to assess . . . what the economic picture looks like." It was familiar ground for the Democrat; born and raised in Flint, he hoped to provoke public debate on how to help his hometown and other crumbling rust belt cities. The first to testify was economics professor and former Michigan State University president Walter Adams. In a blistering critique, Adams decried the U.S. auto industry's "long-run self-destructive, suicidal course of conduct, stubbornly pursued for more than a quarter century . . . [and its] record of innovative lethargy, [having] lagged, not led, in the battle to develop cleaner, safer, more fuel efficient cars." The economist blamed auto industry executives, concluding that in the postwar years, "visionless managers [of the Big Three have] chosen to devote disproportionately massive resources to style and model changes, accompanied by a cacophony of advertising." Witness after witness bemoaned the city and state's "bleak" unemployment outlook and the "immense problems" engendered by the industry's decline.[10]

The hearings did little to slow the city's soaring unemployment rate, which reached nearly 25 percent in 1982 and prompted the out-migration of families by the hundreds, then thousands, from the Flint area. As jobs evaporated, the number of city residents sank below Depression-era levels. In 1960 Flint's population stood at nearly 200,000, reflecting the influx of newcomers responding to the postwar boom in automobile production. By 1980 the population had dropped to less than 160,000; by 1990 to slightly more than 140,000; by 1998 to 131,000, and by 2000 to less than 125,000. Thus in four decades Flint's population had declined by nearly 40 percent. At midcentury the city had ranked fiftieth among the nation's largest urban centers, but by 1990 was no longer in the top 100 and had slid to fourth among Michigan cities.

In 1987 *Money* magazine issued the first of what became an annual list ranking three hundred U.S. cities in terms of livability. By *Money*'s reckoning, Flint ranked dead last: the former "All-American City" had become the nation's most unlivable. In part the ranking reflected the city's unemployment rate, then 27 percent, but it also considered the ripple effects of GM's layoffs that included the widespread closing of retail stores and other businesses, a soaring crime rate, and a slashing of public services: with garbage collected every other week, rats outnumbered people by a growing margin. Some Flint residents raged against the messenger when a local radio station sponsored a public burning of the offending issue in the heart of the boarded-up downtown.[11]

An even greater blow to the city's reputation came in 1989 with the release of Michael Moore's controversial film *Roger & Me,* which turned Flint into America's unofficial unemployment capital.[12] In graphic footage and biting wit, the internationally distributed film portrayed the futile efforts of Flint's boosters and city government to stanch the flow of jobs, end the downward spiral of morale, and address the myriad problems resulting from GM's departure. Writing in 1999, *Flint Journal* reporter James M. Miller looked back at the city during the 1980s: "[R]ecession squeezed the city's economy, and crack cocaine ravaged the streets. . . . Flint seem[ed] like the punchline of a nationwide joke." After 1985, Miller concluded, "employment at Flint area GM factories began the long slide that continues today."[13] In less than fifteen years the booming city had fallen into seemingly irreversible decline.

Even before the release of *Roger & Me,* the dramatic story of Flint's demise drew national media attention. Journalist Daniel Zwerdling's brief account in *The Progressive* magazine, written during the "Reagan recession" of 1981–82, was an especially poignant portrayal. "To see what 25 percent unemployment does to a community, take a stroll down Saginaw Street to the middle of town. It used to be a lovely place, lined with brick buildings. . . . [Now] there is almost nobody and nothing here. Virtually every second store is boarded up with plywood. Some businesses have fled to suburban malls, the rest of them have simply folded. Flint is a 1982 ghost town."[14] Not only the city's downtown area but its once mighty manufacturing zones were devastated. He went on to describe the St. John District and the area to its north, where racial segregation was extreme. In this "black side of town," the neighborhood "looks like the rubble after a riot."[15] Zwerdling's observations on racial segregation were confirmed in an important 1994 study, which found that while residential segregation by race declined in many U.S. cities during the 1980s, in Flint, as throughout much of the rust belt, blacks became more segregated from whites. Of the 232 cities studied, Flint ranked as the eighth most segregated in the nation in 1980; a decade later it had become the sixth most segregated.[16]

Driving north from the Flint River, Zwerdling "passed miles, literally miles, of abandoned stores, closed supermarkets, closed auto body shops, closed fast food restaurants." Along more than half a dozen blocks in this rundown section the city had installed, at a cost of $100,000, "huge, bright-orange metal tubes" that "zigzagged along the sidewalks at waist level."[17] The neon-colored tubes were meant to add aesthetic appeal and visual excitement to the formerly thriving commercial area. Such seemingly bizarre and desperate measures did little to restore business, but some residents did find practical uses for the colorful installations: men and women sat on them, chatting in front of boarded up storefronts as they waited for one of the few city buses to roll by, while children, lacking neighborhood parks, used them as makeshift play stations.[18]

The idea of installing the bright orange metal tubes was one of the most modest in a string of urban revitalization schemes concocted by Flint civic and business leaders. A 1992 study by George F. Lord and Albert C. Price details the attempts to restructure the city's economy after the loss of its industrial base in vehicle production.[19] Beginning in the mid-1970s, the city invested in refurbishing its riverfront, a plan that did prettify the streetscape along a short segment of the Flint River. Complementing the riverside revitalization, the newly expanded regional branch of the University of Michigan moved from near the Cultural Center to the downtown.

Such cosmetic changes did not inject capital or jobs into a flagging economy being steadily drained of its economic lifeblood. City boosters thus seized on the unlikely concept of turning Flint into a tourist center, luring visitors from the millions of travelers zipping along the Interstate 75 corridor running from Michigan to Florida.[20] The first stage in this plan began in 1979 with the construction of a sixteen-floor luxury hotel alongside the river on South Saginaw Street. The Hyatt Hotel, with a price tag of nearly $30 million, was financed largely through federal development funds, plus monies from the Flint-based Mott Foundation, established by GM founder C. S. Mott.[21] From its opening the Hyatt had low occupancy rates; by the end of the 1980s it declared bankruptcy and was later sold for a paltry $8 million.

A much grander and more disastrous white elephant was Autoworld, a combination museum and theme park intended to celebrate "the wonderful world of the automobile." The ungainly building cost $80 million, and two years after opening went bankrupt. Despite the hopes of the local "growth coalition," the boosters and city leaders who had dreamed up the venture, few travelers along the busy interstate chose to stop in decaying Flint to spend an afternoon admiring vehicle engines, car memorabilia, or the chronicle of the horseless carriage, at least as displayed in Autoworld's bewildering exhibits and lackluster rides.[22] After standing empty for several years the cavernous building was demolished and the land became part of the University of Michigan-Flint campus.

Flint's misguided "tourist solution" also included riverfront apartments and a business complex, complete with food court. Dubbed "Windmill Place," perhaps to evoke fond memories of a simpler pre-industrial era, the complex stood next to the Autoworld site along the north bank of the Flint River. More ambitious was the construction of a "festival marketplace" occupying an entire city block across from the ill-fated Hyatt. Developed by James Rouse, a noted proponent of the "malling" of downtowns, "Water Street Pavilion," with its shops, restaurants, and food court proved as economically unviable as Windmill Place.[23] Both went belly-up, the pavilion later remade into university office space. Why these projects failed was obvious even to casual observers of the city's deserted streets: by the mid-1980s, with its sole economic pillar crumbling, Flint simply had too little business downtown to support such enterprises—and the longed-for throngs of tourists never came.

Together, these redevelopment efforts cost over $600 million, a remarkable expenditure of funds for a city of Flint's size, and a painful lesson in how the application of band-aid solutions cannot stanch a hemorrhage of capital. The backers of the revitalization schemes had promised the retention of nearly twelve thousand jobs and the creation of more than sixty thousand others. Instead, in the fifteen years between the construction of the Hyatt and the razing of Autoworld, the city's workforce declined by more than forty thousand.

Flint's fiscal picture got even worse when city leaders implemented the second prong of their redevelopment strategy: tax abatements coupled with infrastructure improvements for GM.[24] In a vain attempt to retain a fraction of the automobile industry, the city granted the corporation generous tax relief while helping it refit some of its plants, retoolings that often spurred further layoffs. The largest Fisher Body plant, for example, avoided nearly $500,000 in taxes between 1977 and 1984, then closed in 1987. GM then convinced the city to help redevelop the site as a technology center, gaining more tax abatements.[25] The "Buick City" project, which turned the massive plant into what was touted as a state-of-the-art, roboticized facility, was the most ambitious redevelopment scheme, with complex financing involving the federal government, the state, the city, and GM.[26] In the 1980s GM received more than $640,000 in tax abatements in Flint. The pace continued into the 1990s and beyond, with city and county officials in 2004 touting the advantages of granting GM a twelve-year, 50 percent tax break in exchange for maintaining the three thousand jobs left at the "Truck and Bus" plant on Flint's western outskirts.[27]

By then there remained a mere fifteen thousand GM jobs, both salaried and hourly, in all of Genesee County. For despite the panoply of generous corporate subsidies, in July 1999 Buick had ceased production of all vehicles in Flint, ending the city's years as a place where automobiles were made. The closure came a year after a strike by 9,200 workers at the local parts plants in a vain struggle to maintain the existing job structure.[28] An article in popular magazine *U.S. News & World Report* declared "The End of an Era for Autos," and asked: "How can a town nicknamed Buick City not make Buicks?"[29] The anachronistic nickname remains a poignant reminder of what Flint once was and what it has become.

History shows how many celebrations and special events were produced in Flint by Chevrolet. What it amounted to was Chevrolet loved Flint and Flint loved Chevrolet. The feelings are still mutual. But as Flint Chamber [of Commerce] President [Larry] Ford pointed out [recently], "These are changing times."

—*Lynn Ruester in* See the U.S.A. in your Chevrolet: Celebrating 85 Years of Tradition, *1996*

In 2002 the vast bulk of the once-mighty Buick facility, reincarnated as the revamped "Buick City," was razed, generating nearly four hundred thousand tons of debris. For many, the demolition represented the destruction of Flint's way of life. As of 2004, the small building left standing on the northern end of the Buick site housed only a "Powertrain" plant, with three thousand workers, and a small firm that supplied frames to the truck plant. Even these few remaining GM jobs were in jeopardy, as the company's relentless "downsizing," or "right-sizing," the company's preferred euphemism, continued.[30] A key component of that "right-sizing" entailed the "spin-off" of units within GM, including the former AC Spark Plug division, which became part of independent Delphi company in 1998, competing with other suppliers worldwide for the business of its former parent company. In the Flint area, Delphi employed some three thousand former GM employees in 2004, with many workers anxious that even more job cuts were just around the corner.[31]

By the end of the century there seemed to be no good news to report about Flint; or rather, for every positive story reported in the news media, more dreadful ones followed. In January 2000, for example, forty-six-year-old African American autoworker Christopher Paul Curtis won the American Library Association's Newberry Medal for the best American children's book for his novel *Bud, Not Buddy*.[32] Yet just a month later this tale of literary triumph was eclipsed by a news item that horrified the nation, when a six-year-old boy shot and killed his classmate in a schoolroom in a poor and largely black school district contiguous to Flint.[33] The shooting revived memories of another notorious case, when in June 1997 six black residents, four of them teenagers, were charged with murder, kidnapping, armed robbery, and sexual assault against three white teens. Quoting Flint Mayor Woodrow Stanley's lament that "This incident is holding the entire city up to national ridicule," *Time* magazine described how "this crime, cloaked sensationally in black-on-white, is quickly escalating into a small-town version of the O. J. Simpson case."[34]

Like many declining industrial centers in the rust belt of the Midwest and Northeast, Flint today is primarily a black city, its population 53 percent African American, 42 percent white, and the remaining 5 percent either of mixed race or Native American or Asian. Less than 3 percent of Flint's population is Hispanic (not defined as a "racial" category by the Census Bureau), and less than 1 percent Jewish. More than a quarter of the population lives below the federal poverty line. Homeownership, achieved by more than three-quarters of the population during Flint's heyday, declined to less than 60 percent in 2000. More alarming is the vacancy rate, with one of every eight structures abandoned, rendering neighborhoods increasingly vulnerable to arson, vandalism, and crime.[35]

Meanwhile outlying areas in Genesee County continued growing at a fairly rapid pace, with even bigger growth on the southern edge of the county, adjoining Oakland County, the recipient of capital and population flight from Detroit. The expansion of Bishop Airport on the city's near western fringe has proved something of an economic boon, as residents of Detroit's northernmost suburbs and exurbs have taken advantage of its relative proximity. At the same time, the establishment of Bishop Airport as a "free-trade zone" under the terms of the North American Free Trade Agreement allowed auto parts manufactured in Mexico or Canada to enter the city with few or no tariffs.[36]

For many of Flint's beleaguered residents the arrangement exudes a bitter irony, as the federal government grants generous tax relief to foreign manufacturers to import products once produced locally. After decades of failed governmental inducements to keep GM jobs in the area, these foreign products become part of the few "American-made" vehicles still produced in Genesee County. Meanwhile, as the process of globalization moves forward, so too does the saga of Flint's descent, the deindustrialized city a shell of its former self.

A MODEL JEWISH COMMUNITY IMPERILED

The same year GM celebrated production of its seventy-millionth Chevrolet in Flint and then abruptly closed a major local plant, Flint Jewry's leading social institution received a prestigious award. In 1970 the National Council of Jewish Federations and Welfare Funds bestowed on the Flint Jewish Community Council its Charles Goodall Award, recognizing its "outstanding achievement and excellence in moving ahead toward becoming a model small Jewish community."[37] Flint's Jews took deserved pride in the recognition and looked forward to an even more vibrant future. Instead, the award came at the peak of the community's strength. The rapid eclipse of the city's auto manufacturing base after 1973 dashed the community's plans, overburdening its institutions, sapping its vitality, undercutting its financial stability, and precipitating its decline. Resilient and adaptable, a dwindling local Jewry continued to add to its record of attainments during these years, but under exceptionally trying conditions. Since the early 1970s, the city's economic and civic crises have defined the parameters in which Flint Jewry have struggled to carve out a viable communal life.

The tale of the imperiled community has several interweaving threads. Demographically Flint Jewry's ranks have thinned, dispersed, and aged. Economically its members have suffered, merchants and professionals hurt especially by the collapse of demand for goods and services. Accompanying these changes have been sustained efforts to rejuvenate a deteriorating communal life, both within the Jewish community and between Jews and other groups. The community's attenuated resource base has prompted institutional reorganization and consolidation, with attendant tensions. Intensified denominational competition has spurred further internal conflict, as Flint has witnessed the emergence of a branch of Orthodox Judaism alongside its Conservative and Reform congregations. Closely linked to these trends has been an increasingly fervent commitment to support Jewry worldwide, expressed both through an extensive resettlement effort for Soviet Jews and greater mobilization for Israel. While this fervor has crosscut internal divisions, it has exacerbated conflicts between Jews and other groups, all of which are struggling within the overarching context of economic decline.

> I was sitting with Mr. Mott and he was telling me about [Autoworld] and I said, "You know, that sounds very interesting, but who the hell is going to come up and watch something about cars? . . . If I were you, I'd build the biggest roller coaster in America—a triple loop-de-loop, and call it the Buick Special. And then people will stop all the time for it."
>
> —*Jack Stanzler, civic activist, recalling a city revitalization plan, 2003*

DOWN AND OUT

The population figures alone tell a grim story. With deindustrialization the Flint area's Jewish population plummeted from roughly 2,700 in 1967, to 2,100 in 1988, to some 1,200 in all of Genesee County in 2004—a 55 percent decrease that exceeds even the steep drop in Flint's overall population.[38] Most of this decline stemmed from out-migration, with families moving away in response to the city's deteriorating economy and civic life. The Jewish population also got older. Many became less active in communal affairs and many others more socially isolated, in part because the area's remaining Jewish population shrank and became less geographically compact.

In 1972, when Congregation Beth Israel (CBI) built a new synagogue beyond the city limits, the ground breaking preceded the departure of most congregants to the suburbs—a pattern contrasting with nearby Detroit, whose major Jewish religious institutions followed the suburban exodus of the majority of their worshipers.[39] After the economy soured, Reform and Conservative households began moving out of Flint, with scattered clusters soon emerging among the subdivisions to the west and south. By 1980 nearly 125 Jewish households resided in the "Western Hills" subdivision only a mile west of the synagogue, while none remained in the neighborhood of the congregation's former synagogue on McFarlan Street.

In 1998 Temple Beth El (TBE) also relocated outside Flint's municipal boundaries, selling the building it had erected in 1950. Attesting to heightened cooperation between the synagogue and the temple in the face of a shrinking Jewish population, CBI sold TBE an adjacent lot on Calkins Road at below market value. Yet while both suburban facilities hosted congregations physically nearer to the bulk of the remaining Jewish population, their numbers kept falling. In the mid 1970s the temple and synagogue together boasted more than 800 families but by 2004 only some 440, with TBE member families numbering just over 200 and CBI slightly more.[40] Even these worrisome figures disguised the net decline in financial support for both congregations, since the rosters at both TBE and CBI included "courtesy members," persons lacking the wherewithal to pay dues, most either elderly, longtime residents or Russian immigrants. For dues–paying members a more realistic figure was roughly 300 to 325 families divided equally between Reform and Conservative congregations.[41] Even more revealingly, one family in seven on the rosters of both CBI and TBE were former or part–time Flint residents: "snowbird" retirees who traveled south for the winter or those who lived out–of–state. Their commitment and material contributions remained important, but these absentee members effectively had become disengaged from much of the community's daily life. The problem of an aging congregation was more severe at CBI, the temple's older membership balanced in part by younger families, most including children, and some drawn from counties adjacent to Flint.

REORGANIZING AND RETRENCHING

In the face of these troublesome demographic trends, a key question confronting Flint Jewry has been how to maintain a strong community life. Working with increasingly limited resources, the community has undertaken structural reorganization, instituted new programs, and, continuing its strong social survey tradition, commissioned two studies to help guide its work. The results have been mixed, the community hard-pressed to meet the needs of its thinning and aging membership much less inject renewed dynamism into cultural activities for area Jews.

The major organizational restructuring occurred in the mid 1980s, with Flint's deindustrialization irretrievable, the local Jewish population sinking, and the need for social services growing in inverse proportion to the economic plunge. By then the Flint Jewish Community Council (FJCC), established during the 1930s, had changed its name to the Flint Jewish Federation (FJF), following a national trend; the group remains the umbrella organization for secular Jewish life in Genesee County.[42] The local federation took a number of steps to try to better the position of Flint Jewry during these trying years. Under the direction of David Nussbaum, the FJF became more active politically, establishing a greater voice in Genesee County's Democratic Party. Similarly the FJF became more visible in larger community affairs, raising the profile of the organization and of Flint Jewry more generally by participating, under FJF auspices, in major civic events.[43]

In 1984 the FJF commissioned a study to examine the problems confronting its growing number of elderly members and suggest solutions.[44] The results were sobering: more than a third of the community's elderly population lived alone, a majority were foreign-born Yiddish speakers, and not even a third visited friends or relatives monthly. While most had substantial financial resources and owned their own homes, many had difficulty with daily activities such as preparing food and obtaining medical care. The report noted the aid provided by the Senior Friendship Club, inaugurated in 1962 by community member Dr. Evelyn Golden, but concluded that Flint's Jewish elderly "lacked *social support systems.*"[45] A follow-up report recommended that the Jewish community construct a forty- to sixty-unit senior housing project, at an estimated cost of more than two million dollars.[46]

The recommendation immediately sparked controversy in the Jewish community. Flint Jewry had never built a Jewish Community Center, despite decades of discussion about the need for such a facility.[47] This proposal, coming in the midst of economic crisis, struck most Flint Jews both as far too expensive and too limited in its prospective clientele. Unwilling to spend so much money on the aged while failing to meet other pressing needs, the community also realized that it could not ignore the problems exposed by the study.

In 1987 the community resolved the dilemma by establishing an independent agency. The Jewish Social Services of Flint (later renamed Jewish Family and Children's Services or JFCS and still later, Jewish Community Services) would provide the social support network the community lacked, not only for the elderly but for all members of the community.[48] Sharing office space with the FJF but with its own full-time director since 1999, the JFCS has raised money within the community and, as an independent agency, also has qualified for grants offered by external private and public funding sources. To serve the aged, the JFCS has launched a wide range of services, from providing kosher meals to sponsoring the Russian Resettlement Senior Social Day club. In addition, the JFCS has offered information and referrals to all community members and developed programs targeted at teens and young adults, in hopes that the next generation will remain active in the Jewish community.[49] It assumed responsibility for maintaining the Camp Maccabee summer day camp, carrying on a tradition of blending education in Jewish culture with recreation until 2002. During these years the camp became increasingly vital as former programs, including federation-sponsored sports teams, were eliminated as the number of young people declined.[50]

A "hootenanny" at Camp Maccabee, 1972. Established in 1954 and held in various locations in the Flint area through 2002, the summer day camp offered Jewish children and teens an array of activities, encouraging them to learn about Jewish culture while sharing good times.

Flint Journal

Sloan Museum

Flint Jewish Federation (FJF) softball team, 1982. By the 1990s the Jewish community no longer had sufficient numbers to field sports teams such as this one, whose teammates wear shirts emblazoned with FJF and the Jewish Star of David. For decades participation in these teams promoted community solidarity and fostered interaction with members of other ethnic, racial, and religious groups. This team played in the so-called church league, organized by the Young Men's Christian Association.

Midwinter's Dream Party, 1980. The Flint Jewish Federation sponsored events like this "shalom swim party" to promote socializing among the area's declining numbers of Jewish young adults. Pictured (*left to right*) are: Debra (Golden) Steinman, Sharon Stein, Marty Natchez, Randy Grossman, and Harold Steinman.

Sloan Museum

Similarly, the JFCS has worked with the federation to encourage young Jewish singles and couples to mingle in informal settings, a high priority in light of climbing intermarriage rates since the 1970s.[51]

Part of the impetus for these JFCS activities stemmed from the findings of another survey, conducted in 1990 to explore the "needs and possibilities" for the Jewish community as it struggled to cope with still further declines in population and resources.[52] Because the federation's budget could not afford a full-blown community survey, this self-study was more limited in scope and method than the one conducted in 1967 and provided less data and analysis.[53] Most critically, the study did not assay the impact of Flint's deindustrialization on Jewish business owners and professionals, though it did find that an extraordinary 97 percent of respondents twenty-five years of age and older believed their children would leave the area, mainly to pursue economic opportunities elsewhere.[54] Related concerns were the dearth of local Jewish marriage partners, the city having few members aged twenty-five to thirty-five, and a growing rate of intermarriage, more than a quarter of all spouses indicating they had not been born Jewish. Spurred by these data, and the projected wholesale departure of respondents' children, the JFCS instituted more programs for youth and young adults.[55] Despite the organizations' efforts, few "young Jewish couples . . . interested in a Jewish life" stay in Flint, notes federation activist Michael Pelavin, "because there's not much of a Jewish community here. For those who . . . are observant and who require kashrut and day schools and things of that kind, it's basically unavailable."[56] Thus the erosion of community life deepens.

Clearly neither the JFCS nor the federation can halt the local economy's decline, the ultimate source of most community members' problems. Instead both have retrenched as the community's economic resources have shriveled, directing more resources into core services and promoting what they view as these organizations' local, national, and international interests. Yet even functions perceived as vital have been threatened by fiscal constraints. In 1999 the federation failed to reach its fund-raising goal, lowering by one-fifth the local budget earmarked for Israel via the United Jewish Appeal.[57] In the 1990s, contributions to the federation fell by more than 20 percent. As federation executive director Gary Alter explained in 2003, "As the population goes down, our campaign goes down," adding that the "bigger givers to local fund-raising were people in industrial and commercial businesses," many of whom have left the area or been "squeezed out" by the decline in Flint's economy.[58]

FEELING THE ECONOMIC CRUNCH

Since the early 1970s, Flint's economic malaise has spilled over into the city's once-thriving Jewish businesses. The story of the Vogue's downward spiral illustrates the eroding viability of downtown retail businesses, a process disproportionately hurting local Jewish families. In 1970 the Vogue opened its large store in Genesee Valley Mall while retaining its flagship store downtown and operating three other outlets in Flint proper. The women's clothing business was hit hard by the city's economic crisis, but high-end buyers, the Vogue's main customers, still had money to spend and for several years the stores managed to stay afloat. However, in the words of Vogue owner Michael Melet, "In 1978 I started for the first time feeling at the Vogue [that] our actual sales figures [showed that] something really bad was happening in Flint. I could see a down-trend. . . . We were one of the last to feel it."[59] Melet then learned to his dismay that the city's only large department store, Smith-Bridgman's, soon would declare bankruptcy and that another downtown mainstay, Montgomery Ward, also planned to shutter. Melet decided to "get out while the getting out [was] good"—in fact rather later than most. In December 1979, at the height of the Christmas season, Melet told his employees that within six months the downtown Vogue would close. He recalled the circumstances: "Interest rates hit 20 percent, unemployment hit 26 percent in Flint. [The city was] on the cover of the *Wall Street Journal,* the *New York Times,* and it looked like Flint was going to be wiped off the map."[60] He then closed the other two Flint stores and "downsized" the mall outlet.

Yet in his father's tradition he placed great faith in municipal commercial ventures, in the mid 1980s pouring his energy and remaining finances into several redevelopment schemes, including ten retail outlets in Water Street Pavilion. When the festival marketplace went belly-up so did Melet's businesses. In 1990 the Vogue declared bankruptcy, ending nearly seventy-five years as a Jewish-owned clothing retailer.

By then two favorite dining spots for local Jews already had gone out of business. In 1980, even as city leaders instituted plans for building the multimillion-dollar Hyatt, the stately Durant Hotel stood empty, and with the Durant's closure came the demise of the Phoenix Club. Housed on the hotel's eighth floor, for a quarter-century the club had served as the leading site for elite Jews to lunch and socialize. Later in the decade, the closure of once-crowded Uncle Bob's Diner, a comfortable delicatessen

Max Wexler (*left*) and Sydney Osher, owners of Cut Rate Auto
Parts, in front of their once-flourishing business at 4026 North Dort
Highway, 1982. Most such enterprises on "Junkyard Alley" closed
with the decline in GM manufacturing.

Flint Journal

that served a diverse clientele, symbolized to many
area Jews the end of an era in the city's downtown.

The scrap business, another mainstay of Jewish
enterprise, similarly fell on hard times. Many of
these small, family-owned firms lined Dort Highway
in northeast Flint, a mile-long stretch dubbed
"Junkyard Alley."[61] By the early 1980s proprietors
like Abraham Natchez, owner of Industrial Iron and
Metal, in business since 1916, saw their customer
base erode, as steel mills stopped buying their junked
cars. The auto industry was partly to blame, with steel
mills needing less scrap as GM and other U.S.
automakers made fewer vehicles and used less steel
and more plastic. Similarly, Max Wexler and Sydney
Osher, co-owners of Cut Rate Auto Parts, saw their
livelihood threatened by the exodus of former
autoworkers. As Wexler explained, "They were the
ones who had two cars, factory workers who could afford to buy new cars and junk the
old ones." With fewer autoworkers, "Business just isn't very good anymore." Plagued
by growing stockpiles, endemic thievery, and multiplying vermin, Osher, Wexler, and
most other Junkyard Alley owners laid off employees, and by the end of the decade
closed. Swimming against this tide, the Natchez family continued, holding on to the
Industrial Iron business as late as 2004.

ZIONIST MOBILIZATION

In autumn 1973 international events again jolted the local community, refortifying
American and Flint Jewry's already strong commitment to Israel.[62] The catalyst was the
Yom Kippur War, launched in early October on the holiest day of the Jewish year.
Egyptian and Syrian forces, backed militarily by Iraq and Jordan and economically by
Saudi Arabia, attacked Israeli positions on the Suez Canal and Golan Heights.[63] Taken
by surprise, Israel suffered a string of initial defeats. Its forces quickly regrouped,
launching offensives on both fronts and receiving crucial aid from a U.S. airlift of
weapons and supplies. In late October a UN-brokered cease-fire helped end continued skirmishing. Israel emerged the clear victor from the short but bloody war, gain-
ing territory from Syria and on the west bank of the Suez.

Members of the Flint delegation of the national *Koach* (mission of strength) parade through an Israeli neighborhood, 1975. Israel's victory in the Yom Kippur War spurred many Flint Jews to undertake such trips and to deepen their financial support for Zionism.

Beyond the legacy of continued conflict between Israel and its Arab neighbors, the Yom Kippur War had two significant effects for Flint Jewry. One was the oil embargo, which dealt a severe blow to the U.S. economy, especially its auto industry. Beyond this economic fallout, Flint Jewry, like Jewish communities elsewhere, experienced the Yom Kippur War as a psychological call to arms. The surprise attack underscored Israel's continuing vulnerability and steeled the determination of American Jewry to press for an even stronger pro-Israeli U.S. foreign policy. Only two days after the war began, Flint Jewry publicly demonstrated its strong support for Israel. With Egyptian and Syrian troops still advancing, the community held a huge rally at CBI. Sponsored by the FJCC, supported by the rabbi of TBE, and attended by then U.S. Representative Donald Riegle, the event proved the most successful fund-raiser in the community's history, pushing the local annual pledge to the "Israel Emergency Fund" to $635,000.[64]

After the Israeli victory, area Jews began traveling to Israel in what were termed "leadership missions." Although some had visited in the 1960s and early 1970s, the missions represented a sustained and institutionalized effort to educate members of the community about Israel and galvanize recruitment efforts for similar journeys. Just months after war's end, the FJCC publicized and urged participation in four upcoming missions. The council also helped defray costs, bringing the price of a two-week "study mission" well within the budget of most area Jews. Thus, after 1973 a visit to Israel became virtually mandatory for local Jewish leaders.[65]

For participants the missions proved deeply meaningful. As one remarked, "The result . . . has been a great emotional experience for all of us from Flint. . . . As a result of being in [Israeli] homes and talking frankly and openly [with Israelis], we have been able to develop a real sense of identification with the people. It's given us a great sense of unity."[66] The missions also spurred greater financial support for Israel and, often, for Jewish communal life in Flint. Women as well as men participated in these missions, with Diane Lindholm, one of the first women to serve as FJF president, coordinating most of the visits.

In order to broaden local support for Israel, in the late 1980s community leaders began sponsoring trips to Israel by clergy, public officials, and business, union, and educational leaders. These largely proved successful. In March 1988, local attorney and Flint Board of Education member Mary Simon participated in "Project Interchange," coming back impressed with "the nature of the Israelis and their determination to maintain the Israeli state."[67] Similarly, U.S. Representative Dale Kildee described his 1993 trip to Israel, part of an official congressional visit, as "both a physical and spiritual journey" that "reaffirmed my belief that we must work toward real peace in the Mid-East." The mission also confirmed Kildee's resolute backing of the Israeli view of the terms of such a hoped-for peace.[68]

Kildee's visit to Israel took place two years after the end of yet another violent Mideast conflict, the Persian Gulf War. Precipitated by Iraq's invasion of Kuwait in August 1990, the brief conflict again aroused local Jews' fears for Israel. Iraqi missile attacks proved ineffectual but showed once again the dangers confronting Israel. More than previous conflicts, the Persian Gulf War allowed Flint Jewry to make common cause with many local Gentiles, many of whom supported U.S. actions and some of whom, like three area Jewish families, had relatives stationed in the Mideast.[69] By then most of Flint Jewry embraced an ardently Zionist position. Almost half of all households surveyed in 1990 had members who belonged to Hadassah, the women's organization that had pioneered Zionist activity in the 1920s.[70] What had been a minority movement before World War II—and one challenged openly by TBE then-rabbi Elmer Berger—had become, in the postwar years, the hegemonic view of Flint's Jewish community.

In the aftermath of the Gulf War, as prospects for peace in the Middle East have dimmed and with Israel increasingly besieged by internal and external foes, local Jewry has remained firm in its commitments to Israeli security. Two Palestinian intifadas, the rise of Hamas and suicide bombings, and the looming prospect of a separate Palestinian state have all served to heighten local support for Israel, as have the aftershocks of the terrorist attacks of September 11, 2001, and the Iraq War from March 2003. With genuine peace in the Middle East seemingly unattainable, and in a local context of continuing economic decline and social malaise, the commitment to Israel has helped unify area Jewry in the face of a range of seemingly intractable problems.

WELCOMING NEW IMMIGRANTS

From the late 1960s, as Flint's Jewish community repeatedly reaffirmed its strong support for Israel, it also mobilized in support of world Jewry, especially Soviet Jews. In 1967, the aftermath of the Six Day War prompted an outpouring of cultural and religious sentiment among Russian Jews, who pressed Soviet officials for permission to emigrate to Israel, the United States, and elsewhere in Europe. Deftly exploiting cold war rivalries, Soviet Jews enlisted the moral and material support of Jews throughout the world.[71] For U.S. leaders, waging a costly and losing war in Vietnam and under mounting criticism, the solicitations of Soviet Jews came at an auspicious moment, providing an opportunity to garner Jewish political support at home and refurbish the nation's image as a beacon of hope for liberty-seekers abroad.

This pattern was clearly evident in Flint, where key public officials strongly endorsed efforts to promote emigration from the USSR and worked to build local interest in the cause. In mid 1971, Genesee County District Attorney Robert Leonard visited the Soviet Union, urging officials to authorize and expedite resettlement efforts.[72] Later that fall, Flint Jewry sponsored the largest rally in the community's history, when more than nine hundred people marched to City Council chambers, demanding greater attention to the plight of Soviet Jewry.[73] In spring 1972, Flint Jews joined a rally at the state capital in Lansing, part of a national action for Soviet Jews.[74]

Local Jewry took particular interest in one Soviet family in the media spotlight, the Fairmarks, launching a letter-writing campaign on their behalf and wearing bracelets bearing their names. Within two years Galena Fairmark and her young daughter immigrated to Flint. Their arrival sparked much celebration, though their quick departure left some feeling disappointed and resentful.[75] The decamping of the Fairmarks and several other Russian families in the early 1970s mirrored an earlier pattern, when Flint Jewry helped resettle refugees after World War II. As before, some members' disappointment did not dampen the larger community endeavor, which resettled nearly a hundred Soviet Jews over the course of the decade, exceeding the quota suggested by the Hebrew Immigrant Aid Society for a city of its size.[76] The JFCS helped new arrivals get medical care, find employment, and learn English, like newcomers Boris and Valentina Bonzaft, he training as a draftsman and she as a cardiology technician.

As elsewhere in the United States, women stood at the forefront of the movement. In early December 1977, Flint women joined with women in fifty cities nationwide to appeal to Soviet authorities to permit increased Jewish emigration, especially of entire families. The current policies, they declared, left "mothers ... separated from parents, daughters separated from parents, wives from husbands, and sisters from

Dr. Jack Stanzler, head of the Flint Jewish Federation's Community Relations Council, addresses a crowd of more than nine hundred demonstrators after a march from downtown to City Council chambers, 1971. Organized to draw attention to the plight of Soviet Jewry, the rally garnered support from the local Interfaith Action Council and represented a key step in building momentum for the cause.

sisters and brothers."[77] The next week, during the height of the Christmas shopping season, the activists erected a small booth at the Genesee Valley Mall, collecting petition signatures calling on Soviet leader Leonid Brezhnev to free all Jews held as "prisoners of conscience," end persecution of Jews, and allow "refuseniks" to leave. This holiday-time informational booth remained an annual tradition through the mid 1980s.[78] The campaign drew support from local Christian clergy and laity, especially women.[79] At Woodside Church, an interdenominational Protestant congregation near the College and Cultural Center, a small group of parishioners, "Woodside Freedom Writers for Soviet Jewry," urged others to join their petition campaign. A high point in the campaign came in January 1978, when father and son Anstel and Leonid Blyakh, separated by Soviet authorities at the Moscow airport in 1975, were reunited in Flint, a reunion for which local activists had toiled for three years.[80]

In the mid 1980s Jewish women redoubled and consolidated their efforts on behalf of Soviet refugees, the TBE and CBI sisterhoods working with Hadassah, B'nai B'rith Women, and two new groups, a Women's Communal Service Committee of the Federation Community Relations Council and a chapter of Women's American Organization through Rehabilitation and Training. The movement was in high gear, with many women committed to feminism and to Judaism providing leadership. In 1988, just before President Reagan's third summit with Soviet President Gorbachev, forty members of Flint's Jewish community joined a huge march in Washington. As a

Sloan Museum

Sloan Museum

Shoppers at the Genesee Valley Mall pause to sign the petition for the release of Soviet Jewry proffered by Esther Price and daughter Rhonda, 1977.

Linda Pinti gathers signatures on a petition calling for the freeing of jailed dissident Soviet mathematician Anatoly Sharansky, a target of anti-Semitism, 1977. A member of an interdenominational church, Pinti helped form the interfaith "Woodside Freedom Writers for Soviet Jewry."

teenage member of the delegation recalled, "What struck me [flying home] was that all those 200,000 [demonstrators] were Jews coming together from all parts of the country, working toward the freedom of fifteen percent of world Jewry, and everyone knowing the words to the same song, *Am Yisreal Chai,* "The People of Israel Live."[81]

In the late 1980s, as Soviet President Gorbachev instituted the glasnost reforms, the flow of emigrés from the USSR increased, the trickle becoming a flood in the wake of the regime's collapse in 1991. Local Jewry enthusiastically endorsed "Operation Exodus," the national campaign to bring Russian refugees to the United States, which brought more than 350 to Flint during the 1990s.[82] In three years the community raised nearly $500,000 to aid the newcomers, establishing a corps of volunteers to greet them at the airport, tutor them in English, and train them in needed skills like shopping and driving, even furnishing them apartments at a complex on the city's west side, accessible to both temple and synagogue. Dozens of local Jewish families participated.[83] Those resettled earlier proved especially willing and capable volunteers. As Ina Alexander, co-chair of the Russian Resettlement Committee, observed, "I know what they will be feeling . . . what their fears will be . . . knowing the language and remembering the position that I was in when I arrived [helps me aid] them."[84] To finance these activities, in July 1990 the FJF instituted a successful annual dinner to honor local Jewish and Gentile civic leaders. Named the Donald Riegle Community Service Award Dinner, the fund-raiser honored former U.S. Senator Donald Riegle, the native son who led Congressional initiatives to try to stem Flint's manufacturing collapse, courted the Jewish vote assiduously throughout his career, supported Israel stalwartly for two decades, and sponsored legislation facilitating Soviet immigration.[85]

Despite these well-funded and extensive initiatives, by the year 2000 more than a third of the Russians resettled to the Flint area had moved away. The city's economic malaise proved reason enough. Yet some newcomers also had clashed with their sponsors. From the volunteers' perspective, some emigrés showed too little connection to Judaism, failing to join either the synagogue or the temple and demonstrating scant interest in community affairs. Some refugees, in turn, suspected volunteers were somehow government agents (as they might have been in the Soviet Union). Many also felt disenchanted, with so little money to buy the abundant consumer goods surrounding them. The downward mobility many experienced, especially those unable to practice professions, compounded their dismay. Some adapted, with considerable community help, like Dina and Anatoly Ionina, sixty-year-old medical doctors who became physician assistants. Others, like Yuliya Gaydayenko, pursued postsecondary education. Immigrating in 1995, she graduated from the University of Michigan–Flint and in 1998 began working in the local Jewish Community Services office, three years later becoming the staff member overseeing senior programs and in 2004 the agency's executive director. Still others adopted new lines of work. Aliya Movsesyan opened a Russian restaurant, succeeded for several years, and then succumbed to the overexpansion common among immigrant businesses.[86]

A family reunion of Soviet Jewish emigrés at Flint's Bishop Airport, 1990. Nick Naroditsky, age four (*right*), gives flowers to his grandparents, Fayvous and Jennie (*left*), while his mother, Inna (*third from left*), and friends look on. Bureaucratic obstacles had delayed the grandparents' immigration for two months.

In all, the thirty-year resettlement effort helped hundreds of individuals while providing a crucial locus for local community organizing. In the midst of economic crisis, declining numbers, and the departure of many young adults who might have become future leaders, aiding the Russian refugees proved a worthwhile and positive endeavor. The community takes pride in what it did for these newcomers, perceiving that in this city built by successive waves of new arrivals, these most recent immigrants represent one hopeful sign for the continued vitality of Flint Jewry.

COMMUNITY RELATIONS

The Jewish community's response to local economic decline and international events also helped shape its relations with Flint's non-Jewish communities, a story of both successes and disappointments. As noted previously, one high point came in 1970, when Flint area Jews received the prestigious Goodall

Sonia Weston, who settled in Flint after World War II, awaits the arrival of cousins from the Soviet Union, 1990.

Flint Journal

Award, this recognition due in part to inauguration of the Community Relations Council (CRC) of the FJCC.[87] The CRC had worked with black leaders to promote entrepreneurship, establish a black/Jewish dialogue, and end "redlining" (realty agencies' and financial institutions' discrimination against prospective black homebuyers).

Jack Stanzler, an osteopath who came to Flint to practice internal medicine in 1955, headed the CRC throughout these years, also serving as a member of the Flint Interfaith Metropolitan Agency for Planning, dedicated to fostering interracial and interfaith dialogue and mobilized especially around issues of racism and police brutality. Stanzler recalled that the most important achievement of the interfaith agency, fully supported by the CRC, was an investigation of the Flint Police Department, which revealed its entrenched racism, blatant sexism, and failure to address citizen complaints on a range of important issues.[88] These and related efforts helped foster cordial relations between the organized Jewish community and such groups as the NAACP and the Urban League, as did individual acts of benevolence by leading Jewish community members toward organizations and institutions serving the broader public.

The atmosphere of mutual trust did not last long, Flint Jewry's intensified support for Israel in the wake of the Yom Kippur War coming at a tricky moment in public sentiment. In vehicle-loving Flint, many residents blamed Arab nations and the oil embargo for the dramatic decline in demand for GM vehicles, the steep jump in fuel prices, and the long gas lines. There was also a sense among some residents that Israel and by extension local Jews bore responsibility for the energy crisis. If a current of anti-Semitism informed this view, it also stemmed from a national preoccupation with locating the source of mounting domestic economic problems anywhere but at home.

Also by the mid 1970s, a range of problems rooted in the declining local economy and exacerbated by national and international issues drove a widening wedge between African Americans and Jews. Middle Eastern developments in particular heightened tensions and undermined dialogue between the two groups. Former Flint Mayor James Sharp Jr., active in the city's African American community, recalled two key events. The first was the revelation in 1979 that U.S. Ambassador to the United Nations Andrew Young, the first African American to hold the post, had held a secret meeting

Sloan Museum

The Schreiber family endows a scholarship for business students at Mott Community College (MCC), 1978. Presenting the check to Edwyna G. Anderson, chairman of the MCC Board of Trustees (*left*), and Dr. Charles N. Pappas, MCC president (*second from left*), are (*left to right*) Edwin Schreiber, Zelma Gottlieb, and Gerald Schreiber, children of Abe and Shirley Schreiber, who founded Royalite Company, supplier of electrical goods to auto factories and consumers. Pappas belonged to Temple Beth El.

with the Palestine Liberation Organization. Young resigned, sparking bitter exchanges between blacks and Jews nationwide.[89] The local dispute intensified when scathing letters between CBI's Rabbi Hillel Rudavsky and local NAACP leader Edgar Holt became public.[90] Relations between the two communities were already strained, as some Flint Jews, including the CBI rabbi, had been vocal opponents of affirmative action, a policy upheld by the Supreme Court the year before.[91] Interactions between Jews and white Christians were more amiable, as shown in March 1979 with a well-attended interfaith meeting at TBE celebrating a peace treaty between Egypt and Israel. Tellingly, local Arab–American leaders, while expressing hopes for peaceful resolution to the Mideast conflict, chose not to attend the event.[92]

In the context of simmering racial and religious conflicts, the 1980s saw some notable successes, including a joint black/Jewish effort to oppose apartheid in South Africa and a large interracial seder held in 1986. At this gathering of more than one hundred blacks and Jews, TBE's rabbi Gerald Schuster, a supporter of the 1968 Fair Housing Ordinance, again appealed to the two groups' shared heritage of oppression: "Tonight, we participate as members of two communities, black and Jewish commu-

Sloan Museum

Members of Flint's Black/ Jewish Dialogue lead the singing of "We Shall Overcome," anthem of the civil rights movement, at a rally in downtown's Riverbank Park, 1986. Pictured (*left to right*) are: Reuben Greenberg (Charleston, SC, police chief and rally speaker), Reverend Granville Smith (Mt. Cavalry Baptist Church), Rabbi Gerald Schuster (Temple Beth El), Peter Goodstein (Flint Jewish Federation), Sylvester Broome (Genesee County Board of Commissioners), and Flint mayor James Sharp Jr.

nities, that have historically struggled for freedom side-by-side. We share a common history of slavery and oppression; we share common dreams of equality, justice, and peace. And so tonight we join together to send out a message of freedom which we hope will ring through the hills of our land and across the seas."[93] In this spirit, several Jewish families established ongoing interfaith and interracial conversations, among them four Jewish couples who met regularly with four Arab American couples to discuss Middle Eastern affairs and work toward a Flint-area Arab/Jewish dialogue.

Similarly, in the mid 1980s the CRC worked with other community agencies to help the city's small Hispanic population establish the Spanish Speaking Information Center. On several occasions the CRC also joined with the political wing of the UAW to support liberal causes, in 1988 collaborating to help defeat a statewide ballot initiative to end Medicaid funding for abortions.[94] Through the 1980s the CRC also launched effective campaigns to modify the weekly schedules of the city's elite cultural institutions that ignored Jewish worship practices. At the CRC's urging, the Flint Institute of Arts ended its customary Friday-night openings of new exhibits, while the Flint Symphony stopped holding concerts on Yom Kippur. The CRC also distributed

Sloan Museum

Double ceremony, 1986. Marking fifty years of organized Jewish communal life in the area, the Flint Jewish Federation dedicates its new home at 619 Clifford Street. Retiring dentist Maurice Taylor (*second from left*) and physician Saul Gorne (*extreme right*) donated the building to the federation. Also pictured (*left to right*) are federation president Natalie Pelavin, Fay Taylor, and Sophie Gorne.

Sloan Museum

Kristallnacht remembered, 10 November 1988. Fifty years after the "Night of Broken Glass," a ceremony commemorates the rampages against European Jewry that marked intensification of Nazism's extreme anti-Semitism. At this candlelight vigil, Clifford Street was renamed to honor Raoul Wallenberg, a Christian Swedish diplomat who saved thousands of Jews from the Nazis' horrific "Final Solution." Huddling under an umbrella are Jewish community leaders Dr. Evelyn Golden (*left*) and Pat Fauer.

calendars to public schools that designated prominent Jewish observances; the Jewish community was duly gratified when the schools renamed their seasonal holiday recesses "winter" and "spring" (rather than "Christmas" and "Easter").[95]

The late 1980s marked the high tide of the CRC's influence in Flint and of cooperative Jewish relations with other community groups.[96] In 1986, demonstrating support for ongoing downtown revitalization efforts, the Flint Jewish Federation (FJF) moved to a building donated by two retiring professionals long active in the Jewish community, physician Saul Gorne and dentist Maurice Taylor. The renovated structure stood on Clifford Street, near the university's downtown campus. Two years later the federation petitioned the city government to change the name of Clifford Street to Wallenberg Street, in honor of Raoul Wallenberg, the Christian Swedish diplomat credited with saving some one hundred thousand Jews from perishing in the Holocaust. Earlier in the decade, the federation had supported renaming streets in honor of two giants of the civil rights struggle, Dr. Martin Luther King Jr. and Cesar Chavez. Black and Hispanic groups reciprocated, supporting the federation's petition.[97] Fifty years after Kristallnacht, a crowd of some 150 people stood in the pouring rain in front of the federation building on renamed Wallenberg Street, to mourn the dead, remember the living, and praise those who risk their lives for others.[98]

Relations between area Jews and Arab Americans, in contrast, tense since the founding of Israel in 1948, deteriorated throughout the 1980s in response to international affairs. In September 1982, following the killing of unarmed civilians in a Lebanese refugee camp, demonstrators marched through downtown protesting Israel's Palestinian policy.[99] Waving an American flag and hoisting banners urging human rights for Palestinians, some demonstrators held blatantly anti-Semitic signs that deeply offended members of the Jewish community. One placard showed a Star of David, a plus sign, a dollar sign, an equal sign, and a swastika. A member of the then-ongoing Arab/Jewish dialogue recalled her anguish when no one from Flint's Arab community, including those with whom she had been meeting regularly, even "picked up the phone" to find out if she was upset by the demonstration, which had occurred outside her husband's office. After this incident, she recalled, the group "just sort of drifted apart."[100] Its demise marked the end of a brief and tentative effort to bridge the gap between local Jews and their Arab American neighbors and demonstrated the fragility of such personal outreach. Over the next two decades relations between the groups grew more hostile. In the late 1990s an effort to reestablish the dialogue failed, relations becoming even more polarized after the U.S. invasion of Iraq in 2003.[101]

Moreover, despite enlisting the aid of Representative Kildee, the CRC failed to convince the Flint Board of Education to adopt its curriculum on the Holocaust. By the late 1980s only two Flint teachers routinely incorporated the CRC materials into their classrooms.[102] A similar effort in the mid 1990s met with little success. Despite failing to convince local educators of the need for materials focusing specifically on the Nazi genocide, the FJF cooperated with many community organizations, from the United

Flint Journal

Pro-Palestinian demonstrators rally outside downtown's Water Street Pavilion (later acquired by the University of Michigan–Flint), 1988. As violence continued in the Middle East, American foreign policy support for Israel, championed by the local Jewish community, faced stiffer opposition by the area's growing Arab American population.

Way to the Girl Scouts, in a series of activities promoting multicultural education and highlighting the Jewish experience. These included extensive programming termed "A World of Difference," beginning in 1988; a 1996 program titled "Youth Working with Cultural Diversity to Create Community"; and various training sessions, theatrical productions, and speaker series, including a presentation by eminent Holocaust survivor Elie Wiesel.[103]

In sum, Flint Jewry's relations with Flint's non-Jews since the early 1970s have been shaped by several contradictory forces. Among the most important have been the Jewish community's commitment to civil rights for all Americans, its desire for dialogue, and its many attempts to forge alliances and find common ground with its neighbors. Yet despite these efforts and the community's genuine goodwill, larger forces have tended to undermine those relations and create barriers between Flint Jewry and other groups. One has been the historic tension between Jewish and African Americans in U.S. history, a complex and difficult topic rooted in the groups' similar yet different histories. Both diasporic groups with long histories of oppression and marginalization, each has been victimized differently, and has responded differently, in ways rooted in distinct cultural traditions and material circumstances. In Flint, exacerbating these larger historic tensions have been differences in social class, with local Jewry wealthier relative to their poorer black neighbors, which also has tended to work against formation of a permanent alliance. Relations with area white Christians have generally improved over time, as they have with the area's small Latino population. Relations with area Arab Americans, in contrast, generally have been stormy and tense, a local division obviously rooted in the Israeli–Palestinian conflict. On the whole, then, the three decades after the mid 1970s present a decidedly mixed picture, as area Jews have worked diligently, and sometimes successfully, to find common ground with many of their neighbors.

TEACHING THE NEXT GENERATION

As intergroup relations presented both successes and disappointments, the same years presented a range of challenges within the Jewish community, among the most prominent the question of religious education. By the late 1970s some Jewish leaders recognized that the community's aging population, dwindling numbers, and increasingly scarce resources made maintaining two separate educational facilities problematic. They also knew that long-standing religious and philosophical differences made bridging the gap difficult, as did simmering animosities between some influential Conservative and Reform members. At the time CBI and TBE each had its own school, conducting classes at the end of the regular school day and on weekends. They cooperated only in offering some joint elective courses for middle and high schoolers. Yet discussions among the synagogue, temple, and FJCC regarding the development of an interdenominational school proved contentious, with disagreements on matters ranging from curriculum to finance.

Reform member Clifford Hart, a self-described "leading opponent" of the joint school idea, recalled, "[W]e had very, very heated meetings, I mean heated. One of my contemporaries took a poke at me." Believing that "a strong shul is good for the community and a strong temple [also is] good for the community," Hart feared an intercongregational school would dilute differences between the Reform and Conservative branches to the detriment of each and Flint Jewry as a whole.[104] TBE member Natalie Pelavin, in contrast, strongly promoted a joint school, hoping it would cement ties across Jewish institutions, especially for young people who did not otherwise cross paths. Yet she agreed with Hart that negotiations involved "a very long process . . . because there was so much resistance."[105] In the early 1980s, as population loss accelerated, the parties resolved to move forward despite continuing friction. The joint school, named Ivriah (place of Hebrew), began operation in 1982, using classrooms at both the temple and synagogue.[106]

When founded, Ivriah was an institutional "odd duck," in the words of the school's longtime director Emily Bank Alter.[107] Most other Jewish communities that had combined schools in response to declining enrollments had consolidated along denominational lines. Alternatively, in cities too small to support more than one congregation of each tradition, local Jewish community centers usually had established a classroom wing for students of both denominations, giving the community center

Sloan Museum

At Temple Beth El, Rabbi Gerald Schuster (*left*) instructs Ben Roberts in studying a sacred Hebrew text in preparation for his bar mitzvah.

considerable authority over the school. In Flint, without a community center, the FJF assumed a lesser role, providing only monetary support. Instead, the congregations controlled the school, CBI and TBE forced to work through thorny problems directly, with the federation mediating only informally.

Although the decision to pursue this joint educational venture did not quell controversy between advocates of a more strictly Reform or Conservative training, Ivriah generally has proven successful. Students share much of the curriculum while focusing on denominational particulars. Some blending of the two religious forms has resulted, diluting each, as some opponents of the school had feared. Yet given the decreasing numbers of students in the Flint area, the establishment of Ivriah likely averted a severe crisis that would have reverberated throughout the community.

A key sign of the school's acceptance by both congregations came in the late 1990s. TBE's new facility, built next to CBI, was designed to have only a few classrooms, the majority of Ivriah's activities taking place at CBI's educational wing. By eliminating duplicate classroom space the two congregations acknowledged the continued downward trend in enrollment of local Jewish youth. When it opened in 1982, Ivriah had 185 students, most from CBI. Twenty years later enrollment stood at about 85.[108] Reflecting the age structure of the two congregations and perhaps the erosion of Conservatism in the community, three-fourths of the children enrolled were from Reform families, while in consequence of growing intermarriage between Jews and non-Jews, more had parents in "mixed" marriages.[109]

In thinking creatively and working cooperatively to educate the next generation, Flint Jewry has demonstrated its resolve to confront one of the most serious problems of a deteriorating communal life. The evidence strongly supports the conviction of Emily Bank Alter that despite dwindling numbers the Flint Jewish community is "blessed" with an abiding commitment to Jewish education.[110]

RESURGENT ORTHODOXY AND CHANGING RELIGIOUS LIFE

Ever since 1927, when Reform-minded dissidents at Conservative Congregation Beth Israel began fund-raising to begin what became Temple Beth El, these two congregations constituted the twin pillars of organized Judaism in Flint. Orthodox families, numbering at most a score throughout the early twentieth century, had met in private homes but played virtually no role in the area's communal life. In Flint's booming postwar years there is no evidence of continued Orthodox practice, the local pattern paralleling what many observers believed would emerge as the contours of Judaism in a modernizing America: a steady drift toward less traditional forms of practice and belief, thickening the ranks of the Reform branch and further liberalizing Conservatism, a phenomenon some referred to as the "Protestantization of Judaism."[111] Yet while this trend did emerge nationally and locally, so did an important countertrend: the renaissance of Orthodoxy. This "supposedly ossified" branch of Judaism "experienc[ed] a surprising rebirth after 1945," partly a reaction to the horrors of the Holocaust, and partly because of the emigration of Orthodox Europeans to the United States during and after World War II.[112] While some Conservative and Reform clergy and practitioners greeted this development in Judaism warmly, for many the rise of Orthodoxy proved discomfiting, destabilizing community relations and reinserting into the American mainstream the visible signs of an old-world Judaism they believed was better left behind.

Rabbi Yisroel Weingarten and his wife, Shainie Chana Weingarten, emissaries of resurgent Orthodoxy, appeared in Flint in 1986, four years after the opening of Ivriah. The congregation they founded altered the religious landscape of Flint Jewry, establishing a denominational competitor just as Conservative and Reform members had begun administering the joint school.

The Weingartens represented the Chabad-Lubavitch movement, a mystical branch of Orthodoxy distinguished by its fervent messianism, its conviction that the messiah would soon appear, and its belief that heightened fervor among the faithful would hasten the messiah's coming. Consequently Lubavitch followers have sought first to redeem themselves and then, through proselytizing, to prepare other Jews for redemption. In order to strengthen Jewish consciousness the Lubavitch movement has launched drives by missionary married couples such as the Weingartens, established "Chabad" houses for worship and community activities, developed their own "Torah schools," and frequently held public demonstrations of their commitment to Jewish traditions. Likened by some to Mormons in their missionizing style and success, by 2002 the Lubavitch movement boasted hundreds of thousands of supporters worldwide, with institutions in forty-five U.S. states and sixty-five nations.[113] By the 1970s the expansion of the Chabad-Lubavitch movement represented an especially vivid demonstration of the reascendance of an important strand of Orthodox Judaism.[114]

In Flint many synagogue and temple members viewed the establishment of Chabad House of Eastern Michigan, as the Lubavitch center formally was called, with trepidation, concerned about losing adherents to the group's energetic proselytizing.[115] Many also expressed discomfort at the reassertion of strict Orthodox modes of life, the Lubavitchers adopting many practices that even the grandparents of TBE and CBI members had not followed. Congregation members maintained stringent kosher foodways. Men sported beards and wore dark suits and large hats; women covered their hair with wigs and their limbs with long skirts and long-sleeved blouses. Rigid gender segregation characterized the congregation's worship services, men and women seated separately and only men counting for a minyan (prayer quorum).

In stark contrast, women at both TBE and CBI had become increasingly active in leadership positions and at worship services. Both congregations had elected female presidents to their boards of directors.[116] Since the 1970s the Conservative synagogue had incorporated women into the prayer quorum, following the pattern of the Reform, if with considerable reluctance. As CBI member Esther Price recalled, "When we decided to count women in the minyan, it was pretty traumatic around here. . . . Some women didn't want to be counted. . . . But the men were most vocal. We had a man that actually walked out of a minyan because there [were] nine men there, and then a woman [came in]."[117] By the 1980s women also held positions of authority in the FJF, JFCS, Ivriah, the Russian resettlement movement, and other lay organizations as well as serving on the boards of such citywide organizations as Planned Parenthood. Those supporting the expanding role of women in Conservative and Reform Judaism thus looked askance at the Lubavitchers, who advocated vociferously for the patriarchal family, believed women should serve as helpmates to their husbands and fathers, and praised mothers who bore as many children as possible.

Chabad House also distressed some area Jews by violating the community's long-standing efforts to discourage public religious celebrations, especially the display of nativity scenes during Christmastime in public spaces like the city council and county courthouse grounds. In December 1988, during Hanukkah, Rabbi Weingarten and Chabad House members erected a large, electrically lit menorah (candelabrum) at

Rabbi Yisroel Weingarten, Chabad House, Lubavitch of Eastern Michigan, lighting a large menorah erected at an auto dealership on a major thoroughfare on Flint's outskirts, December 2004.

Flint Journal

Windmill Place, the glass–and–brick business and shopping center then in operation on the north side of the Flint River. Though the menorah was on private property, many Flint Jews believed the display might unleash a backlash by local Christians opposing the ban on public display of religious symbols and undermine the strict separation of church and state so many local Jews regarded as critical for maintaining civil liberties.[118] Disregarding his critics, Rabbi Weingarten has persisted in installing a giant candelabrum to celebrate Hanukkah, the lot of a large auto dealership on Flint's outskirts providing the setting in 2004. Such concerns were tempered by some community members' admiration for the rigorous educational programs in Hebrew language sponsored by Chabad House and appreciation for the energetic work of both Shainie and Yisroel Weingarten to minister to the infirm, elderly, and poor. For some, these positive assessments came to predominate. As Peter Goodstein, FJF president when Chabad House was established, remarked: "[T]hey are very focused and committed to what they do . . . [and] anybody who is pushing for Jewish sorts of values, [that's] a positive thing."[119]

A few community members actively supported Chabad House from its inception, helping to found this first Orthodox institution in the city. Even earlier, in the 1960s, several Flint families affiliated with CBI and TBE had agreed to help underwrite a Chabad summer camp near Fenton, some twenty miles south of Flint. Donations by the Kasle and Pelavin households for the camp helped foster a relationship between the leaders of Michigan's Lubavitch movement, centered in Oak Park, near Detroit, and the Flint community. When the regional Chabad office decided to open a house in

Flint, it received seed money from these and other area Jewish families, then obtained further funding to expand the missionary congregation.[120] From the point of view of Yisroel and Shainie Weingarten, the local community was "welcoming" to them, with members of both CBI and TBE offering them encouragement as well as financial aid. Both born into the large Orthodox community in Brooklyn and having spent years in the smaller but still substantial Orthodox community in Oak Park, the Weingartens described Flint's small Jewish community as "loving," impressed particularly with the "outreach . . . to new Americans." Here they referred to the Russian immigrants settling in the area at about the same time they did, some of whom were attracted by Chabad House's messianism, energetic proselytizing, and communal orientation.[121]

The number of adherents at Chabad House remains unclear, although the 1990 community self study suggests that Lubavitch adherents account for less than 10 percent of area Jewry who claim a denominational affiliation.[122] The small congregation draws from a four-county area and has enough adherents to constitute a minyan twice daily for worship services, thus having at least ten adult men attending regularly. In addition to a kitchen where food can be prepared according to strict dietary rules of kashrut, Chabad House includes a *mikveh,* a pool of water where women can take ritual baths. As in other Lubavitch congregations, the Hebrew day school at Chabad House has proved attractive to Jewish families, whatever their denominational affiliation, who wish their children to have a traditional religious education at a very reasonable cost.[123]

The Lubavitch movement, including Chabad House of Eastern Michigan, is unequivocally Zionist. This vocal and uncompromising advocacy of the need to secure Israel as a homeland for Jews and to support its policies in the Mideast may have contributed in some measure to the increasing trend toward Zionism within Flint Jewry as a whole. It certainly provided one salient point of convergence for some CBI and TBE members as well as for the FJF leadership. In turn, the Chabad's unflinching commitment to Zionism may have been a major appeal for at least one prominent CBI family who converted to the Lubavitch movement through the Weingarten's missionizing. Soon after the founding of Chabad House, ophthalmologist Jerome Kasle, an avid Zionist and the son of Lou Kasle, perhaps the city's premier fund-raiser for Israel, and his wife Sherry joined the Lubavitch movement. Becoming ever more engaged in Chabad activities, in the 1990s the couple and their children left Flint to live among the sizeable Lubavitch settlement in Oak Park. In this case, increased devotion led the family to relocate to a more devout environment; for Flint Jewry it amounted to yet another diminution in its ranks.[124]

Notably, Chabad House was built across the street from the synagogue. Since 1998, when TBE built their new facility next to CBI, the three Jewish religious facilities have stood as a group, a close physical proximity symbolizing both Judaism's distinctiveness relative to other religious traditions in Flint and the divisions internal to the local Jewish community. Despite the vicissitudes suffered by Flint Jewry, its decline in numbers and its aging membership, the three congregations attest to the efforts of their congregants to retain a vital Judaism in the area. In general, relations between the Conservative and Reform congregations have become more cordial, and of necessity must become more so if each is to survive. The installation of a concrete walkway between CBI and TBE in 1999 offers tangible proof that the two denominations realize that in the future they must cooperate even more closely.[125] As CBI lay leader Leonard Meizlish remarked, "Just as we've created Ivriah, which was designed to allow each institution to have its kids educated but maintain the identity of each institution, I would assume that through creative thinking [we can] maintain the identity of [both CBI and TBE] but yet at the same time derive some economies of scale."[126]

SHARING AUTHORITY, GIVING VOICE

Fireworks burst overhead and a crowd lining Saginaw Street applauded a parade of cars, as the city held yet another gala for a milestone in Flint's automotive history, the celebration of Buick's centennial. Yet in July 2003 the star attraction of so many other similar occasions was missing: a vehicle fresh from a Flint assembly line. Instead, the 1,500 cars cruising down the street were vintage, some dusted off and pulled out of museums. The two Buick engine–powered World War II B-24 Liberator bomber planes and the M18 "Hellcat" tank destroyer on display had been built sixty years before. Their place of origin, the giant Buick factory in the city's St. John District, the home of GM's Buick division, had been demolished the year before. Despite the fireworks and the festive atmosphere, this commemoration was a bittersweet exercise in nostalgia, for Flint no longer made Buicks.[127]

Later that fall the city reached still further back in time, honoring its bygone era of carriage making. After an intense private fund–raising drive, Flint installed replicas of the seven "Vehicle City" signs that had arched over Saginaw Street from 1899 to 1919. In time for the city to celebrate the winter holidays, the arches, like the originals each fitted with fifty bulbs, lit up the downtown. Yet the scene they illuminated had changed dramatically from the days when Billy Durant's company had manufactured buggies and carts. The streets, once bustling with shoppers and workers, now stood eerily quiet, the sidewalks nearly empty.[128] Looking up at the signs, H. L. Weatherford, who brought his restored blue 1949 Chevy downtown to join a parade of vintage autos, commented, "I think Flint is too far gone to be helped, but you never know, [the arches] just might help," adding, "They sure look good."[129]

Looks indeed can be deceiving, the surface obscuring the substance beneath. In 1955 William Attwood wrote in *Look* magazine that "Flint, Michigan is a good place for Americans to live. It is a prosperous auto–manufacturing town of 165,000. Among its people are 800 Jewish families."[130] Were he to have returned to Flint half a century later, what would he have written? Perhaps that Flint, Michigan, is a very hard place to live—a deindustrialized former autotown of 125,000 whose Jewish population has

Flint Journal

In another effort to revitalize downtown Flint, replicas of the turn-of-the-century "Vehicle City" arches were installed across South Saginaw Street, 2003.

declined by half. As this book has shown, much in Flint has changed since Attwood's brief visit in 1955. The city has imploded, gone from boom to bust within a generation. Yet some things have changed very little. As before, Flint's people, including its Jewry, continue to struggle to make a better life for themselves, their children, and the larger society, albeit under very difficult circumstances.

Surveying his subjects from a determinedly distant stance, William Attwood included in his *Look* magazine story the voice of not a single Jewish resident of Flint. The Jewish community remained wholly silent, interpreted only through the author's imperious and patronizing gaze. In this book we have pursued a different narrative approach. We have tried to give voice to members of Flint's Jewish community, to tell the story of Flint Jewry against the backdrop of a boom-to-bust town in our own way, using our own analytic framework and interpretive lens, but using the community's words and perceptions to help guide the analysis, inform the interpretation, and give shape and substance to the story. The book's Epilogue continues in this spirit, giving "shared authority" to several women and men of Flint's Jewish community to reflect on Flint's Jewish past and project into its future, offering readers a sense of where Flint Jewry sees itself going from here.[131] The history of Jewish life in this former industrial promised land is still being written, as the following pages make clear.

Epilogue

To offer first-person perspectives on the past and future of Flint Jewry, we turn to five current members of this community. All came to Flint as adults, the first arriving in 1962 and the most recent four decades later. We present excerpts of their remarks, grouped around three themes: memories of joining the Flint community, experiences of communal life, and thoughts about the future of Flint Jewry. Each voice adds to the portrait of Jewish life in Flint during the last decades, and together they raise important questions about the community's evolution in the twentieth-first century.[1]

JOINING THE FLINT COMMUNITY

Leonard Meizlish

I was raised in a predominantly Jewish neighborhood in the Detroit area. My folks were mostly observant, so I attended the yeshiva and orthodox shuls in Detroit. In 1962 I was offered a job at Flint Junior Community College, now Mott Community College, and have been teaching there for over forty years. In Flint I met Naomi Lande, a high school teacher who later became my wife. Her family belonged to Temple Beth El (TBE). We were married in Congregation Beth Israel (CBI) and we both became involved in CBI, but our friends and family were from both the temple and the shul.

David Leyton

I arrived in Flint from Boston in 1975 to gather, write, edit, and broadcast the news on two radio stations. My first contact with the Flint Jewish community came when I met the overnight disc jockey, Marty Natchez. Marty invited me to his parents' home in Grand Blanc for Shabbat dinner. Two years later Marty's mother insisted we attend a "Shalom" group gathering of young singles and married couples at CBI. At the event I met the most beautiful girl I had ever seen, Therese Kaufman. Marrying Therese more fully introduced me to Flint's warm, wonderful Jewish community. Her parents were cornerstones of Genesee County's professional and cultural life. Dr. Benjamin Kaufman was Flint's first Jewish orthodontist, and his wife Estelle was a leader in B'nai B'rith, CBI sisterhood, and Pioneer Women. Therese and I married in 1980 at CBI, and I remember feeling how, in just a few short years, I had been accepted into the community. I'm not sure that would have been possible anywhere else

Mitchell Weiss

My wife Lynne and I were born on Chicago's west side, and my high school was more than 90 percent Jewish. It was a very insulated life. I did not come into contact with Gentiles in large numbers until I went to college at the University of Illinois campus in the city. We came to Flint in 1972 when I took a job at Mott Community College. I was going to be there for three years but because of my good job and benefits, we decided to remain. We tried to integrate ourselves into Flint's Jewish community but at first found it very cliquish. We had to fight our way in. After we met some other Jewish families we formed the Newcomers Association. Then we joined Temple Beth El, while Rabbi Jerry Schuster was there. He put a human face on the rabbinate for me. When my son was in religious school I volunteered as a teacher's aide, serving bagels and cream cheese. In 1977, I joined TBE's board of directors and remained on it for twenty-two years.

Yuliya Gaydayenko

I was born in Moscow, Russia, in 1970. I graduated from the Moscow Pedagogical University with a degree in Russian language and literature. I wanted to go to the Moscow State University, but it was basically prohibited for Jews to study there. The situation in Russia for Jews was becoming very bad. In 1995 I came from Moscow straight to Flint with my husband, son, and mother. I was twenty-five and pregnant with my second child. I had never heard of Flint. We had an uncle in New York City, but we did not want to join him because we felt that raising two children there would be difficult.

We had a great reception when we arrived in Flint. We were met at the airport, then taken to an apartment that was ready for us. We did not expect this treatment because we heard stories about people who went to New York City who had nothing waiting for them. Here we had everything: food in the refrigerator, furniture, our kids had new beds, and the apartment was clean and nice. Volunteers took us to the grocery store. Our host family introduced us to the community. I was overwhelmed with our new life here. Only later I understood all they did for us, and I really appreciated it.

Rabbi Karen Companez

I have been a resident of Flint since 2002, during which time I have had the privilege of functioning as the rabbi of Temple Beth El. The Flint Jewish community is very close-knit and even now, I am still discovering connections between people—these links form a multilayered mesh. I can only compare Flint with the Melbourne, Australia, Jewish community in which I was born and raised. There my primary congregation consisted of two thousand households. The feeling of intimacy and mutual responsibility was not like it is here in Flint.

EXPERIENCES OF COMMUNITY LIFE

Mitchell Weiss

After the great recession in the early 1980s, we began to wonder how cooperative a community we were going to be. That I think was the impetus to merge the two schools and found the Ivriah. It's an achievement that very few Jewish communities, especially in large cities, could ever accomplish. Then TBE left its old building in 1997 and moved into the new temple, right next door to CBI. That move was deliberately designed to heal the breach between the congregations, physically and tangibly.

> One of the secrets of Jewish survival has been [the] ability to face the future and seek out meaning in choosing values and directions.
>
> —*Rabbi Gerald Schuster, Temple Beth El, 1970*

Leonard Meizlish

Historically there was a deep split between the Reform and the Conservative congregations: the temple looked upon the shul as somewhat antiquated and the synagogue looked upon the temple as something less than fully Jewish. I think those views were fairly typical among American Jews at the time. Over the years a number of efforts to overcome this split have paid off, including the creation of the Ivriah. I was involved with that because I was chairman of CBI's religious school at the time. There are still institutional differences between the Reform and Conservative congregations, but not the deep animosities and hostilities there used to be.

David Leyton

My wife Therese and I have tried to carry on the Flint Jewish community's spirit of voluntarism and public service. I became an attorney and recently was elected Genesee County Prosecuting Attorney. She is a member of CBI's sisterhood, has chaired many fund-raising events, and created a video series on health topics based on interviews held at Jewish Community Services. We have often talked about how participation at the synagogue shaped our lives and fostered special feelings toward Judaism among our four children. Like so many others educated at Ivriah, our kids have a remarkable knowledge of Torah, daily rituals, traditions, and the Shabbat service. It shows the dedication of the Hebrew school's teachers and the youngsters' parents who make a concerted effort for their children to learn about our religion. That dedication is due, in part, to the small and close-knit nature of the community. To be Jewish in Flint and maintain a Jewish identity takes effort and a special feeling. We have that here.

Yuliya Gaydayenko

When we first arrived, we experienced culture shock moving to a small place from a large city. Compared to Moscow there wasn't much to do in Flint. On the other hand, I think it was beneficial to my family. Here we were pressed to learn English right away and embrace being American. In New York there are Russian stores, everything is in Russian. For our kids, it was better because we had a quiet, spacious apartment. Jewish Community Services helped us to get our social security cards, medical care, and gave us support for the first few years while we got on our feet. We had a chance to go to school to learn English and American culture and to gain training. My husband was able to choose a good profession as a computer programmer, and I was able to complete graduate school. For nearly two years I have been executive director of Jewish Community Services, an agency that offers a variety of services and programs for families, youth, and children. We provide transportation for clients to medical appointments, casework coordination, and information and referral services to older adults, and several programs for Russian-speaking immigrants. Most who come to our Senior Nutrition Program luncheons are really aging; the average age is over eighty. Flint lost many Russian immigrants who moved to Detroit, Ann Arbor, New York, Arizona, or wherever they had relatives or were offered a job. Yet we have retained a large percentage, too. We offer citizenship preparation, and I am proud to say that all but three in our Russian community are American citizens.

Rabbi Karen Companez

The first and enduring thing that struck me about members of the Flint Jewish community was their boundless spirit of volunteerism. I was staggered by the number of people who are always prepared to "step up to the plate" in whatever capacity they are needed, in order to make things happen in this community. People come together to celebrate communal seders, to ensure a meaningful and memorable High Holy Day season, to organize attendance at cultural events, to welcome new immigrants to the community and make sure they have whatever they need to start their new lives in Flint, to rejoice at *smachot* (happy occasions), and to grieve together at times of sadness.

THE FUTURE OF FLINT'S JEWISH COMMUNITY

Leonard Meizlish

The decline in the number of kids in the Ivriah is an indication of where the community is headed. We have fewer kids in the school because we don't have that many young families in the community and we don't have that many young families because either the people aren't staying or they aren't moving in. At both the shul and temple we are confronted with demographic and financial difficulties. We are getting older and smaller, and the financial base is decreasing. At one time at High Holidays you would fill the sanctuary at CBI plus the social hall. We can hold services in the sanctuary now and have room left over. The pressure is on to get the individual congregations to engage in some form of cooperative activity.

Yuliya Gaydayenko

As for the future of Flint, I would like to stay optimistic. But looking at the size of the community and how it is constantly shrinking, it is hard to predict. I hope we can pull together and make sure that our community has resources for those in need. What if at some point we only have poor people left? About four years ago, we explored the possibility of becoming a satellite operation of the Detroit Federation and its related social services agencies. This idea was not widely accepted because Flint community members wanted to keep their own identity. But if we do not work together it might be inevitable. The positive vision for our community is that we develop a shared facility, that we pool together our resources and provide for the needs of our community as long as we have Jewish people in Flint.

Rabbi Karen Companez

Today the Flint Jewish community stands at a crossroads. Discussions are currently under way between Congregation Beth Israel, Temple Beth El, the Flint Jewish Federation, and the Ivriah about the possibility of sharing a common facility. I hope that the community will be able to find a way to make this innovative idea a reality.

Mitchell Weiss

I have two competing visions of the future of the Flint Jewish community. One is very pessimistic—that we will not be able to overcome our difficulties. The synagogue will slowly but surely atrophy, and I don't see that much better for us at the temple. The other vision I have is that we will overcome this divide, and we will see that by cooperating that we can overcome our financial and demographic problems. In the future, the shul and temple should pool their resources but remain separate entities and maintain their own religious ideologies.

After my wife, Lynne, died, people asked if I was moving back to Chicago. I am not leaving Flint because the members of this community know my day-to-day life better than my family members in Chicago. People here really care about people, and over the years that idea of being cliquish totally disappeared. In part Flint's Jewish community welcomes people because we need to have people, I won't argue that. But we welcome people sincerely—we are good at it.

Notes

PREFACE

1. Hasia R. Diner, *The Jews of the United States, 1654 to 2000* (Berkeley: University of California Press, 2004), 1.
2. Diner, *Jews of the United States*, 1. For an excellent account of Jewish experience in small communities see Lee Shai Weissbach, *Jewish Life in Small Town America: A History* (New Haven: Yale University Press, 2005).
3. Jonathan D. Sarna, "American Jewish History: A Chance to Reflect," *Chronicle of Higher Education* 51 (1 October 2004), B9; Diner, *Jews of the United States*, 259.
4. Jonathan D. Sarna, *American Judaism: A History* (New Haven: Yale University Press, 2004), xx.

INTRODUCTION

1. This is the common paraphrase of a statement by a prior head of General Motors, Charles E. Wilson, as reported in *New York Times*, 24 February 1953.
2. "Harlow Curtice," *Time*, 2 January 1956.
3. Ronald Edsforth, *Class Conflict and Cultural Consensus: The Making of a Mass Consumer Society in Flint, Michigan* (New Brunswick, N.J.: Rutgers University Press, 1987), 217.
4. Edward S. Shapiro, *A Time for Healing: American Jewry since World War II* (Baltimore: Johns Hopkins University Press, 1992), 60–61.
5. William Attwood, "The Position of the Jews in America Today," *Look* 19 (29 November 1955): 27–35.
6. Ibid., 28.
7. Will Herberg, *Protestant, Catholic, Jew: An Essay in Religious Sociology* (Garden City, N.Y.: Doubleday, 1955).
8. *Gentleman's Agreement* was produced by Darryl Zanuck for Twentieth Century Fox and directed by Elia Kazan, with a screenplay written by Moss Hart and based on the novel by Laura Z. Hobson.
9. Sociologist Milton Gordon, for example, examined different forms of assimilation, presenting his full taxonomy in the prize-winning book *Assimilation in American Life: The Role of Race, Religion, and National Origins* (New York: Oxford University Press, 1964).
10. Many standard biographical sources on twentieth-century Americans include information on Attwood; see, for example, *The Scribner Encyclopedia of American Life*, v. 2, s. v. "Attwood, William

Hollingsworth," and *Current Biography Yearbook 1986*, s. v. "Attwood, William (Hollingsworth)."

11. William Attwood, *The Twilight Struggle: Tales of the Cold War* (New York: Harper and Row, 1987).

12. Art Hurand, interview by Nancy Hanflik, tape recording, Flint, Mich., 10 June 1999.

13. Ibid.

14. The phrase derives from sociologist Steven P. Dandaneau's book *A Town Abandoned: Flint, Michigan, Confronts Deindustrialization* (Albany: State University of New York Press, 1996).

15. The quoted phrase is from Jon C. Teaford, *Cities of the Heartland: The Rise and Fall of the Industrial Midwest* (Bloomington: Indiana University Press, 1993), 227. *Roger & Me* was written, produced, and directed by Michael Moore for Dog Eat Dog Productions; Moore was raised in Davison, a small community contiguous to Flint.

16. The darkly satirical and autobiographical account of Flint autoworker Ben Hamper, a longtime associate of Moore, also gained a large national audience; Hamper, *Rivethead: Tales from the Assembly Line* (New York: Warner, 1991).

17. A fine critical discussion of the city's economic problems and the ill-considered efforts to deal with them is George F. Lord and Albert C. Price, "Growth Ideology in a Period of Decline: Deindustrialization and Restructuring, Flint Style," *Social Problems* 39 (May 1992): 155–69. See also Steven Dandaneau and George Lord, "Hit or Miss for Flint," *In These Times* 16 (April 15–21, 1992), 2. On Autoworld see especially Daniel Zwerdling, "And Then There's the Disneyland Solution," *Progressive*, July 1982, 34–35; and *Autoworld: Deconstructing Ideologies of Labor, Gender, Race, Class, and Consumerism in Flint, Michigan's Automobile Theme Park and Museum*, videotape and text exhibit produced and directed by Connie Samaras, 1989.

18. Don Terry, "A City Where Hope Runs on Empty," *New York Times*, 26 February 1992, sec. A, p. 8, Midwest edition.

19. See the important work by Michael Frisch, *A Shared Authority: Essays on the Craft and Meaning of Public History* (Albany: State University of New York Press), 1990.

20. Gilbert Rubenstein, interview by Nancy Hanflik, tape recording, Flint, Mich., 28 June 1999.

CHAPTER ONE. *SETTLERS TO THE CITY*

1. For a brief historical overview of Jewish life throughout the state see Judith Levin Cantor, *Jews in Michigan* (East Lansing: Michigan State University Press, 2001); on the mid- to late-nineteenth-century settlements see esp. pp. 6–20. Significantly, Cantor's book omits discussion of Jewish life in Flint. Flint also is not included in Lee Shai Weissbach's *Jewish Life in Small Town America: A History* (New Haven, Conn.: Yale University Press, 2005). See also Jacob R. Marcus, *A History of Jews in Michigan Before 1850* (Detroit: Wayne State University Press, 1955).

2. Biographical information on Henry Brown derives from his obituaries; see "Life of Ald. Henry Brown," *Flint (Michigan) Sunday Democrat*, 10 February 1877, 1; and "Death of Hon. Henry Brown," *Flint (Michigan) Wolverine Citizen*, 10 February 1877, 5.

3. Hasia R. Diner, *A Time for Gathering: The Second Migration, 1820–1880* (Baltimore: Johns Hopkins University Press, 1992), 15–16.

4. See the graduation report card for thirteen-year-old Heinrich Braun, Walsdorf, Germany, 4 May 1843, tr. Markus Muennix, Flint Jewish History Collection, Sloan Museum, Flint, Michigan.

5. Diner, *A Time for Gathering*, 76–80. See also Nancy L. Green, *Ready-to-Wear and Ready-to-Work: A Century of Industry and Immigrants in Paris and New York* (Durham: Duke University Press, 1997).

6. Edwin O. Wood, *History of Genesee County, Michigan: Her People, Industries and Institutions. With Biographical Sketches of Representative Citizens and Genealogical Records of Many of the Old Families* (Indianapolis: Federal Publishing Company, 1916), 1: 534–35.

7. See "Death of Hon. Henry Brown."

8. On the connection between Jews and fraternal organizations, especially the Masons, see Diner, *A Time for Gathering*, 160–62.

9. Flora Winton, letter to Nancy Hanflik, 29 April 1999.

10. Wood, *History of Genesee County*, 534–35.

11. Bess Krolik, interview by Nancy Hanflik, tape recording, West Bloomfield, Mich., 9 June 1999.

12. Robert G. Schafer, *Producing a Human Mosaic: Immigration and Economic Change in the Development of Genesee County's Population, 1820–1987* (Flint: University of Michigan–Flint Archives in cooperation with the Genesee County Historical Society, 1989), 21–22; Franklin Ellis, *The History of Genesee County, Michigan: Its Prominent Men and Pioneers* (Philadelphia: Everts, 1879), 130–31; Wood, *History of Genesee County*, 772–73.

13. Wood, *History of Genesee County*, 512–13; Ronald Edsforth, *Class Conflict and Cultural Consensus: The Making of a Mass Consumer Society in Flint, Michigan* (New Brunswick, N.J.: Rutgers University Press, 1987), 55. The story of cigar making in Flint merits further attention.

14. For further discussion see Nancy Hanflik, "150 Years of Jewish Life in Flint: 1850–2000" (master's thesis, University of Michigan–Flint, 2000), 16–17.

15. Information on individuals and businesses derives from city directories. See the bibliography for complete listing of directories consulted.

16. During this period a minyan was defined as the presence of at least ten males over the age of thirteen.

17. For a synthetic overview of the background and workings of the vast Eastern European Jewish immigration see Gerald Sorin, *A Time for Building: The Third Migration, 1880–1920* (Baltimore: Johns Hopkins University Press, 1992), 12–68. Sorin also discusses the discriminatory attitudes some German Jews had toward their Eastern European counterparts and the efforts by the earlier immigrants variously to assist, accommodate, or Americanize the Russian and Polish newcomers; see, for example, pp. 86–88, 146–47, 162–63.

18. Gilbert Rubenstein, interview by Nancy Hanflik, tape recording, Flint, Mich., 28 June 1999.

19. For an account of Durant's life and the formation of the carriage and automobile industries see Lawrence R. Gustin, *Billy Durant: Creator of General Motors* (Grand Rapids, Mich.: Eerdmans, 1973).

20. Demographic data derive from the 1910 federal census.

21. Data on occupations are from census and city directory sources.

22. See Ewa Morawska, *Insecure Prosperity: Small-Town Jews in Industrial America, 1890–1940* (Princeton, N.J.: Princeton University Press, 1996). See also, for example, Joel Perlmann, *Ethnic Differences: Schooling and Social Structure Among the Irish, Italians, Jews, and Blacks in an American City, 1880–1935* (Cambridge: Cambridge University Press, 1988), on Providence, Rhode Island; and for midwestern comparison see the briefer account of Jewish life in Muncie, Indiana, home of the Ball Corporation, famous for the glass home canning jars it once produced: Dan Rottenberg, ed., *Middletown Jews: The Tenuous Survival of an American Jewish Community* (Bloomington and Indianapolis: Indiana University Press, 1997).

23. Information on Julius Hurand from son Art Hurand, interview by Nancy Hanflik, tape recording, Flint, Mich., 10 June 1999.

24. "Flint College and Cultural Developments: Sponsor Recalls Start in Scrap Business," *Flint (Michigan) Journal*, 2 March 1956, 1.

25. Industrial Removal Office to Frank V. V. Swan, 1 March 1910, Industrial Removal Organization Collection, American Jewish Historical Society, Newton Centre, Mass. (hereafter cited as IRO File), first half of I-91, Box 48, Flint, Mich., 1908–17, Manufacturers Association.

26. Robert A. Rockaway, *Words of the Uprooted: Jewish Immigration in Early 20th Century America* (Ithaca, N.Y.: Cornell University Press, 1998), esp. 5.

27. David Handler to Gentlemen of Hebrew Relief Society, 5 February 1906, Flint IRO File. The umbrella organization of which the IRO was a part had several names over the years, and those writing to the IRO referred to it by still other names, including the "Hebrew Relief Organization."

28. Henry P. Goldstein to David Bressler, 1 July 1908, IRO File, I-91, Box 19, Flint, Mich., 1908–17, Manufacturers Association.

29. W. H. Little to David M. Bressler, 17 April 1909, IRO File, I-91, Box 19, Flint, Mich., 1908–17, Manufacturers Association.

30. Swan to IRO, 24 May 1909, IRO File, second half of I-91, Box 19, Flint, Mich., 1908–17, Manufacturers Association.

31. IRO to Swan, 28 May 1909, IRO File, second half of I-91, Box 19, Flint, Mich., 1908–17, Manufacturers Association.

32. Swan to IRO, 3 August 1912, IRO File, second half of I-91, Box 48, Flint, Mich., 1908–17, Manufacturers Association.

33. Other manufacturers, of course, had encountered resistance from Jewish workers they recruited. See, for example, the discussion of the immigrant cigarette workers James Duke brought from New York to Durham in 1881; Leonard Rogoff, *Homelands: Southern Jewish Identity in Durham and Chapel Hill, North Carolina* (Tuscaloosa: University of Alabama Press, 2001).

34. Swan to IRO, 18 July and 3 August 1912, IRO File, I-91, Box 48, 1908–17, Flint, Mich., Manufacturers Association.

35. Bressler to Swan, 5 August 1912, IRO File, I-91, Box 48, 1908–17, Flint, Mich., Manufacturers Association.

36. For a fine overall account see David Montgomery, *The Fall of the House of Labor: The Workplace, the State, and American Labor Activism* (New York: Cambridge University Press, 1987).

37. On Menton and the 1912 campaign see Edsforth, *Class Conflict and Cultural Consensus*, 54–64.

38. *Flint: City of Industrial Peace* (Flint, Mich.: Board of Commerce, 1910). Flint IRO file, first half of I-91, Box 48, 1908–17, Flint Mich., Manufacturers Association.

39. Mott's philanthropy and civic-mindedness are stressed in the sympathetic biography by Robert G. Schafer, *Charles Stewart Mott of Applewood: A Memoir* (Flint Mich.: University of Michigan–Flint Archives, in cooperation with the Genesee County Historical Society, 1984). In 1918 Mott again became mayor but resigned soon after election to serve in the Army's Quartermaster Corps.

40. Swan to IRO, 15 August 1912, IRO File, first half of I-91, Box 48, 1908–17, Flint, Mich., Manufacturers Association.

41. Swan to IRO, 26 May 1915 and 10 July 1916, IRO File, second half of I-91, Box 48, 1908–17, Flint, Mich., Manufacturers Association.

42. IRO to Swan, 5 April 1910, and Swan to IRO, 15 May 1911, IRO File, first half of I-91, Box 48, 1908–17, Flint, Mich., Manufacturers Association. Desertion of their wives by immigrants was prevalent throughout America, prompting the development of the Jewish National Desertion Bureau. See Paula Hyman, "Gender and the Immigrant Jewish Experience in the United States," in *Jewish Women in Historical Perspective*, ed. Judith R. Baskin (Detroit: Wayne State University Press, 1991), 230.

43. Gilbert Rubenstein, interview by Nancy Hanflik, tape recording, Flint, Mich., 28 June 1999.

44. After several years of factory work, Gold combined his savings with a loan from his brother to open a coal and scrap iron business. See Diane Roark, "Remembering Our Jewish Heritage: Dora (Laks) and Morris Gold." *Flint (Michigan) Jewish Reporter*, 12 September 1997, 3.

45. HIAS was founded in 1892 by Eastern European Jews in New York; its original purpose was to raise funds for a burial society, but by the early twentieth century it had become a highly successful international relief organization. See Sorin, *A Time for Building,* 48–50.

46. Dr. Sam Sorscher, "Remembering our Heritage: History of Machpelach Cemetery in Flint," *Flint*

(Michigan) Jewish Reporter, 24 November 1994, 9. Note that the spelling of the cemetery varies in different accounts and over time; we have used "Machpelah" consistently in the text, except when quoting from sources that use alternate spellings. See also "Remembering Our Heritage: The Hoffman Family," *Flint (Michigan) Jewish Reporter*, 16 June 1995, 6.

47. This discussion draws in particular on Paul Robert Magosci, *Historical Atlas of East Central Europe*, vol. 1 (1995; repr., Seattle: University of Washington Press, 1993); and Wladyslaw Czaplinski and Tadeusz Ladogórski, eds., *The Historical Atlas of Poland* (Wroclaw: Department of the State Cartographical Publishers, 1981).

48. Saul Gorne, interview by Nancy Hanflik, tape recording, Flint, Mich., 22 June 1999.

49. Gorne maintains that Communists were not responsible for the pogroms in his village, asserting instead that after the Communists gained control, "[w]e were safe."

50. Descendants of Joseph and Ida Linder have lived in Flint for five generations. Esther (Linder) Harris and her husband Louis, for example, opened Louie's General Store, where the couple sold dry goods and groceries.

51. See article on Miriam Lebster, entitled "Bubbe," loose newspaper clipping, 16 May 1923; in possession of authors. "Bubbe" means grandmother in Yiddish.

52. See the announcement of the "2nd Annual Purim Ball," held on 27 February 1918, Flint Jewish History Collection of the Sloan Museum, Flint, Michigan.

53. See the announcement of the "Progress Club of Flint, Mich." in the Flint Jewish History collection of the Sloan Museum, Flint, Michigan. The club met in rented quarters above a downtown candy store. Officers included Benjamin F. Weiner, president, owner of "The Flint," a dressy men's clothing store on South Saginaw Street, and S. S. Pearlstine, secretary, who moved to Flint from Charleston, South Carolina. Pearlstine became one of the city's first Jewish attorneys, joining a firm with two non-Jewish partners.

54. *Congregation Beth Israel Dedication Book* (Flint, Mich.: n.p., 1952), 8–9, Congregation Beth Israel, Flint, Michigan, Collection and Clippings File; hereafter Congregation Beth Israel is abbreviated as CBI.

55. Lee Bernstein Frank, telephone interview by Nancy Hanflik, 9 September 2004; "Future Affairs Engage Interest of Beth Israel," *Flint (Michigan) Journal*, n.d., ca. September 1923, clipping file, CBI, Flint, Michigan.

56. We do not discuss the emergence of Reconstructionism, a small but significant fourth movement that emphasizes "Jewish organic communalism." Reconstructionism began in 1922 when Mordecai Kaplan founded the Society for the Advancement of Judaism in New York. The movement seems to have had no appreciable following in Flint. See Henry L. Feingold, *Entering the Mainstream, 1920–1945* (Baltimore: Johns Hopkins University Press, 1992), 111–17, quote, 113.

57. *Congregation Beth Israel Dedication Book* (Flint, Mich.: n.p., 1972), 9, Congregation Beth Israel, Flint, Michigan, Collection and Clippings File.

CHAPTER TWO. *CREATING A COMMUNITY*

1. P. J. Hammond, "Flint," (Flint, Mich.: P. J. Hammond, 1922), Flint Jewish History Collection, Sloan Museum, Flint, Michigan.

2. Lawrence R. Gustin, ed., *The Flint Journal Centennial Picture History of Flint* (Flint, Mich.: William B. Eerdmans and Flint Bicentennial Commission, 1976), 164–66; Robert G. Schafer, *Producing a Human Mosaic: Immigration and Economic Change in the Development of Genesee County's Population, 1820–1987* (Flint, Mich.: University of Michigan–Flint Archives in cooperation with the Genesee County Historical Society, 1989), 37–39. On Southern white migrants see Chad Berry, *Southern Migrants, Northern Exiles* (Chicago: University of Illinois Press, 2000), especially the narrative of Tennessee-born Orbie Berry, 24–28, 34–37.

3. More than seven hundred Flint families lived in tents after World War I. To ease the crisis, in 1919 GM embarked on a pioneering home–building project in "Civic Park," an area annexed to the city in a special election. Using mass production techniques, workers toiled around the clock and built nearly a thousand homes in less than three months. See Jay Hicks, "Houses Built by General Motors: The Flint Housing Crisis and GMC," *Michigan History* 71 (March/April 1987): 32–39.

4. See *Flint, Michigan, Polk City Directory* (Taylor, Mich. R. L. Polk and Company, 1919–20); hereafter *1920 City Directory*. The names of Jewish World War I veterans are derived from a plaque that hung for many years at Temple Beth El, Flint.

5. *1920 City Directory.* According to the 1916 *Flint, Michigan, Polk City Directory* (Taylor, Mich.: R. L. Polk and Company, 1916), the Vogue incorporated with a capital of $9,000; its financial backers included two non–Jewish women from outside Flint (Elizabeth Porter of Kalamazoo, Michigan, and Mrs. O. M. Thornton, of St. Louis).

6. Information on Jewish–owned businesses after World War I derives principally from the *1920 City Directory*. E. Hyman and Rose Leff owned the Square Deal Clothier, located at 412–414 North Saginaw Street.

7. Kenneth Waltzer, "East European Jewish Detroit in the Early Twentieth Century," *Judaism* 49 (Summer 2000): 291–309, quote, 292. Waltzer draws from, synthesizes, and interprets an impressive body of literature in this essay, including three key works: Olivier Zunz, *The Changing Face of Inequality: Urbanization, Industrial Development, and Immigrants in Detroit* (Chicago: University of Chicago Press, 1982); Robert Rockaway, *The Jews of Detroit* (Detroit: Wayne State University Press, 1986); and Sidney Bolkosky, *Harmony and Dissonance: Voices of Jewish Identity in Detroit, 1914–1967* (Detroit: Wayne State University Press, 1991).

8. Diane Roark, with Dr. Lou Hurwitz, "Remembering Our Heritage: Drs. Samuel and Louis Hurwitz, Father and Son," *Flint (Michigan) Jewish Reporter*, 26 September 1997, 3.

9. "Joe Schiller: B'nai B'rith 1979 Man of the Year," Flint Chapter, B'nai B'rith, n.d., 6, in possession of authors.

10. See the recollection of Jack Rosenberg in Diane Roark, "Our Heritage: Memories of Flint Park," *Flint (Michigan) Jewish Reporter*, 29 June 1999, 7.

11. "Chapters in American Jewish History, Chapter 120: Lending a Helping Hand," *Forward*, 16 July 1999, 9. Free loan societies began with donated capital; *aktsiyes* paid interest to all members who deposited money into savings accounts and loaned a portion of their total deposits to those members starting businesses. See Shelley Tenenbaum, *A Credit to Their Community: Jewish Loan Societies in the United States, 1880–1945* (Detroit: Wayne State University Press, 1993).

12. The organization, known variously as the Flint Loan Association and the Flint Free Loan Society, appears to have developed from a free loan society into an *aktsiye*. In the early 1940s the Internal Revenue Service ruled that the association was not a nonprofit entity because it charged interest to some of its customers. The society disbanded, donating the remaining monies to charity. By then local banks were more willing to extend business loans, including to Jewish community members. Gilbert Rubenstein, interview by Nancy Hanflik, tape recording, Flint, Mich., 28 June 1999; and Ellis Warren, dictation to Jennie Krasnick, n.d., in possession of authors.

13. "Remembering Our Heritage: Henry Schafer," *Flint (Michigan) Jewish Reporter*, 15 August 1997, 3. The cooperative stored their bulk purchases in the basement of D&H Market, 2224 North Street.

14. "Remembering Our Heritage: Jewish Businesses in St. John Industrial District," *Flint (Michigan) Jewish Reporter*, 23 August 1996, 2; Robert Himelhoch, interview by Nancy Hanflik, tape recording, Flint, Mich., 28 June 2004. Industrial Market was at 3101 Industrial Avenue; Joseph Himelhoch's store was at 3401 St. John Street; 1930 *Flint, Michigan, Polk City Directory* (Taylor, Mich.: R. L. Polk and Company, 1930). At Industrial Market, Aaron Himelhoch ran the meat department, Julius ran the grocery section, and Isadore handled the finances. Other leading members of the

grocer's association were brothers David and Henry Schafer, who owned D&H Market, their initials giving the store its name. Reuben Himelhoch, Joseph's brother, also owned a grocery store, but it was located in the southern section of the city, near an auto body plant.

15. See, for example, the full-page advertisement for Kobacker's in *Flint (Michigan) Daily Journal*, 15 November 1921, in which the store promotes an "Original Furniture Style Show" featuring "a rare collection of arts and crafts and all period designed furniture" and to which it invites leading public officials and corporate heads. Kobacker's called itself " 'The Store Ahead' in the City Ahead."

16. "Remembering Our Heritage: The Beginnings of Temple Beth El," *Flint (Michigan) Jewish Reporter*, 13 January 1995, 7.

17. The women were proud of their accomplishments. See, for example, the newspaper clipping titled "Women of Flint," ca. 1923, which begins: "Communities which have experienced unusual growth due to great industrial activity are often slow to keep pace with cultural and organization activities. This cannot be said of Flint, especially the Jewish women of that municipality." Clipping file, Congregation Beth Israel, Flint, Michigan. More generally on Jewish women's activism in the early twentieth century, see Beth S. Wenger, "Jewish Women and Voluntarism: Beyond the Myth of Enablers." *American Jewish History* 79 (Autumn 1989): 16–36; Wenger, "Jewish Women of the Club: The Changing Public Role of Atlanta's Jewish Women (1870–1930)." *American Jewish History* 76 (March 1987): 311–33; and Sydney Stahl Weinberg, "Jewish Mothers and Immigrant Daughters: Positive and Negative Role Models," *Journal of American Ethnic History* 9 (Spring 1987): 39–55.

18. *Temple Beth El 1950 Dedication Book* (Flint, Mich.: n.p., 1950), Temple Beth El, Flint, Michigan, Collection and Clippings File; *Temple Beth El 50th Anniversary Book, 1927–1977* (Flint, Mich.: n.p., 1977), Temple Beth El, Flint, Michigan, Collection and Clippings File.

19. See Kenneth B. West, "Standard Cotton Products and the General Motors Sit-Down Strike: Some 'Forgotten Men' Remembered," *Michigan Historical Review* 14 (Spring 1988): 59.

20. Rubenstein, interview by Hanflik, 28 June 1999.

21. See the announcement of the formation of the Young Judean Club, "Jews of Flint!" *Flint (Michigan) Community Herald*, 12 September 1920, 1.

22. Gerald Sorin, *A Time for Building: The Third Migration, 1880–1920* (Baltimore: Johns Hopkins University Press, 1992), 225–26.

23. On Ann (Shapiro) Lebster, see " "Flint Profile: Mrs. Louis Lebster and Mrs. Israel Sendler," *Flint (Michigan) Reporter*, December 1950, 3, 5–6; and "Remembering Our Heritage: Hadassah," *Flint (Michigan) Jewish Reporter*, 24 February 1995, 6.

24. See the loose clipping, "Zionists Gather at Chicago Convention," 31 December 1917, unknown newspaper, copy in possession of the authors; pictured among the "[p]rominent Zionists from all over the country" who participated in the "Federated Zionists Societies of the Middle West" convention were two Flint women, "Mrs. Louis Lebster" and "Mrs. Harry Winegarten" [*sic*].

25. On Ida (Lifschitz) Sendler, see " Flint Profile: Mrs. Louis Lebster and Mrs. Israel Sendler"; "Remembering Our Heritage: Hadassah"; and Reva (Sendler) Ratner, interview by Diane Roark, tape recording, Flint, Mich., 18 July 1999.

26. See, for instance, "Donor Dinner of Hadassah Attended by 250 Guests," *Flint (Michigan) Journal*, 12 December 1932, 9; untitled item under "Clubs," *Flint (Michigan) Sunday Journal*, 29 January 1932, 15; and "Remembering Our Heritage: Hadassah."

27. Lou Kasle and Charlotte (Lewis) Kasle, interview by Nancy Hanflik, tape recording, Flint, Mich., 15 June 1999.

28. See *Third Annual Purim Subscription Banquet*, Congregation Beth Israel (Flint, Mich.: n.p., 1934), Congregation Beth Israel, Flint, Michigan, Collection and Clippings File.

29. See *Congregation Beth Israel Dedication Book* (Flint, Mich.: n.p., 1952), Congregation Beth Israel, Flint, Michigan, Collection and Clippings File.

30. "Raids on Reds Land 32 Men in Jail Here," *Flint (Michigan) Daily Journal*, 3 January 1920, 1.

31. The literature on Ford's anti-Semitism is substantial. See especially Neil Baldwin, *Henry Ford and the Jews: The Mass Production of Hate* (New York: Public Affairs, 2001).

32. See Alan Brinkley, *Huey Long, Father Coughlin, and the Great Depression* (New York: Knopf, 1982). The Catholic hierarchy did not silence Coughlin until 1940.

33. The Klan had as many as ninety thousand members in Michigan; see Kenneth T. Jackson, *The Ku Klux Klan in the City, 1915–1930* (New York: Oxford University Press, 1967), 127–43.

34. Ronald Edsforth, *Class Conflict and Cultural Consensus: The Making of a Mass Consumer Society in Flint, Michigan* (New Brunswick, N.J.: Rutgers University Press, 1987), 111–13.

35. Ibid., 104.

36. "Remembering Our Heritage: My Town, by Joseph L. Laro, Part 1," *Flint (Michigan) Jewish Reporter*, 7 December 2004, 6–7. Shedlische is about forty miles west of Lublin.

37. Art Hurand, interview by Nancy Hanflik, tape recording, Flint, Mich., 10 June 1999; Esther (Silver) Price, interview by Nancy Hanflik, tape recording, Flint, Mich., 23 June 1999.

38. The restriction of immigration had profound effects on American Jewry. According to Henry L. Feingold, "Only 73,000 Jewish immigrants settled in the United States between 1924 and 1931, a small fraction of the 656,000 who had come between 1907 and 1924." See Feingold, *A Time for Searching: Entering the Mainstream* (Baltimore: Johns Hopkins University Press, 1992), 29. Another estimate puts the number of Eastern European immigrants arriving in the United States between 1880 and 1914 at nearly two million; Andrew Godley, *Jewish Immigrant Entrepreneurship in New York and London, 1880–1914*, Enterprise and Culture, Studies in Modern History (New York: Palgrave, 2001), 80.

39. Dr. Nelson Schafer, "Remembering Our Heritage: Henry & Rae Schafer," *Flint (Michigan) Jewish Reporter*, 3 May 1996.

40. Hasia R. Diner, *A Time for Gathering: The Second Migration, 1820–1880* (Baltimore: Johns Hopkins University Press, 1992), 132–33.

41. Diane Roark, with Esther Price, "Our Heritage: The Silver Family," *Flint (Michigan) Jewish Reporter,* 30 March 1999, 4.

42. See Sidell Sorscher's comments in *You're a Wonderful Person* (Detroit: Harlo Press, 1985), 111.

43. See the advertisement for C&C Sanitary, 709 Dayton St. (near Industrial Avenue), Flint Jewish History Collection, Sloan Museum, Flint, Michigan.

44. This discussion of the impact of the Depression on Flint draws especially on the detailed analysis by Edsforth, *Class Conflict and Cultural Consensus*, 127–56.

45. Ibid., 136–37.

46. See especially the oral history testimony discussed in Kenneth B. West, "'On the Line': Rank and File Reminiscences of Working Conditions and the General Motors Sit-Down Strike of 1936–37," *Michigan Historical Review* 12 (Spring 1986): 57–82.

47. Edsforth, *Class Conflict and Cultural Consensus*, 138.

48. See, for example, Beth S. Wenger, *New York Jews and the Great Depression: Uncertain Promise* (New Haven, Conn.: Yale University Press, 1996.)

49. Charlotte (Lewis) Kasle, interview by Nancy Hanflik, tape recording, Flint, Mich.., 15 June 1999.

50. "Our Heritage: Hyman Podolsky—Salesman Extraordinaire," *Flint (Michigan) Jewish Reporter*, February 1999, 10.

51. Gilbert Rubenstein, "Remembering Our Heritage: Rubenstein and Hauser Families," *Flint (Michigan) Jewish Reporter*, 24 January 1997, 5.

52. Art Hurand, interview by Hanflik, 10 June 1999. Julius Hurand's very friendly interactions with non-Jewish Polish immigrants were exceptional; he was so welcomed by this immigrant community that he became a member of Flint's chapter of *Dom Polski* (the city's Polish center). For a succinct discussion of Jewish-Polish relations see, for example, John J. Bukowczyk, *And My Children*

Did Not Know Me: A History of the Polish Americans (Bloomington and Indianapolis: Indiana University Press, 1987), esp. 111–15.

53. Roark, with Price, "Silver Family"; Price, interview by Hanflik, 23 June 1999.

54. Edsforth believes that this strike has not received adequate attention; he sees it as a pivotal moment in the city's history because it "reflected an indigenous response to the Great Depression" that prefigured later activism. Edsforth, *Class Conflict and Cultural Consensus*, 127–35, quotes, 134 and 135.

55. See Nora Faires, "Transition and Turmoil: Social and Political Development in Michigan, 1917–1945," in Richard J. Hathaway, ed., *Michigan: Visions of Our Past* (East Lansing: Michigan State University Press, 1989), 200–217.

56. Edsforth, *Class Conflict and Cultural Conflict*, 149. Electoral politics in Flint during the late 1920s and early 1930s are complex, involving changes in the form of government; the establishment of a "Civic League" supported by major industrialists and financiers; the determined opposition to this group by a "machine" politician, William McKeighan, who garnered substantial working-class support; and a series of campaign and voting irregularities. Furniture dealer Maurice Rosenblum, who ran for city commissioner on the Civic League slate in 1930, was the victim of a complicated election eve effort, involving a deceptive radio broadcast that sought to provoke anti-Semitism. Rosenblum lost the election, and GM magnate C. S. Mott issued a public statement deploring the scheme. See *Flint (Michigan) Daily Journal*, 7 April 1930, 1, and 14 April 1930, 1.

57. On the effect of New Deal programs see William H. Chafe, "Flint and the Great Depression," *Michigan History* 53, no. 3 (1969): 224–39.

58. See the *Flint (Michigan) Daily Journal* photograph of the crowds lining South Saginaw Street as the Roosevelt motorcade passed by, the large sign for Winegarden's Furniture visible above the skyline; reprinted in Gustin, *Centennial Picture History of Flint*, 193.

59. For a detailed and thoughtful account by the editor of the union's newspaper in Flint see Henry Kraus, *The Many and the Few: A Chronicle of the Dynamic Auto Workers*, 2nd ed. (Chicago: University of Illinois Press, 1985). See also especially Sidney Fine, *Sit-Down: The General Motors Strike of 1936–37* (Ann Arbor: University of Michigan Press, 1969); Fine, "The General Motors Sit-Down Strike: A Re-examination," *American Historical Review* 70 (April 1965): 691–713; and Edsforth, *Class Conflict and Cultural Consensus*, 170–83.

60. Edsforth, *Class Conflict and Cultural Consensus*, 139.

61. Price, interview by Hanflik, 23 June 1999; "Schiller: B'nai B'rith Man of the Year"; and Esther Fineberg, interview by Dale Cyran, tape recording, Flint, Mich., 30 June 1978, and Joseph Schiller, interview by Dale Cyran, tape recording, Flint, Mich., 4 July 1978, both in Labor History Project Interview Transcripts, Frances Willson Thompson Library, Genesee Historical Collections Center, University of Michigan–Flint. At the time of the strike Joseph Schiller and his brother Charles co-owned Field's Clothing Store, 526 South Saginaw Street, which normally had a cash-only policy.

62. Fineberg, interview by Cyran, 30 June 1978.

63. Saul Gorne, interview by Nancy Hanflik, tape recording, Flint, Mich., 22 June 1999.

64. Fay (Laro) Alfred, interview by Nancy Hanflik, tape recording, Flint, Mich., 29 October 2002.

65. West, "Standard Cotton Products," 59. Discussion of this company, its workers, and the strike relies on this article.

66. West, "Standard Cotton Products," 60–63; see Schiller, interview by Cyran, 4 July 1978; and also the detailed contemporary study by Erdmann Doane Beynon, "The Southern White Laborer Migrates to Michigan," *American Sociological Review* 3 (June 1938): 333–43.

67. For example, it may be that two members of Flint's Jewish community who had secured city jobs during the mid-1930s acted on behalf of the local government against the sit-down: Hy Hoffman, a lawyer who became assistant city attorney; and William Lewis, the shop owner turned shoe repairman who became a city policeman.

68. Gilbert Rubenstein, who attended law school at the University of Michigan while continuing to work at his father's clothing store, recalls the formation there of a casual group of Jewish law students from Flint. Some rode back and forth together. Rubenstein, interview by Hanflik, 28 June 1999.

69. Fay (Laro) Alfred, interview by Hanflik, 29 October 2002; on the Zipperstein Resort in South Haven, Michigan, see Judith Levin Cantor, *Jews in Michigan* (East Lansing: Michigan State University Press, 2001), 40.

70. Based on a comparison of the 1930 *Flint, Michigan, Polk City Directory* (Taylor, Mich: R. L. Polk and Company, 1930) and the 1940 *Flint, Michigan, Polk City Directory* (Taylor, Mich.: R. L. Polk and Company, 1940).

71. Diane Roark, "Our Heritage: Bessie Shapiro Feldman, *Flint (Michigan) Jewish Reporter*, 17 December 1998, 6.

72. Rubenstein, "Remembering Our Heritage: Rubenstein and Hauser Families"; Gilbert Rubenstein, telephone interview by Nancy Hanflik, 9 September 2004.

73. *Congregation Beth Israel Dedication Book*, (Flint, Mich., n.p., 1972), 11, Congregation Beth Israel, Flint, Michigan, Collection and Clippings File; *Temple Beth El 50th Anniversary Book*, 10.

74. Price, interview by Hanflik, 23 June 1999; Clifford Hart, interview by Nancy Hanflik, tape recording, Flint, Mich.., 16 July 1999; Paula Hyman, "Gender and the Immigrant Jewish Experience in the United States," in Judith R. Baskin, ed., *Jewish Women in Historical Perspective* (Detroit: Wayne State University Press, 1991), 232–34.

75. Feingold, *Time for Searching*, 118–20.

76. See, for example, *Flint (Michigan) Daily Journal*, 12 December, 1932, 9; 19 January 1933, 11; and 26 November 1935, 10.

77. *Flint (Michigan) Daily Journal*, 1 January 1937, G-3.

78. For an account that places Berger in the context of anti-Zionist activity see Monty Noam Penkower, "The Genesis of the American Council for Judaism: A Quest for Identity in World War II," *American Jewish History* 86, no. 2 (1998): 167–94.

79. Elmer Berger, *Why I Am a Non-Zionist* (Flint, Mich., n.p., 1942); Berger, *The Flint Plan: A Program of Action for American Jews* (Flint, Mich., n.p., 1942).

80. See Penkower, "Genesis of the American Council for Judaism," 189–91.

81. Quote from Price, interview by Hanflik, 23 June 1999; Rubenstein, interview by Hanflik, 28 June 1999.

82. For a discussion of contention within Detroit's Jewish community in the 1930s and early 1940s, especially concerning how to address growing anti-Semitism in Europe, see Sidney M. Bolkosky, "Detroit's Reaction to the Holocaust and the New Immigrants," *Judaism* 49 (Summer 2000): 309–15.

83. Neither the federation's successor organization nor any other local body can locate a copy of the self-study.

84. Mimi (Gruner) Hanflik, interview by Nancy Hanflik, tape recording, Hallandale, Fla., 31 May 1997; see also the recollections of one of her older sisters, Anna (Gruner) Berg, interview by Nancy Hanflik, tape recording, Hallandale, Fla., 1 June 1997.

85. Charles Weinstein, "Remembering Our Heritage—The Weinstein Family," *Flint (Michigan) Jewish Reporter*, 13 August 2002, 7.

86. Those killed were Gilbert Himelhoch, Milton I. Fineberg, Arthur L. Benison, and Jack M. Laro. Army lieutenants Benison and Laro were killed simultaneously when the Japanese ship on which they were being transported as prisoners of war was sunk in October 1944. See "We Remember Our War Casualties: In Memory of Those We Lost in World War II," *Flint (Michigan) Jewish Reporter*, 17 January 1992, 7.

87. Gorne, interview by Hanflik, 22 June 1999; Rubenstein, interview by Hanflik, 28 June 1999.

88. *Congregation Beth Israel Dedication Book*, 1952, Congregation Beth Israel, Flint, Michigan, Collection and Clippings File.

89. Edsforth, *Class Conflict and Cultural Consensus*, 199; Gustin, *Centennial Picture History of Flint*, 205–10.

90. "Return to Tent City," Flint Jewish History Collection, Sloan Museum, Flint, Michigan.

91. There is considerable debate about the extent, nature, and evolution of anti-Semitism in the United States in the late 1930s and through the war years. See Edward S. Shapiro, *A Time for Healing: American Jewry since World War II* (Baltimore: Johns Hopkins University Press, 1992), 250–53.

92. *Temple Beth El 1950 Dedication Book*, 22.

93. Rubenstein, interview by Hanflik, 28 June 1999.

CHAPTER THREE. *A GOLDEN AGE?*

1. Carl Crow, *The City of Flint Grows Up: The Success Story of an American Community* (New York: Harper and Brothers, 1945), 208.

2. Ibid., 211.

3. Ibid., vii.

4. As reported in the *New York Times*, 24 February 1953. Wilson was testifying before a U.S. Senate committee, as newly elected President Dwight Eisenhower's selection for secretary of defense; Wilson held the post from 1953 to 1957. See also the article published five years later: James A. Maxwell, "What's Bad for General Motors Is Bad for Flint," *Reporter*, March 20, 1958.

5. Lou Kasle, interview by Nancy Hanflik, tape recording, Flint, Mich., 15 June 1999.

6. Crow, *City of Flint Grows Up*, 205.

7. See Ronald Edsforth, *Class Conflict and Cultural Consensus: The Making of a Mass Consumer Society in Flint, Michigan* (New Brunswick, N.J.: Rutgers University Press, 1987), 202–5. Edsforth emphasizes that longtime UAW president Walter Reuther embraced anti-Communism and consolidated his power within the UAW, in part, by attacking his opponents as "Reds." For a perspective that stresses Reuther's broader vision of labor, see Nelson Lichtenstein, *The Most Dangerous Man in Detroit: Walter Reuther and the Fate of American Labor* (New York: Basic Books, 1995).

8. By the mid-1960s, General Motors had 127 manufacturing plants in the United States and five more in Canada, plus operational works in twenty-two other countries. The corporation produced "cars, trucks, engines, household appliances, defense products, and heavy equipment," and had its own consumer finance and insurance departments. See Flint Board of Education, "Buick Motor Division, General Motors Corporation," *The World We Live By*, rev. ed., vol. 12 (1964): 2.

9. See, for example, the coverage of Flint as a model of modern labor-management relations: "Labor Peace: It's Wonderful," *U. S. News and World Report*, July 1950.

10. *Flint, Michigan: The Vehicle City* (Flint, Mich.: Flint Chamber of Commerce, 1955), n.p.

11. The photograph on page 2 depicts the 1954 parade celebrating production of GM's fifty-millionth car. See *General Motors Golden Carnival: Celebrating Its First 50 Million Cars* (Flint, Mich.: Flint Journal, 1954) and "Salute to General Motors on the Completion of 50,000,000 Automobiles," special edition, *Flint (Michigan) News-Advertiser*, 23 November 1954.

12. *Flint, Michigan: The Vehicle City*, n.p. GM added nearly seven million square feet of production facilities in Flint and its immediate fringe area between 1950 and 1954. The Fisher Body plant, at two-and-a-half million square feet, was the largest auto plant in the world.

13. Flint Board of Education, "The Background Story of Flint and Transportation," *The World We Live By*, rev. ed., vol. 5 (1965): 7.

14. Flint Board of Education, "Your City Government," *The World We Live By*, vol. 17 (1961): 13.

15. *Flint, Michigan: The Vehicle City*, n.p.

16. Michael Melet, interview by Nancy Hanflik, tape recording, Flint, Mich., 17 June 1999. Michael Melet, son of Sidney Melet, provides a detailed account of how his father, who moved to Flint from Minneapolis as the representative of a large clothing company, became a partner in both stores. In 1956 Sid Melet sold his share in Maas Brothers and became the sole owner of the Vogue. Born in 1940, Michael was active in the business from his boyhood.

17. Jennifer Walkling, "Yankee Was a Dandy Chain of Stores Back When," *Flint (Michigan) Journal*, 19 October 1998, B1, B10.

18. On average, Megdell opened one store per year between 1948 and 1967. The store situated downtown on South Saginaw Street is visible in the background of the photograph on page 2.

19. With his wife, Fanny Newblatt, Robert Newblatt previously had co-owned the successful Fanny's Hollywood Grill at 527 North Saginaw Street. She continued to operate the restaurant after they separated.

20. The Hebrew Immigrant Aid Society also extended help to non-Jews. See, for example, Michael W. Evanoff, *St. John St.: A Remembrance*, 3rd ed., rev. of *Through the Melting Pot and Beyond* (1979; repr., Flint, Mich.: Edelweiss Press, 1986), 249. Evanoff describes how his Macedonian family received help in New York City from HIAS, learning their "first ethnic custom" in America when the boys in the family were asked to wear yarmulkes during meals.

21. "Flint Jewish Council Resettles Families," *Flint (Michigan) Jewish Reporter*, January 1952, 3. Chairing this committee represented an extension of efforts Schafer made during the 1930s, when she and her husband, grocer Henry Schafer, collected and shipped clothes to Jews in Europe; Dr. Nelson Schafer, "Remembering Our Heritage: Henry and Rae Schafer," *Flint (Michigan) Jewish Reporter*, 3 May 1996, 2. Laura Bayliss, who headed FJCC's social committee, was also very active in the resettlement. See also "Federation Continues Long-Time Local Commitment," *Flint (Michigan) Jewish Reporter*, 12 June 1986, 3.

22. "Remembering Our Heritage: Our Heritage Tributes Solomon Saltiel," *Flint (Michigan) Jewish Reporter*, 2 April 1998, 3.

23. See Hastaoglou-Martinidis Vilma, "A Mediterranean City in Transition: Thessaloniki between the Two World Wars," *Facta Universitatus, Architecture and Civil Engineering* 1 (1997): 493, 502.

24. "Remembering Our Heritage: Sarah Feldman," *Flint (Michigan) Jewish Reporter*, 22 March 1997, 5; Betty Brenner, "Combination of Luck, Contacts, Brains Helped Flint Woman Survive Holocaust," *Flint (Michigan) Jewish Reporter*, 12 May 1995, 1, 3.

25. Ron Krueger, "Filling Others' Urgent Needs Help Block Memories of Nazism," *Flint (Michigan) Journal*, 3 April 1983, B1, B3.

26. As quoted in ibid., B1.

27. Anna (Gruner) Berg, interview by Nancy Hanflik, tape recording, Hallandale, Fla., 1 June 1997. Some moved to Detroit, where the population of survivors numbered between 3,400 and 4,000 by the mid-1950s; see Sidney M. Bolkosky, "Detroit's Reaction to the Holocaust and the New Immigrants," *Judaism* 49 (Summer 2000): 315–18.

28. Reva (Sendler) Ratner, interview by Diane Roark, tape recording, Flint, Mich., 18 July 1999.

29. *Congregation Beth Israel Dedication Book* (Flint, Mich.: n.p., 1952), Congregation Beth Israel, Flint, Michigan, Collection and Clippings File.

30. Jonathan D. Sarna, *American Judaism: A History* (New Haven, Conn.: Yale University Press, 2004), 278–79.

31. On the Rabbinical Assembly rulings see Edward S. Shapiro, *A Time for Healing: American Jewry since World War II* (Baltimore: Johns Hopkins University Press, 1992), 171–73.

32. *Congregation Beth Israel Dedication Book*, 1952, Congregation Beth Israel, Flint, Michigan, Collection and Clippings File. The first recorded bat mitzvah was held in August 1956 for Barbara Gellis, Susan Goldberg, Sally Sorscher, and Sandra Sorscher.

33. *Temple Beth El 1950 Dedication Book* (Flint, Mich.: n.p., 1950), Temple Beth El, Flint, Michigan, Collection and Clippings File.

34. Like the fund-raising effort to build CBI, the campaign for donations to build TBE was intense. The congregation went ahead with construction despite not having enough money to install air conditioning; not until several years after the building's dedication could the congregation afford the installation. Clifford Hart, telephone interview by Nancy Hanflik, 15 June 2004.

35. Sarna indicates that in the two decades after the war more than a thousand temples and synagogues were rebuilt or constructed, and that more than three-quarters of Jewish children received some regular religious education, a substantial increase over prewar rates; *American Judaism,* 279.

36. The letter from Truman is reproduced in *Temple Beth El 1950 Dedication Book.*

37. "Eleanor Roosevelt Calls for Arab-Israel Peace," *Flint (Michigan) Jewish Reporter*, February 1954, 1.

38. Clifford Hart, interview by Nancy Hanflik, tape recording, Flint, Mich., 16 July 1999.

39. Saul Gorne, interview by Nancy Hanflik, tape recording, Flint, Mich., 22 June 1999.

40. Caroline (Wise) Panzer, interview by Nancy Hanflik, tape recording, Flint, Mich., 24 October 2002.

41. Natalie Pelavin, interview by Nancy Hanflik, tape recording, Flint, Mich., 15 June 1999. The issue of foodways was and remains a delicate issue within American Judaism. Sarna discusses a defining incident, the so-called *trefa* (non-kosher) banquet held in Cincinnati in 1883. Ostensibly hosted in a spirit of goodwill and with the hope of unifying the diverse tendencies within Judaism, the banquet had a menu that included foods that broke the Jewish dietary code, infuriating the Conservatives. The banquet became a touchstone in Conservative/Reform relations. Sarna, *American Judaism,* 144–45.

42. Reva (Sendler) Ratner, for instance, used the term "uppity" to describe the attitude of some Reform members. See Ratner, interview by Roark, 18 July 1999. These sentiments are echoed by Gilbert Rubenstein, interview by Nancy Hanflik, tape recording, Flint, Mich., 28 June 1999.

43. In 1957, CBI organizations included a sisterhood, men's club, and junior sisterhood; TBE had a sisterhood, brotherhood, teen group, and the dramatic club for young adults.

44. "Joint School Chanukah Party a Howling Success," *Flint (Michigan) Jewish Reporter*, December 1954, 3. Usually celebrated in December, Hanukkah (also transliterated as "Chanukah") commemorates the rededication of the temple in Jerusalem in 165 B.C.E. by Judas Maccabaeus, following its use for worship by the Greeks.

45. "Aleph Zadik Aleph" are Hebrew letters that stand for the words "*Ahavah*" (brotherly love), "*Tzedakah*" (charity), and "*Achoos*" (harmony). A.Z.A. began in 1923 in Omaha, Nebraska, when a group of Jewish young men were denied admission to a high school fraternity; it became a national affiliate of B'nai B'rith two years later. Local organizations for girls followed shortly thereafter, and in 1944 the national organization recognized B'nai B'rith Girls.

46. See, for example, "B'nai B'rith Beats A.Z.A.," *Flint (Michigan) Jewish Reporter*, April 1951, 3; see also the announcement of the "Second Annual All-Jewish Basketball Jamboree," 20 February [1939?], pitting Aleph Zadik Aleph against the older men of B'nai B'rith, and featuring a "preliminary" event between "Jr. [Temple Beth El] Sisterhood" and "Jr. Hadassah"; Flint Jewish History Collection, Sloan Museum, Flint, Michigan.

47. Because the Jewish community lacked a pool, for example, members of the girls' club had less chance to make their mark in swimming, a sport in which Jewish women had been prominent since World War I. On the topic of Jewish women and sport, see especially the work of Linda J. Borish, including "Women, Sports, and American Jewish Identity in Late Nineteenth and Early Twentieth Centuries," in *With God on Their Side: Sports in the Service of Religion,* ed. Tara Magdalinksi and Timothy J. L. Chandler (London: Routledge, 2002), 71–98; and on swimming, "'The Cradle of American Champions, Women Champions . . . Swim Champions': Charlotte

Epstein, Gender and Jewish Identity, and the Physical Emancipation of Women in Aquatic Sports," *International Journal of the History of Sport* 21 (March 2004): 197–235.

48. Art Hurand, interview by Nancy Hanflik, tape recording, Flint, Mich., 10 June 1999; see the discussion in the Introduction.

49. Lou Kasle, interview by Hanflik, 15 June 1999.

50. Elmer Berger, *The Flint Plan: A Program of Action for American Jews* (Flint, Mich., n.p., 1942); see Chapter Two for a discussion of Elmer Berger's views. More than fifty years after Berger left Flint, one community member called the rabbi's anti-Zionism "the most divisive thing" that ever occurred among Flint Jewry; another stated flatly, "we do not mention Elmer Berger's name in our house"; quotes from Hurand, interview by Hanflik, 10 June 1999, and Ratner, interview by Roark, 18 July 1999.

51. Flint Jewish Community Council, "Notes for Dr. Golden," Flint, Mich., 28 November 1972, 2, Flint Jewish Federation, Flint, Michigan, Collections and Clippings File.

52. *Flint (Michigan) Jewish Reporter*, May 1950:,1–3; see also "1950 United Jewish Appeal, " *Flint (Michigan) Jewish Reporter*, September 1950, 1.

53. See "1950 United Jewish Appeal"; "Youth Division of Flint United Jewish Appeal Organized, " *Flint (Michigan) Jewish Reporter*, May–June 1954, 3; and "Joseph Megdell General Chairman 1957 UJA Drive," *Flint (Michigan) Jewish Reporter*, January–February 1957, 1. In 1957, the women's division raised $17,000, 11 percent of the FJCC's total annual contribution to UJA.

54. "Flint Profile: Mrs. Louis Lebster and Mrs. Israel Sendler," *Flint (Michigan) Jewish Reporter*, December 1950, 3, 5–6.

55. On women's roles in the analogous Detroit organization, see Sidney Bolkosky, *Harmony and Dissonance: Voices of Jewish Identity in Detroit, 1914–1967* (Detroit: Wayne State University Press, 1991), 450.

56. "Flint Commitments for Bond Purchases Reach $125,000," *Flint (Michigan) Jewish Reporter*, May 1951, 1.

57. Lou Kasle, interview by Hanflik, 15 June 1999.

58. *Flint (Michigan) News–Advertiser*, 23 June 1953.

59. Lawrence R. Gustin, ed., *The Flint Journal Centennial Picture History of Flint* (Flint, Mich.: William B. Eerdmans and Flint Bicentennial Commission, 1976), 230; Betty Brenner, "Comeback from Disaster Can't Blot Out Memories of Tornado," *Flint (Michigan) Journal*, 8 August 1999, H2.

60. William Attwood, "The Position of the Jews in America Today," *Look* 19 (29 November 1955): 27–35.

61. Individual members of Flint's Jewish community long had supported the city's Red Feather Fund Campaign (later to become the United Way), but an editorial in the FJCC *Reporter* less than a year before Attwood's visit testifies to the significance that community leaders placed on the drive: "The 1954 Red Feather Fund Campaign gets under way on October 1st in our community. . . . We shall welcome the solicitors who approach us, considering that they are volunteers in a common front. Let us open our hearts when we are called upon and give generously for the betterment of our community." "Red Feather Merits Your Support," *Flint (Michigan) Jewish Reporter*, September 1954, 2 The editorial also extolled the value of the local blood drive, the FJCC contributing through its own "blood drive committee," whose membership included the wives of nine prominent men.

62. Attwood, "Position of the Jews in America," 27. Attwood introduced the Hurands to his readers this way: "A bustling American family in Michigan prospers and maintains its faith in Judaism."

63. The phrase is from the title of a sociological investigation: James B. Ringer, *The Edge of Friendliness: A Study of Jewish-Gentile Relations* (New York: Basic Books, 1967). On Detroit see Gerhard Lenski, *The Religious Factor: A Sociologist's Inquiry* (New York: Anchor, 1963).

64. "Study Committee Is Appointed," *Flint (Michigan) Journal*, 2 June 1954, 23; "Sub-Committee Begins Planning," *Flint Michigan) News–Advertiser*, 4 June 1954, 16.

65. Flint Board of Education, "Buick Motor Division," 8; Betty Brenner, "Culture: Residents' Money, Time Were at Center of It All," *Flint (Michigan) Journal*, 8 August 1995, H5. Art Hurand reported that Abe Schreiber, owner of Royalite company, a supplier of electrical equipment to General Motors, felt obliged to become a sponsor; Hurand, interview by Hanflik, 10 June 1999.

66. *Flint, Michigan: The Vehicle City*, n.p.; quote is from the foreword.

67. See the photograph on page 10.

68. "Albert Harris," (1987–89), 536, Robert Schafer Oral Histories Collection, Genesee Historical Collections Center, Frances Willson Thompson Library, University of Michigan–Flint, Flint, Mich. Harris often attended committee meetings as part of his job.

69. Hart, interview by Hanflik, 16 July 1999.

70. Ibid.

71. Melet, interview by Hanflik, 17 June 1999.

72. Ibid.

73. "Our Heritage: Willowood," *Flint (Michigan) Jewish Reporter*, 27 January 1999, 4.

74. Natalie Pelavin, interview by Hanflik. 1999; and Melet, interview by Hanflik, 17 June 1999.

75. "Happiest Town in Michigan," *Coronet*, June 1956.

76. Steve Lee, "Stag Reports on a Wide-Open Town," *Stag* 7 (March 1956): 11–15, 66–67.

77. Ibid., 66.

78. Meyer's data are drawn from GM and Ford shops outside Flint, but particularly given the huge size of the Chevrolet and Buick plants it seems highly unlikely that Flint factories were less conflictual sites. See Stephen Meyer, "Work, Play, and Power: Masculine Culture on the Automotive Shop Floor, 1930–1960," *Men and Masculinities* 2 (October 1999): 115–34. Essays by Flint autoworker Ben Hamper provide ample evidence of such behavior in later years; see Hamper, *Rivethead: Tales from the Assembly Line* (New York: Warner Books, 1991). See also Steve Meyer, "Rough Manhood: The Aggressive and Confrontational Shop Culture of U.S. Auto Workers during World War II," *Journal of Social History* 36 (Fall 2002): 126–24. For a nuanced study of gender and shop floor culture at a Lansing, Michigan, auto company see Lisa M. Fine, *The Story of Reo Joe: Work, Kin, and Community in Autotown, U.S.A.* (Philadelphia: Temple University Press, 2004); see also Nancy F. Gabin, *Feminism in the Labor Movement: Women and the United Auto Workers* (Ithaca, N.Y.: Cornell University Press, 1990).

79. Tim Retzloff, "Cars and Bars: Assembling Gay Men in Postwar Flint, Michigan," in *Creating a Place for Ourselves: Lesbian, Gay, and Bisexual Community Histories,* ed. Brett Beemyn (New York: Routledge, 1997), 226–52.

80. Ibid., quote, 231; map, 226.

81. Rhonda Sanders, *Bronze Pillars: An Oral History of African-Americans in Flint* (Flint, Mich.: Flint Journal and Alfred P. Sloan Museum, 1995), 265–66.

82. Betty Tableman, *Intra-Community Migration in the Flint Metropolitan District* (Ann Arbor, Mich.: Institute for Social Adjustment, Social Sciences Research Project, University of Michigan, 1948), 13–15.

83. On Southern whites' migration to Flint, see Chad Berry, *Southern Migrants, Northern Exiles* (Chicago: University of Illinois Press, 2000); on the backgrounds of Flint's black residents see Sanders, *Bronze Pillars*.

84. I. Harding Hughes Jr., *Local Government in the Fringe Area of Flint, Michigan* (Ann Arbor, Mich.: Institute for Social Adjustment, Social Sciences Research Project, University of Michigan, 1947), 1.

85. Flint Board of Education, "Your Public Schools," *The World We Live By*, rev. ed., vol. 11 (1964): 8.

86. For Manley's account of the program's achievements after twenty-five years, see F. J. Manley, B. W. Reed, and R. K. Burns, *The Community School in Action: The Flint Program* (Chicago: University of Chicago Press, 1961); see also William Fred Totten and Frank J. Manley, *The Community School: Basic Concepts, Function, and Organization* (Galien, Mich.: Allied Education Council, 1969).

87. Another large backer of the Community Schools Program was the Ballenger Trust Fund, established by William S. Ballenger, who began as a bookkeeper and rose to an executive position at Chevrolet.

88. Flint Board of Education, "Your Public Schools," 8.

89. Lee, "Wide-Open Town," 66.

90. See Deborah Dash Moore, "Jewish GIs and the Creation of the Judeo-Christian Tradition," *Religion and American Culture* 8 (Winter 1998): 31–53 and Deborah Dash Moore, *GI Jews: How World War II Changed a Generation* (Cambridge, Mass.: Harvard University Press, 2004). .

91. Will Herberg, *Protestant, Catholic, Jew: An Essay in Religious Sociology* (Garden City, N.Y.: Doubleday, 1955); Will Herberg, "The 'Triple Melting Pot,'" *Commentary* 20 (August 1955): 101–8. Herberg drew on Ruby Jo Reeves Kennedy, "Single or Triple Melting Pot? Intermarriage Trends in New Haven, 1870–1940," *American Journal of Sociology* 49 (January 1944): 331–39. For a skeptical contemporary view of Herberg's work by a prominent Jewish scholar, see Marshall Sklare, "Protestant–Catholic–Jew: An Essay in Religious Sociology," *Commentary* 21 (February 1956): 195–98. See also Shapiro, *Time for Healing*, 16–18, and Moore, "Jewish GIs."

92. Hurand, interview by Hanflik, 10 June 1999; Michael Pelavin, interview by Nancy Hanflik, tape recording, Flint, Mich., 15 June 1999.

93. "Mayor's Commission on Human Relations," *Flint (Michigan) Jewish Reporter*, editorial, January 1952, 2.

94. "Flint Profile: B. Morris Pelavin," *Flint (Michigan) Jewish Reporter*, November 1950, 3; Michael Pelavin, interview by Hanflik, 15 June 1999.

95. "Beth Israel Sisterhood Discusses Social Action," *Flint (Michigan) Jewish Reporter*, February 1951, 3; see also "Beth Israel Sisterhood 'Town Hall' Is Inspiring," *Flint (Michigan) Jewish Reporter*, January 1951, 3.

96. "Stimulating Discussion at Beth El Interfaith Luncheon," *Flint (Michigan) Jewish Reporter*, January 1952, 3.

97. See the series of articles in the *Flint Journal* during and after the HUAC subcommittee hearings, including: "House Detroit Probe Awaits Red Trial End," 7 January 1954; "Union Heads Worried Over Work Stoppages: Accused Chevrolet Worker Elected and Mauled by Crowd of 500," 17 June 1954; "Borod Ousted at Chevrolet: Falsification of Job Application Charged," 22 June 1954; "Red Suspect Fights Firing: Injunction Sought by Detroit Teacher," 24 June 1954; "Clardy Finds New Source on Communist Cell at MSC," 26 June 1954; "Action Set for Thursday: Clardy Says Former Resident Involved," 20 July 1954; "27 Red Colonizers Found in Flint Plants, House Probers Report," 5 September 1954; and "Congressional Committee Reveals Witness X Testimony: Young Labor League Here Held Up as a Model for Other Branches in Michigan," 11 September 1954. Also see Clardy's obituary: "Kit Clardy, Ex-Congress Member Dies," *Flint (Michigan) Journal*, 6 September 1961. For the text of the hearings held in Flint, see House Committee on Un-American Activities, *Investigation of Communist Activities in the State of Michigan: Hearings before the United States House Committee on Un-American Activities*, 83rd Cong., 2nd sess., parts 8 (12 May 1954), 9 (13 May 1954), 10 (14 May 1954), and 11 (17 November 1954).

98. See Hart, interview by Hanflik, 16 July 1999. The case was *Baxter v. General Motors.* Baxter had applied for employment under her maiden name and was discharged from GM after her husband's brother was called before HUAC. The Michigan Employment Security Administration ruled that Baxter's use of her maiden name did not constitute falsification and required that she be paid unemployment compensation. See National Lawyers Guild, *Civil Liberties Docket* 1 (April 1956): 75, case number 255.4.

99. "FEPC Proposed to City Commission," *Flint (Michigan) Jewish Reporter*, January 1955, 1.

100. Esther (Silver) Price, interview by Nancy Hanflik, tape recording, Flint, Mich., 23 June 1999; Robert Himelhoch, interview by Nancy Hanflik, tape recording, Flint, Mich., 28 June 2004; Jack

Stanzler, interview by Nancy Hanflik, tape recording, Ann Arbor, Mich., 28 October 2002; Esther Fineberg, interview by Dale Cyran, tape recording, Flint, Mich., 30 June 1978, in Labor History Project Interview Transcripts, Frances Willson Thompson Library, Genesee Historical Collections Center, University of Michigan–Flint.

101. "Urban League President Joins in Condemnation of Persecution," *Flint (Michigan) Jewish Reporter*, January–February 1957, 1.

102. "Rev. Lloyd Channels New Chairman," *Flint (Michigan) Jewish Reporter*, January–February 1957, 2.

103. "Mayor Proclaims April 13ᵗʰ–20ᵗʰ 'Israel Independence Week,'*Flint (Michigan) Jewish Reporter*," April–May 1956, 3.

104. Shapiro, *Time for Healing*, 201.

105. FJCC, "Notes for Dr. Golden," 28 November 1972, n.p.

106. "Human Relations Commission," *Flint (Michigan) Jewish Reporter*, May–June 1960, 1.

107. See "Yankee Stores Now Prime Target of Group Seeking Free Enterprise Control," *Flint (Michigan) Weekly Review*, 20 December 1962, 1; "Card Party Finally Hits in Michigan," *Flint (Michigan) Weekly Review*, 11 January 1963, n.p. The *Flint (Michigan) Journal* editorialized against Megdell's boycott: "Community Not Responsible for Ill-Conceived Boycott," *Flint (Michigan) Journal*, 15 January 1965, 10; Megdell's response, including the quoted material, is in letter to the editor, *Flint (Michigan) Journal*, 20 January 1965, 2.

108. Melet, interview by Hanflik, 17 June 1999; Stanzler, interview by Hanflik, 28 October 2002.

109. Thomas J. Sugrue, *The Origins of the Urban Crisis: Race and Inequality in Postwar Detroit* (Princeton, N.J.: Princeton University Press, 1996), 259.

110. The "Sugar Hill" neighborhood was along Lapeer Road, west of Dort Highway. See Sanders, *Bronze Pillars*, esp. 17–20, 261.

111. These patterns can be seen in data outlined in a series of studies conducted by the University of Michigan's Institute for Human Adjustment, as part of its Social Science Research Project during the late 1940s and 1950s; remarkably, race is rarely a category of analysis in the studies. See especially Hughes, *Local Government in the Fringe Area of Flint, Michigan*; Robert C. Schmitt, *The Future Population of Metropolitan Flint* (Ann Arbor, Mich.: Institute for Social Adjustment, Social Sciences Research Project, University of Michigan, 1947); Mary Elizabeth Dunlap, *The Urban and Metropolitan Status of the City of Flint* (Ann Arbor, Mich.: Institute for Social Adjustment, Social Sciences Research Project, University of Michigan, 1948); John Kantner, *The Relationship between Accessibility and Socio-Economic Status of Residential Lands, Flint, Michigan* (Ann Arbor, Mich.: Institute for Social Adjustment, Social Sciences Research Project, University of Michigan, 1948); J. D. Carroll Jr., *Urban Land Vacancy: A Study of Factors Affecting Residential Building on Improved Vacant Lots in Flint, Michigan* (Ann Arbor, Mich.: Institute for Social Adjustment, Social Sciences Research Project, University of Michigan, 1953); Dell S. Wright, *Central Business District of Flint, Michigan: Changes in the Assessed Valuation of Real Property, 1930-1951* (Ann Arbor, Mich.: Institute for Social Adjustment, Social Sciences Research Project, University of Michigan, 1953); Thelma F. Batten, *Flint and Michigan: A Study in Interdependence* (Ann Arbor, Mich.: Institute for Social Adjustment, Social Sciences Research Project, University of Michigan, 1955); Basil G. Zimmer, *Demographic Handbook of Flint Metropolitan Area* (Ann Arbor, Mich.: Institute for Social Adjustment, Social Sciences Research Project, University of Michigan, 1955), esp. 11; and Tableman, *Intra-Community Migration*. See also Walter Firey, *Social Aspects to Land Use Planning in the Country-City Fringe: The Case of Flint* (East Lansing: Michigan State College, Agricultural Experiment Station, Section of Anthropology, 1946).

112. Christopher Machniak, "Racial Issues Were Battles Hard Fought," *Flint (Michigan) Journal*, 12 September 1999, G5.

113. For examples of episodes of harassment and formal discrimination, see Sanders, *Bronze Pillars*,

249–309; see also the report of a special task force on financial lending appointed by Republican governor William Milliken: Michigan, Governor's Task Force on Redlining, *Final Report of the Governor's Task Force on Redlining* (Lansing: State of Michigan, 1976), 51–58.

114. See Richard Hébert, "Flint: GM's Mark of Excellence," in *Highways to Nowhere: The Politics of City Transportation* (New York: Bobbs-Merrill, 1972), 6–8.

115. Wright documented this pattern in his 1953 study; see *Central Business District,* 1. See also Hébert, who contends that "Flint began feeling the full brunt of suburbanization of its tax base sooner than most cities. As early as 1960 some 56 percent of its urbanized land area was outside the thirty square miles of the city limits, and the suburbs accounted for almost 52 percent of the population in the Standard Metropolitan Statistical Area, already twice the national average in 1960."

116. See Zimmer, *Demographic Handbook,* 8, 11; Hughes, *Local Government,* 3, 5–6.

117. Hébert, "Flint: GM's Mark of Excellence," 9.

118. Gilbert Rubenstein, telephone interview by Nancy Hanflik, 9 September 2004.

119. The executive director of the Greater Flint Downtown Corporation, Saul Siegel, believed his agency only helped slow the process of suburban flight. See Hébert, "Flint: GM's Mark of Excellence," 16. Moreover, while the Mott Foundation supported the Downtown Corporation's mission of trying to solve the city's commercial crisis it also backed a Flint Board of Education publication that couched the shift in retail trade in a language of progress, an inevitable shift toward a more rational economy and more comfortable way of life. The school publication explained that "Retailing is a flexible changing business," adding that because "most people have at least one car . . . [t]hey no longer depend on a handy neighborhood store for the things they need," instead shopping in suburban discount stores or shops in "an enclosed mall, air conditioned center" where they are "not exposed to the elements as they walk from one store to another." Such sentiments were hard to swallow for both Flint merchants and the city's black residents, unwelcome in the suburbs. See Flint Board of Education, "Retailing in Flint," *The World We Live By,* vol. 19 (1963): 11; see also the photograph of downtown Flint at night, p. 2, juxtaposed with the daylight aerial view of a suburban shopping center, p. 3.

120. See especially the planning document that shows maps of the proposed routes and provides a rationale for the location of both expressways: Office of Planning, Michigan State Highway Department, *Freeways for Flint: A Statement of the Michigan State Highway Department. Proposals for Location of I-475, M78/21 Freeways in Flint.* Presented to the Flint City Commission by the Office of Planning, Michigan State Highway Department, 17 January 1963.

121. See the discussion of removals and displacement in the St. John neighborhood in Evanoff, *St. John St.: A Remembrance;* the Himelhoch Grocery is pictured on p. 311.

122. Hébert, "Flint: GM's Mark of Excellence," 21.

123. Gustin, *Centennial Picture History of Flint,* 166–68; Michael Pelavin, interview by Hanflik, 15 June 1999; Christopher Machniak, "The Journal of the Twentieth Century, 1960–69," *Flint (Michigan) Journal,* 12 September 1999, 1; Sanders, *Bronze Pillars,* 140, 143, 287–88.

124. Hart, interview by Hanflik, 16 July 1999.

125. Jack Minore, "Champions of Justice," *Forum Magazine,* May 1998, 10–11. The case was: U.S. Supreme Court, *Harper et al., v. Virginia Board of Elections et al.,* Appeal from the United States District Court for the Eastern District of Virginia, no. 48. Argued January 25–26, 1966. Decided March 24 1966. Together with N. 655. *Butts v. Harrison, Governor of Virginia, et al.,* from the same court. Segar was appealing *Butts v. Harrison.* The majority opinion was offered by Justice William Douglas.

126. *Spencer v. Flint Memorial Park Association,* Docket No. 318, Court of Appeal of Michigan, 4 Mich, App. 157; 144 N. W. 2d 622. April 6, 1966, Submitted. September 13, 1966, Decided.

127. Krueger, "Filling Others' Urgent Needs."

128. Albert J. Mayer, *Flint Jewish Population Study 1967* (Flint, Mich.: Flint Jewish Community Council, 1969).

129. Ibid., 1.

130. Ibid., 16.

131. In 1960, 17 percent of Flint's overall population were employed as professionals, business owners, or executives; in 1967, 82 percent of Flint's Jews were employed in the professions or business; Ibid., 16.

132. Ibid., 21–22.

133. Ibid., 12–13.

134. Ibid., 26.

135. Ibid., 58–67.

136. Ibid., 85–89.

137. Ibid., 89.

138. Ibid., 4.

139. Melet, interview by Hanflik, 17 June 1999.

CHAPTER FOUR. *HARD TIMES*

1. Data provided by Janis Karcher, Flint Chamber of Commerce, telephone interview by Nancy Hanflik, 3 November 2004. See also Danny Hakim, "G.M. Will Reduce Hourly Workers in U.S. by 25,000," *New York Times,* 8 June 2005.

2. For discussions of national trends, see Jon C. Teaford, *Cities of the Heartland: The Rise and Fall of the Industrial Midwest* (Bloomington: Indiana University Press, 1993, and Steven High, *Industrial Sunset: The Making of North America's Rust Belt, 1969–1984* (Toronto: University of Toronto Press, 2003); see also Jefferson Cowie and Joseph Heathcott, eds., *Beyond the Ruins: The Meanings of Deindustrialization* (Ithaca, N.Y.: ILR Press, 2003).

3. See figures in David Harvey, *The Condition of Postmodernity: An Enquiry into the Origins of Cultural Change* (Oxford: Basil Blackwell, 1989), 167–69.

4. Harvey, *Condition of Postmodernity,* 193.

5. The roots of the oil embargo lie in a complicated pattern of international relations, the immediate catalyst for the embargo the 1973 "Yom Kippur War" waged between Egypt and Syria against Israel. Consequently, as we discuss in the following, the oil crisis had special salience for Flint's Jewish community; here we focus on its economic impact on Flint and the nation.

6. Ralph Nader, *Unsafe at Any Speed: The Designed-In Dangers of the American Automobile* (New York: Grossman Publishers, 1965).

7. Harvey Swados, *Unsafe at Any Speed,* by Ralph Nader; and *Safety Last,* by Jeffrey O'Connell and Arthur Meyers, *Commentary* 41 (June 1966): 88–91; John Keats, *The Insolent Chariots* (Philadelphia: Lippincott, 1958).

8. "Flint—A City Fighting Back," *U.S. News and World Report,* 7 July 1975.

9. James M. Miller, "80's Decade One of Flint's, GM's Toughest," *Flint (Michigan) Journal,* 14 November 1999, A13; and Miller, "Oil Embargo, Rises of Imports Gave GM a Jolt," *Flint (Michigan) Journal,* 10 October 1999, G4. More generally see Steven P. Dandaneau, *A Town Abandoned: Flint, Michigan, Confronts Deindustrialization* (Albany: State University of New York Press, 1996).

10. Senate Committee on the Budget, *Regional Impact of an Economic Slowdown: The Michigan Picture, Hearings before the Committee on the Budget, United States Senate,* 96th Cong., 1st sess., February 1980 (Washington, D.C.: U.S. Government Printing Office, 1980), 161 ff.

11. Carla Fried, with Leslie M. Marable and Sheryl Nance-Nash, "Best Places to Live in America," *Money* 25 (July 1996): 66–85, 88–95; and Michael Moore, "Flint and Me," *Money* 25 (July 1996): 86–87.

12. *Roger & Me* was written and directed by Michael Moore and produced by his company, Dog Eat Dog Productions.

13. Miller, "80's Decade," A13.

14. Daniel Zwerdling, "And Then There's the Disneyland Solution," *Progressive* (July 1982): 34.

15. Ibid.

16. Reynolds Farley and William H. Frey, "Changes in the Segregation of Whites from Blacks During the 1980s," *American Sociological Review* 59 (February 1994): 23, 33–35.

17. Zwerdling, "Disneyland Solution," 34–35.

18. Ibid., 34.

19. George F. Lord and Albert C. Price, "Growth Ideology in a Period of Decline: Deindustrialization and Restructuring, Flint Style," *Social Problems* 39 (May 1992): 155–69. Lord, a sociologist, and Price, a political scientist, faculty members at the University of Michigan–Flint, followed the unfolding of these events firsthand.

20. For insights into this "tourist solution" see the remarks of Deborah Kelly, president of the Flint Area Convention and Tourist Council, Senate Committee on the Budget, "The Michigan Picture," 1980, 288–92.

21. In 1992 the Mott Foundation had a capital base of some $750 million. Lord and Price, "Growth Ideology," 158; see also Zwerdling, "Disneyland Solution," 35, and Charles Stewart Mott Foundation, "Report to the People: The Flint Process: A Look at Our Community" (Flint, Mich.: Charles Stewart Mott Foundation, n.d., ca. 1978.)

22. These aspects are highlighted in the 1989 video *Autoworld: Deconstructing Ideologies of Labor, Gender, Race, Class, and Consumerism in Flint, Michigan's Automobile Theme Park and Museum*, produced and directed by Connie Samaras, with script and narration by Nora Faires.

23. J. W. Rouse, "Must Shopping Centers Be Inhuman?" *Architectural Forum* (June 1962): 105–7, 196. For an assessment of Rouse and his ideas see Nicholas Dagen Bloom, *Merchant of Illusion: James Rouse, America's Salesman of the Businessman's Utopia* (Columbus: Ohio State University Press, 2004). Bloom lists Flint's festival marketplace as one of Rouse's "now famous flops"; see 92 (quote), 177–78. See also Jon Goss, "The 'Magic of the Mall': An Analysis of Form, Function, and Meaning in the Contemporary Retail Built Environment," *Annals of the Association of American Geographers* 83, no. 1 (March 1993): 18–47; on the Water Street Pavilion see D. S. Sawicki, "The Festival Marketplace as Public Policy: Guidelines for Future Policy Decisions," *American Planning Association Journal* (Summer 1989): 347–61.

24. Lord and Price, "Growth Ideology," 160.

25. Ibid.

26. Ibid., 161; see also Bryan D. Jones and Lynn W. Bachelor, "Flint: Political Maneuvering and Buick City," in *The Sustaining Hand: Community Leadership and Corporate Control* (Lawrence: University of Kansas Press, 1986), 179–236.

27. Christopher Machniak and Todd Seibt, "GM Tax Break," *Flint (Michigan) Journal*, 12 October 2004, 1.

28. Kim Moody, "On the Line in Flint," *Nation* 28 (13 July 1998).

29. Warren Cohen, "The End of an Era for Autos," *U.S. News & World Report* 127 (12 July 1999): 46.

30. Karcher, telephone interview by Hanflik, 3 November 2004; "Demolition Begins on 96-Year-Old Buick City Complex," *Detroit News*, 25 August 2001.

31. See Danny Hakim, and Jeremy W. Peters, "Tough Times at U.S. Makers of Auto Parts," *New York Times*, 12 December 2004.

32. "Best Buddy," *Time* 155 (31 January 2000): 68.

33. See for example, "Six-Year-Old Boy Shoots Classmate; Man, 19, Charged with Involuntary Manslaughter for Possessing the Gun," *Jet* 97 (20 March 2000): 17–18.

34. Ron Stodghill, "A Train Hop to Tragedy," *Time* (21 July 1997): 30–33.

35. See "Analysis: Cleaning Up Abandoned Property in Flint, Michigan," National Public Radio, 21 October 2003; report by Cheryl Corley, to Bob Edwards. Corley interviewed Genesee County

treasurer Dan Kildee, who headed the effort to gain control of abandoned property through tax foreclosures. As of that date, the county had acquired more than 2,100 properties in Flint, some to remodel and most to raze.

36. Lord and Price, "Growth Ideology," 161.

37. "Flint Named Model Small Jewish Community," Flint Jewish Federation Archives, Flint, Michigan, November 1970.

38. Recall that the Jewish population of Flint, like that in other U.S. cities, is difficult to pinpoint because these figures are not included in the decennial census. On population change, see George Jaksa, "Community Thinning as Young Follow Jobs," *Flint (Michigan) Journal*, 20 December 2003.

39. Sidney Bolkosky, *Harmony and Dissonance: Voices of Jewish Identity in Detroit, 1914–1967* (Detroit: Wayne State University Press, 1991), 298–99.

40. Gary Alter, Flint Jewish Federation, interview by Nancy Hanflik, Flint, Mich., 3 November 2004; data in *2004 [5764] Temple Beth El Directory* (Flint, Mich.: n.p., 2004), author's personal copy, and *Beth Israel Sisterhood 2004 Donor Book* (Flint, Mich.: n.p., 2004), author's personal copy.

41. Mitchell Weiss, interview by Nancy Hanflik, Flint, Mich., 4 November 2004. Weiss served as 2004 membership and dues chairman at TBE.

42. To avoid confusion and streamline the text, in this chapter we sometimes use the names interchangeably, referring to the organization as the Flint Jewish Federation or FJF, rather than the Flint Jewish Community Council or FJCC, before the renaming took place.

43. Weiss, interview by Hanflik, 4 November 2004.

44. Dr. Milan J. Dluhy, *Preliminary Report—The Jewish Aged in the Flint/Genesee Area—A Population in Need* (Flint, Mich., 30 Nov. 1984), 7–10; quote, 11 (emphasis in original).

45. Ibid. (emphasis in original).

46. Dr. Milan J. Dluhy, *Improving Housing Choices for the Jewish Aged in the Flint Area*, Flint, Mich., 1 November 1985, 5.

47. See, for example, Flint Jewish Community Council, "Minutes," 29 November 1978 and 21 June 1979, Flint Jewish Federation, Flint, Michigan, Collections and Clippings File.

48. Jewish Family and Children's Services, *Annual Report, 1998–1999* (Flint, Mich., n.p., 1999), Flint Jewish Federation, Flint, Michigan, Collections and Clippings File. The renaming occurred in 1992.

49. See *Jewish Community Services: Annual Report 2003–2004 [5764]* (Flint, Mich., 2004), Flint Jewish Federation, Flint, Michigan, Collections and Clippings File; Jaksa, "Community thinning."

50. Directors of Camp Maccabee have included Marshall Cossman, Judy Kasle, Joan Hallem Schafer, Judy Biesman, Sherri Dickinson, and Debrah Chimovitz.

51. On national trends see Laurie Goodstein, "Survey Finds Slight Rise in Jews' Intermarrying," *New York Times*, 11 September 2003.

52. Daniel Steinmetz, *1990 and Beyond: Needs and Possibilities Facing the Greater Flint Area Jewish Communities,* Project for Urban and Regional Affairs, University of Michigan–Flint, July 1990.

53. The survey was conducted by mail, questionnaires sent to all 821 households receiving the Flint Jewish Federation's newspaper, the *Reporter*; only 300 households responded.

54. Steinmetz, *1990 and Beyond*, 4–5, 12.

55. Ibid., 4–5, 7–8. The problem of too few Jewish marriage partners, due to the small size of the community and the outmigration of young adults, had concerned members of Flint Jewry for years.

56. Michael Pelavin, interview by Nancy Hanflik, tape recording, Flint, Mich., 15 June 1999.

57. "Flint Jewish Federation Board Sets 2000 Allocations to Agencies," *Flint (Michigan) Jewish Reporter*, 22 February 2000, 1. The gap at first was $60,000, with only $365,000 raised of a projected budget of $425,000; extraordinary appeals, including to retired members of the community living out-of-state, helped narrow the deficit.

58. Alter quoted in Jaksa, "Community Thinning."

59. Michael Melet, interview by Nancy Hanflik, tape recording, Flint, Mich., 17 June 1999.

60. Ibid.

61. Cathy M. Jackson, "'Junkyard Alley' Feeling Economic Crunch," *Flint (Michigan) Journal*, 28 November 1982, A1.

62. Analysis of community events between 1967 and 1974 is hampered because the *Flint Jewish Reporter* did not publish during these years. Instead, the Flint Jewish Community Council agreed to have the *Detroit Jewish News* run special issues for Flint subscribers to cover Genesee County stories. This coverage, however, was extremely limited, and in 1975 the *Flint Jewish Reporter* resumed publication. Between 1967 and 1974, however, the Flint Jewish community occasionally issued a newsletter that covered Mideast news. Titled *Operation Masada*, the bi-weekly newsletter's name referred to the mountain fortress built by Judean king Herod the Great in the first century, B.C.E. Unfortunately only a few copies of this newsletter are extant. "Memo—Operation Masada," *Flint (Michigan) Operation Masada*, 7 December 1970, 1.

63. The war began during the Jewish celebration of Yom Kippur and the Muslim celebration of Ramadan; the conflict thus is known to Muslims as the "Ramadan War"; it also is referred to as the "October War."

64. "Flint Jews Give Funds for Israel," *Flint (Michigan) Journal*, 9 October 1973, B1; "Summary of the Flint Jewish Federation Campaigns," 17 July 1975, Flint Jewish Federation. The "Israel Emergency Fund" was established after the Six Day War; pledges for 1973, made before the Yom Kippur War, totaled $284,750. The total cited here ($635,000) is for 1974, the year that includes pledges paid after the October 1973 war. Personal copy of authors.

65. "Missions to Israel," *Flint (Michigan) Operation Masada*, 7 December 1973, 1. With subsidies, the study missions cost only about $1,000.

66. "Flint Participates in Unique Mission," Collections and Clippings File, Flint Jewish Federation, Flint, Michigan.

67. As quoted in "Face to Face: Flint Area Leaders Meet Israeli Government Leaders," *Flint (Michigan) Jewish Reporter*, 9 April 1993, 6.

68. Dale E. Kildee, "Highlights of Congressional Mission to Israel," *Flint (Michigan) Jewish Reporter*, 11 February 1994, 1.

69. See "One of Ours Is in the Military," *Flint (Michigan) Jewish Reporter*, 21 September 1990, 5; "Pray for Their Safe Return," *Flint (Michigan) Jewish Reporter*, 23 January 1991, 1; and "One of Ours Is Over There," *Flint (Michigan) Jewish Reporter*, 26 July 1991, 5.

70. Steinmetz, *1990 and Beyond*, vii, 11.

71. Historian Jonathan Sarna notes that in the two decades after 1967, some 1.5 million Soviet Jews emigrated, truly a mass exodus. Sarna, *American Judaism: A History* (New Haven, Conn.: Yale University Press, 2004), 318–19.

72. *Flint (Michigan) Operation Masada*, 14 May 1971.

73. "900 at Flint Soviet Jewry March," *Flint (Michigan) Operation Masada*, 10 October 1971, 1.

74. "What to Do until Nixon Goes," *Flint (Michigan) Operation Masada*, 14 May 1972, 1.

75. "The Fairmark Family," *Flint (Michigan) Operation Masada*, 10 August 1973, 2; see also Natalie Pelavin, interview by Nancy Hanflik, tape recording, Flint, Mich., 15 June 1999.

76. Minutes of the Executive Committee, Flint Jewish Community Council, 16 August 1979, Flint Jewish Federation, Flint, Michigan, Collections and Clippings File.

77. "Women Appeal in Behalf of Soviet Jewry," *Flint (Michigan) Jewish Reporter*, 16 December 1977, 3.

78. "Women Take Plea for Soviet Jewry to Public," *Flint (Michigan) Jewish Reporter*, 23 December 1977, 3.

79. "Sister Ann Gillen: Letters Are Important," *Flint (Michigan) Jewish Reporter*, 3 June 1977, 2. Sister Ann Gillen, executive director of the National Interreligious Task Force on Soviet Jewry, led a citywide rally at Temple Beth El in May 1977, galvanizing non-Jews to join local Jews in this effort.

80. "A Father–Son Reunion," *Flint (Michigan) Jewish Reporter*, 20 January 1978, 1; "Welcome to Flint," *Flint (Michigan) Jewish Reporter*, 17 February 1978, 4.

81. "The People of Israel Live," *Flint (Michigan) Jewish Reporter*, 4 February 1988, 1.

82. Betty Brenner, "Flint Jewish Community Prepares Welcome Mat for Resettling Soviets," *Flint (Michigan) Journal*, 19 March 1990.

83. "FJF/JSS Boards Endorse Operation Exodus," *Flint (Michigan) Jewish Reporter*, 20 February 1990, 1; "Campaign 1990: Exciting," *Flint (Michigan) Jewish Reporter*, 20 June 1990, 1.

84. "Resettlement Chairs Alexander and Miller Named, *Flint (Michigan) Jewish Reporter*, 20 February 1990, 1; see also "Flint Welcomes Russian Families," *Flint (Michigan) Jewish Reporter*, 13 April 1990, 1; "Super Soviet Volunteers," *Flint (Michigan) Jewish Reporter*, 30 July 1990, 1; and "Summer English Tutoring Program," *Flint (Michigan) Jewish Reporter*, 12 August 1994, 1. Among the earlier arrivals who worked extensively with the newcomers were Dora, Sam, and Emily Lumar and Lia, George, and Julie Salk. Others heading the volunteer services included Delores Rosenberg, Caroline (Wise) Panzer, and Kathy Weiner.

85. The 1991 dinner, for example, raised over $60,000 and attracted 450 attendees. "July 15 Riegle Dinner Planned," *Flint (Michigan) Jewish Reporter*, 22 June 1990, 1; "Riegle Dinner Outstanding," *Flint (Michigan) Jewish Reporter*, 26 July 1991, 1. Riegle did not run for reelection to the Senate in 1994, having been implicated in a massive savings and loan scandal.

86. "Surgical Staff Moves from Russia to Flint," *Flint (Michigan) Jewish Reporter*, 15 October 1993, 5.

87. "Flint Named Model Small Jewish Community," Flint Jewish Federation Archives, November 1970.

88. Jack Stanzler, interview by Nancy Hanflik, tape recording, Ann Arbor, Mich., 28 October 2002. These investigations were prompted in part by the shooting of a young black man, Billy Taylor. See "Complaints against Police Aired," *Flint (Michigan) Journal*, 17 August 1970. The investigation revealed that of some 240 to 250 police officers less than a dozen were African American.

89. James Sharp Jr., telephone interview by Nancy Hanflik, 14 April 2000. See also Jack Nelson, "Young Affair Fuels Jewish, Black Rift," *Detroit News*, 26 August 1979; Edgar Holt Collection, Genesee Historical Collections Center, Frances Willson Thompson Library, University of Michigan–Flint; hereafter, Holt Collection.

90. See the correspondence in the Holt Collection: Olive Beasley, memo to Edgar Holt, undated; Rabbi Hillel Rudavsky, letter to Dr. Benjamin Hooks, 27 August 1979; and Edgar Holt, letter to Rabbi Hillel Rudavsky, 30 August 1979.

91. U.S. Supreme Court, *University of California Regents v. Bakke,* 438 U.S. 265 (1978).

92. "Interfaith Service Heralds Peace Treaty," *Flint (Michigan) Jewish Reporter*, 13 April 1979, 4.

93. Peter Goodstein, interview by Nancy Hanflik, tape recording, Flint, Mich., 2 September 1999; "Blacks, Jews Recall Heritage at Passover Seder," *Flint (Michigan) Jewish Reporter*, 11 May 1987, 7.

94. "Federation, CRC Call for 'No' Vote on Proposal A," *Flint (Michigan) Jewish Reporter*, 30 September 1988, 1; "Vote 'No' on Proposal A," *Flint (Michigan) Jewish Reporter*, 4 November 1988, 1.

95. Michael Pelavin, interview by Hanflik, 15 June 1999; Natalie Pelavin, interview by Hanflik, 15 June 1999.

96. FJF executive directors Richard Krieger and David Nussbaum are credited by community members for their leadership in promoting relations with other civic groups.

97. The Greater Flint Council of Churches, the *Flint Journal*, and Congressman Kildee also joined the effort. "New Name Suggested," *Flint (Michigan) Journal*, 28 September 1988, 1; "Here's What Community Leaders, Groups Say about Wallenberg Street Proposal," *Flint (Michigan) Jewish Reporter*, 4 November 1988, 10.

98. Betty Brenner, "Interfaith Gathering Recalls *Kristallnacht*," *Flint (Michigan) Journal*, 10 November 1988, B1.

99. Betty Brenner, "Arabs Here Blame Israelis for Massacre, Set Protest . . . While Area Jews Lament

Killings, with Truth Sought," *Flint (Michigan) Journal*, 23 September 1982, A3.

100. Natalie Pelavin, interview by Hanflik, 15 June 1999.

101. Leonard Meizlish, interview by Nancy Hanflik, tape recording, Flint, Michigan, 10 July 2003.

102. Betty Brenner, "Holocaust Survivor Tells Students in Flint: 'We Were Just Like You,'" *Flint (Michigan) Journal*, 8 May 2000, C4.

103. Peter Gluck, a professor of political science at the University of Michigan–Flint and Jewish community member, oversaw the "World of Difference" program. See "Flint Groups Seek to Make a 'World of Difference, '" *Flint (Michigan) Jewish Reporter*, 28 October 1988, 1; "Youth Working with Cultural Diversity," *Flint (Michigan) Jewish Reporter*, 22 November 1988, 9; "Why a 'World of Difference' Is So Important," *Flint (Michigan) Jewish Reporter*, 12 December 1988, 2.

104. Clifford Hart, interview by Nancy Hanflik, tape recording, Flint, Mich., 16 July 1999.

105. Natalie Pelavin, interview by Hanflik, 15 June 1999.

106. "Combined School Nears Final Approval," *Flint (Michigan) Jewish Reporter*, 19 February 1982, 1.

107. Emily Bank Alter, interview by Nancy Hanflik, tape recording, Flint Mich., 21 March 2000; Betty Brenner, "Newly Opened Flint Jewish School So Rare It May Be a Signal of the Future," *Flint (Michigan) Journal*, 10 October 1982.

108. Meizlish, interview by Hanflik, 10 July 2003.

109. Emily Bank Alter, interview by Hanflik, 21 March 2000.

110. Ibid.; see also Rabbi James Michaels, interview by Nancy Hanflik, tape recording, Flint, Mich., 30 September 1999.

111. Edward S. Shapiro, *A Time for Healing: American Jewry since World War II* (Baltimore: Johns Hopkins University Press, 1992), 167.

112. Ibid., 171.

113. See Sarna, *American Judaism*, 297–300.

114. See the discussion in Shapiro, *A Time for Healing*, 184–85. Compare also the discussion of Orthodoxy in two editions of an influential text, Marshall Sklare's *Conservative Judaism: An American Religious Movement* (1955; repr., Glencoe, Ill.: Free Press, 1972).

115. In 1990, four years after the founding of Chabad House, two-thirds of the respondents in the federation survey reported "negative experiences" with the Lubavitch congregation; Steinmetz, *1990 and Beyond*, vii.

116. The first women so elected were Frumeth Hirsh-Polasky at CBI and Natalie Pelavin at TBE.

117. Esther (Silver) Price, interview by Nancy Hanflik, tape recording, Flint, Mich., 23 June 1999.

118. "Area Jews Prepare for Hanukkah," *Flint (Michigan) Journal*, 2 December 1988, B1.

119. Goodstein, interview by Hanflik, 2 September 1999.

120. Louis Kasle, interview by Nancy Hanflik, tape recording, Flint, Mich., 15 June 1999; comments by Rabbi Yisroel Weingarten, Yisroel and Shainie Weingarten, interview by Nancy Hanflik, tape recording, Flint, Mich., 6 January 2000.

121. Quotes from Rabbi Yisroel Weingarten, Yisroel and Shainie Weingarten, interview by Hanflik, 6 January 2000.

122. Asked about membership figures, Rabbi Weingarten replied: "We don't have numbers . . . Or if we do have numbers, my response to everybody is . . . every Jew in the community by the mere fact of being Jewish is a member of Chabad House." Rabbi Yisroel Weingarten, Yisroel and Shainie Weingarten, interview by Hanflik, 6 January 2000.

123. See E. J. Kessler, "The Lubavitch Factor," *Forward*, 14 January 2000, 13.

124. For some years after moving to Oak Park Dr. Jerome Kasle maintained his eye clinic on Flint's west side. Yisroel and Shainie Weingarten, interview by Hanflik, 6 January 2000; see also "Congressman Kildee Honors Dr. Jerome and Sherry Kasle—Hon. Dale E. Kildee (Extension of Remarks) 103rd Cong., 2nd sess. *Congressional Record* 140, no. 11 (8 Feb. 1994): E125.

125. Rabbi Michaels, interview by Hanflik, 30 September 1999; Rabbi Michaels served at CBI. For a

similar perspective by the rabbi who served at TBE during the same period see Rabbi Mark Goldfarb, interview by Nancy Hanflik, tape recording, Flint, Mich., 12 October 1999. Both since have left Flint.

126. Meizlish, interview by Hanflik, 10 July 2003.

127. Tony Swan, "Buick Celebrates 100 Years of Tasteful, Not Crass, Automobiles," *Detroit Free Press*, 17 July 2003.

128. Joe Lawlor, "The Vehicle City Arches Are Back," *Flint (Michigan) Journal*, 30 November 2003, A1.

129. As quoted in Lawlor, "Vehicle City Arches," A1.

130. William Attwood, "The Position of the Jews in America Today," *Look* 19 (29 November 1955): 32.

131. The phrase is from Michael Frisch, *A Shared Authority: Essays on the Craft and Meaning of Public History* (Albany: State University of New York Press, 1990).

EPILOGUE

1. The following commentaries are excerpted, with minor editorial changes, from remarks made to Nancy Hanflik. See Rabbi Karen Companez, personal communication to Nancy Hanflik, 29 December 2004; Yuliya Gaydayenko, interview by Nancy Hanflik, Flint, Mich., 9 November 2004; David Leyton, personal communication to Nancy Hanflik, 31 January 2005; Leonard Meizlish, interview by Nancy Hanflik, tape recording. Flint, Mich., 10 July 2003; and Mitchell Weiss, interview by Nancy Hanflik, Flint, Mich., 4 November 2004.

Glossary

Agudas Achis Hebrew for "United Sisters"; the name of a women's fundraising organization at Flint's Congregation Beth Israel during the 1920s.

Aktsiye A cooperative that operated like a credit union: individual members deposited money into savings accounts and were paid interest. The *aktsiye* then loaned a portion of the deposits to members who wanted to start enterprises.

Aliyah Hebrew for "ascent"; refers to an individual who is called up to read the Torah or recite a blessing before and after the Torah reading in the synagogue. This also has come to refer to one who immigrates to Israel.

Ashkenazi Biblical name referring to Germany which became applied to those who followed the religious and cultural traditions originating among German Jews.

AZA Abbreviation for letters of the Hebrew alphabet, *Aleph Zadik Aleph*. The name of the boy's club sponsored by B'nai B'rith.

Bar Mitzvah Hebrew for "son of the commandment"; ceremony at which a thirteen-year-old Jewish boy becomes an adult member of the community.

Bat Mitzvah Hebrew for "daughter of the commandment"; ceremony at which a Jewish girl, aged twelve or older, becomes an adult member of the community.

Beth El Hebrew for "House of God"; adopted as the name for Flint's Reform congregation.

Beth Israel Hebrew for "House of Israel"; adopted as the name for Flint's Conservative congregation.

B'nai B'rith Hebrew for "Sons of the Covenant"; an organization founded in 1843 to unify and strengthen relationships among Jewish men in the United States through social, cultural and religious programs. Today B'nai B'rith is an international organization that includes women.

Developed in consultation with Rabbi Karen Companez, Temple Beth El, Flint, Michigan. Sources consulted include R. J. Zwi Werblowsky and Geoffrey Wigoder, eds., *The Oxford Dictionary of the Jewish Religion* (New York: Oxford University Press, 1997) and Jonathan D. Sarna, *American Judaism: A History* (New Haven, Conn.: Yale University Press, 2004).

Cantor An individual who is primarily responsible for performing vocal music in the synagogue or temple. He or she (except in Orthodoxy) also may act in pastoral and educational roles.

Chabad Hebrew acronym for "wisdom, comprehension, and knowledge"; part of the name of an Orthodox congregation in Flint, indicating its connection to the Lubavitch movement.

Hadassah A Women's Zionist Organization of America composed of volunteers dedicated to the promotion of health care, education, and youth institutions in Israel, founded by activist and scholar Henrietta Szold in 1912.

Hanukkah Hebrew for "dedication"; known as the Festival of Lights, this eight-day Jewish holiday celebrated by lighting candles; commemorates the rededication of the temple in Jerusalem in 165 B.C.E. after its desecration by the Greeks.

HIAS Initials for Hebrew Immigrant Aid Society, an agency founded in 1881 by Jewish immigrants who found sanctuary in the United States. HIAS offers food, shelter and aid to Jewish refugees around the world.

Ivriah Hebrew for "Place of Hebrew"; adopted as the name of Flint Jewry's combined religious school.

Kaddish Aramaic prayer praising God; best known as a mourner's prayer, but also recited during worship services.

Kashrut (Kosher) The system of food preparation according to Jewish dietary laws.

Kristallnacht German for "Night of the Broken Glass"; refers to the anti-Jewish riots launched by the Nazis in Germany and Austria on 9 November 1938. A thousand synagogues were burned, thousands of Jewish businesses destroyed, and many Jews were injured, sent to concentration camps, or killed.

Latkes Potato pancakes traditionally served during Hanukkah.

Lubavitch Belorussian town where Hasidism (a movement for Jewish mystical renewal) was founded and seat of the Schneerson family, leaders of Chabad Hasidism until 1915, when the rabbis were exiled. The sixth rabbi of Lubavitch arrived in the United States in 1940.

Matzah Unleavened bread that according to the biblical book of Exodus was hurriedly baked by the Jewish people as they escaped from Egypt. During Passover, the holiday commemorating this event, matzah is the only bread permitted.

Menorah Hebrew for "candelabrum"; has seven branches. The Hanukkah menorah (Chanukiyah) has eight lights, one for each night of the holiday, plus a ninth used to kindle the lamp.

Minyan Hebrew for "prayer quorum"; the number of Jewish adults (males only for Orthodox) required to recite certain communal prayers. At least ten adults must be present.

Mitzvah (plural, **mitzvot**) Hebrew for "commandment"; there are 613 biblical commandments that form the basis for Jewish law and behavior. The term *mitzvah* also has come to mean "good deed."

Mohel A person who is authorized and trained to perform the ritual circumcision which traditionally takes place on the eighth day after the birth of a male child.

Passover The eight-day Jewish holiday that commemorates the exodus of the children of Israel from Egypt, during which Jewish dietary laws prohibit the eating of leavened bread.

Purim Festival of Lots, commemorating the deliverance of the Jews from the Persian empire; celebrated on 14 Adar of the Hebrew calendar. The biblical book of Esther tells the story of Purim relating the courageous actions of Queen Esther.

Rosh Hashanah The Jewish "new year" celebrated in the fall; in Judaism, on this day God judges humankind for the coming year. Its celebration marks the beginning of ten days of penitence that culminates in Yom Kippur.

Sefer Torah A Torah scroll handwritten on parchment that contains the first five books of the Bible; also known as the Pentateuch or Torah.

Shabbat Hebrew for "Sabbath"; begins approximately at sundown Friday and continues until sundown Saturday.

Shohet Butcher who performs ritual slaughter required for kosher poultry and meats.

Shul Yiddish for "school" and used by Ashkenazi Jews to refer to the synagogue.

Sukkot A harvest festival that also commemorates the forty years of wandering in the wilderness by the Jewish people as recounted in the Bible. Traditionally, celebrants eat meals and spend their days in a temporary sukkah (booth) structure often decorated with the produce from the season.

Talmud The collections of the teachings of Jewish scholars who lived between 200 and 500 B.C.E.

Tefillin Leather boxes containing words of the Torah handwritten on parchment, worn on the arm and forehead, and used primarily by adult Jewish men while reciting the daily morning service from the prayer book.

Torah Hebrew for "instruction or guidance"; refers to the first five books of the Bible and the body of sacred Jewish literature.

Yeshiva An academy or school of higher learning in Judaism that focuses on the study of Talmud.

Yiddish The language of Ashkenazic Jews from Central and Eastern Europe. Originating about one thousand years ago, Yiddish is primarily a blend of German, Hebrew, Aramaic, and Slavic languages and is still spoken by several million people throughout the world.

Yom Kippur Hebrew for "the Day of Atonement"; the most solemn occasion for Jews throughout the world, it is observed by a twenty-five hour fast. In Judaism, God seals the fate of every individual for the coming year on Yom Kippur; prayer and repentance can moderate a severe judgment.

Bibliography

MANUSCRIPT AND ARTIFACT COLLECTIONS

American Jewish Archives, Cincinnati
- Jacob Rader Marcus Center

American Jewish Historical Society, Newton Centre, Massachusetts
- Industrial Removal Organization Collection

Congregation Beth Israel, Flint, Michigan
- Collection and Clippings File

Flint Jewish Federation, Flint, Michigan
- Collections and Clippings File

Flint Public Library, Flint, Michigan
- Michigan Room Collection
- Genesee County Biography File

Genesee Historical Collections Center, Frances Willson Thompson Library, University of Michigan–Flint, Flint, Michigan
- Edgar Holt Collection
- Labor History Project Interview Transcripts
- Robert Schafer Oral Histories Collection

Scharchburg Archives, Kettering University, Flint, Michigan
- Crooks Collection

Sloan Museum, Flint, Michigan
- Flint Jewish History Collection,
- Nineteenth and Twentieth Centuries Collection

Temple Beth El, Flint, Michigan
- Collection and Clippings File

NEWSPAPERS

Flint (Michigan) Journal, 1903–2005 (title changes from *Flint Daily Journal* in 1936)
Flint (Michigan) Jewish Reporter, 1950–1970; 1974–2005
Flint (Michigan) Operation Masada, 1970–1974
Flint (Michigan) Wolverine Citizen, 1854–1900

INTERVIEWS AND PERSONAL COMMUNICATIONS

Alfred, Fay (Laro). Interview by Nancy Hanflik. Tape recording. Flint, Mich. 29 October 2002.

Alter, Emily Bank. Interview by Nancy Hanflik. Tape recording. Flint Mich. 21 March 2000.

Alter, Gary. Interview by Nancy Hanflik. Flint, Mich. 3 November 2004.

Berg, Anna (Gruner). Interview by Nancy Hanflik. Tape recording. Hallandale, Fla. 1 June 1997.

Companez, Rabbi Karen. Personal communication to Nancy Hanflik. 29 December 2004.

Fineberg, Esther. Interview by Dale Cyran. Tape recording. Flint, Mich. 30 June 1978. Labor History Project Interview Transcripts, Frances Willson Thompson Library, Genesee Historical Collections Center, University of Michigan–Flint.

Frank, Lee Bernstein. Telephone interview by Nancy Hanflik. 9 September 2004.

Gaydayenko, Yuliya. Interview by Nancy Hanflik. Flint, Mich. 9 November 2004.

Goldfarb, Rabbi Mark. Interview by Nancy Hanflik. Tape recording. Flint, Mich. 12 October 1999.

Goodstein, Peter. Interview by Nancy Hanflik. Tape recording. Flint, Mich. 2 September 1999.

Gorne, Saul. Interview by Nancy Hanflik. Tape recording. Flint, Mich. 22 June 1999.

Hanflik, Mimi (Gruner). Interview by Nancy Hanflik. Tape recording. Hallandale, Fla. 31 May 1997.

———. Telephone interview by Nancy Hanflik. 15 March 2000.

Hart, Clifford. Interview by Nancy Hanflik. Tape recording. Flint, Mich. 16 July 1999.

———. Telephone interview by Nancy Hanflik. 15 June 2004.

Himelhoch, Robert. Interview by Nancy Hanflik. Tape recording. Flint, Mich. 28 June 2004.

Hoffman, Shelly. Personal communication to Nancy Hanflik. 3 April 2000.

Hurand, Art. Interview by Nancy Hanflik. Tape recording. Flint, Mich. 10 June 1999.

Kaplan, Joel. Telephone interview by Nancy Hanflik. 22 March 2000.

Karcher, Janis. Telephone interview by Nancy Hanflik. 3 November 2004.

Kasle, Lou, and Charlotte (Lewis) Kasle. Interview by Nancy Hanflik. Tape recording. Flint, Mich. 15 June 1999.

Kasle, Noreen. Personal communication to Nancy Hanflik. 4 September 1999.

Krolik, Bess. Interview by Nancy Hanflik. Tape recording. West Bloomfield, Mich. 9 June 1999.

Leyton, David. Personal communication to Nancy Hanflik. 31 January 2005.

Meizlish, Leonard. Interview by Nancy Hanflik. Tape recording. Flint, Mich. 10 July 2003.

Melet, Michael. Interview by Nancy Hanflik. Tape recording. Flint, Mich. 17 June 1999.

Michaels, Rabbi James. Interview by Nancy Hanflik. Tape recording. Flint, Mich. 30 September 1999.

Panzer, Caroline (Wise). Interview by Nancy Hanflik. Tape recording. Flint, Mich. 24 October 2002.

Pelavin, Michael. Interview by Nancy Hanflik. Tape recording. Flint, Mich. 15 June 1999.

Pelavin, Natalie. Interview by Nancy Hanflik. Tape recording. Flint, Mich. 15 June 1999.

Price, Esther (Silver). Interview by Nancy Hanflik. Tape recording. Flint, Mich. 23 June 1999.

Ratner, Reva (Sendler). Interview by Diane Roark. Tape recording. Flint, Mich. 18 July 1999.

Rubenstein, Gilbert. Interview by Nancy Hanflik. Tape recording. Flint, Mich. 28 June 1999.

———. Personal communication to Nancy Hanflik. 29 June 1999.

———. Telephone interview by Nancy Hanflik. 9 September. 2004.

Schiller, Joseph. Interview by Dale Cyran. Tape recording. Flint, Mich. 4 July 1978. Labor History Project Interview Transcripts, Frances Willson Thompson Library, Genesee Historical Collections Center, University of Michigan–Flint.

Sharp, James, Jr. Telephone interview by Nancy Hanflik. 14 April 2000.

Silverman, Gail. Interview by Nancy Hanflik. Tape recording. Flint, Mich. 16 March 2000.

Silverman, Ronald. Interview by Nancy Hanflik. Tape recording. Flint, Mich. 17 March 2000.

Stanzler, Jack. Interview by Nancy Hanflik. Tape recording. Ann Arbor, Mich. 28 October 2002.

Warren, Ellis. Dictation to Jennie Krasnick. N.d., ca. 1999.

Weingarten, Rabbi Yisroel and Shainie. Interview by Nancy Hanflik. Tape recording. Flint, Mich. 6 January 2000.

Weiss, Mitchell. Interview by Nancy Hanflik. Flint, Mich. 4 November 2004.

Winton, Flora. Personal communication to Nancy Hanflik. 29 April 1999.

OTHER SOURCES

Angervine and McCormick's General Directory of the City of Flint, 1872–1873. Flint, Mich.: Angervine and McCormick., 1873.

Attwood, William. "The Position of the Jews in America Today." *Look* 19 (29 November 1955): 27–35.

———. *The Twilight Struggle: Tales of the Cold War*. New York: Harper and Row, 1987.

Autoworld: Deconstructing Ideologies of Labor, Gender, Race, Class, and Consumerism in Flint, Michigan's Automobile Theme Park and Museum. Produced and directed by Connie Samaras. Videocassette, 1989.

Baldwin, Neil. *Henry Ford and the Jews: The Mass Production of Hate*. New York: Public Affairs, 2001.

Batten, Thelma F. *Flint and Michigan: A Study in Interdependence*. Ann Arbor, Mich.: Institute for Social Adjustment, Social Sciences Research Project, University of Michigan, 1955.

Baxter v. General Motors, National Lawyers Guild, *Civil Liberties Docket* 1 (April 1956): 75, case number 255.4.

Berger, Elmer. *The Flint Plan: A Program of Action for American Jews*. Flint, Mich., n.p., 1942.

———. *Why I Am a Non-Zionist*. Flint, Mich., n.p., 1942.

Berry, Chad. *Southern Migrants, Northern Exiles*. Chicago: University of Illinois Press, 2000.

"Best Buddy." *Time* 155 (31 January 2000).

Beynon, Erdmann Doane. "The Southern White Laborer Migrates to Michigan." *American Sociological Review* 3 (June 1938): 333–43.

Bloom, Nicholas Dagen. *Merchant of Illusion: James Rouse, America's Salesman of the Businessman's Utopia*. Columbus: Ohio State University Press, 2004.

Bolkosky, Sidney M. "Detroit's Reaction to the Holocaust and the New Immigrants." *Judaism* 49 (Summer 2000): 309–15.

———. *Harmony and Dissonance: Voices of Jewish Identity in Detroit, 1914–1967*. Detroit: Wayne State University Press, 1991.

Borish, Linda J. "'The Cradle of American Champions, Women Champions . . . Swim Champions': Charlotte Epstein, Gender and Jewish Identity, and the Physical Emancipation of Women in Aquatic Sports." *International Journal of the History of Sport* 21 (March 2004): 197–235.

———. "Women, Sports, and American Jewish Identity in Late Nineteenth and Early Twentieth Centuries." In *With God on Their Side: Sports in the Service of Religion*, edited by Tara Magdalinksi and Timothy J. L. Chandler. London: Routledge, 2002.

Brinkley, Alan. *Huey Long, Father Coughlin, and the Great Depression*. New York: Knopf, 1982.

Bukowczyk, John J. *And My Children Did Not Know Me: A History of the Polish Americans*. Bloomington: Indiana University Press, 1987.

Butts v. Harrison, et al. 382 U.S. 806; 86 S. Ct. 94 (1965).

Cantor, Judith Levin. *Jews in Michigan*. East Lansing: Michigan State University Press, 2001.

"Card Party Finally Hits In Michigan." *Flint Weekly Review*. 11 January 1963.

Carroll Jr., J. D. *Urban Land Vacancy: A Study of Factors Affecting Residential Building on Improved Vacant Lots in Flint, Michigan*. Ann Arbor, Mich.: Institute for Social Adjustment, Social Sciences Research Project, University of Michigan, 1953.

Chafe, William H. "Flint and the Great Depression." *Michigan History* 53, no. 3 (1969): 224–39.

"Chapters in American Jewish History, Chapter 120: Lending a Helping Hand." *Forward*. 16 July 1999.

Charles Stewart Mott Foundation. "Report to the People: The Flint Process: A Look at Our Community." Flint, Mich.: Charles Stewart Mott Foundation. N.d., ca. 1978.

Cohen, Warren. "The End of an Era for Autos." *U.S. News & World Report* 127 (12 July 1999).

"Congressman Kildee Honors Dr. Jerome and Sherry Kasle--Hon. Dale E. Kildee (Extension of Remarks)." 103rd Cong., 2nd sess. *Congressional Record* 140, no. 11 (8 February 1994): E125.

Corley, Cheryl. "Analysis: Cleaning Up Abandoned Property in Flint, Michigan." National Public Radio. Morning Edition. 21 October 2003.

Cowie, Jefferson, and Joseph Heathcott, eds. *Beyond the Ruins: The Meanings of Deindustrialization.* Ithaca, N.Y.: ILR Press, 2003.

Crow, Carl. *The City of Flint Grows Up: The Success Story of an American Community.* New York : Harper and Brothers, 1945.

Czaplinski, Wladyslaw, and Tadeusz Ladogórski, eds. *The Historical Atlas of Poland.* Wroclaw: Department of the State Cartographical Publishers, 1981.

Dandaneau, Steven P. *A Town Abandoned: Flint, Michigan, Confronts Deindustrialization.* Albany: State University of New York Press, 1996.

Dandaneau, Steven, and George Lord. "Hit or Miss for Flint." *In These Times* 16 (April 15–21, 1992).

"Demolition begins on 96-year-old Buick City complex." *Detroit News*, 25 August 2001.

Diner, Hasia R. *A Time for Gathering: The Second Migration, 1820–1880.* The Jewish People in America 2. Baltimore: Johns Hopkins University Press, 1992.

———. *The Jews of the United States, 1654 to 2000.* Jewish Communities in the Modern World 4. Berkeley: University of California Press, 2004.

Dluhy, Milan J. *Improving Housing Choices for the Jewish Aged in the Flint Area.* Flint, Mich., 1 November 1985.

———. *Preliminary Report--The Jewish Aged in the Flint/Genesee Area--A Population in Need.* Flint, Mich., 30 November 1984.

Dunlap, Mary Elizabeth. *The Urban and Metropolitan Status of the City of Flint.* Ann Arbor, Mich.: Institute for Social Adjustment, Social Sciences Research Project, University of Michigan, 1948.

Edsforth, Ronald. *Class Conflict and Cultural Consensus: The Making of a Mass Consumer Society in Flint, Michigan.* New Brunswick, N.J.: Rutgers University Press, 1987.

1860 Census of Genesee County. Transcribed and indexed by the Flint Genealogical Society. Flint Mich.: Flint Genealogical Society, 1982.

Eisen, Arnold M. *The Chosen People in America: A Study of Jewish Religious Ideology.* Bloomington: Indiana University Press, 1983.

Ellis, Franklin. *The History of Genesee County, Michigan: Its Prominent Men and Pioneers.* Philadelphia: Everts, 1879.

Evanoff, Michael W. *St. John St.: A Remembrance*, 3rd ed., rev. of *Through the Melting Pot and Beyond.* 1979; Flint, Mich.: Edelweiss Press, 1986.

Faires, Nora. "Transition and Turmoil: Social and Political Development in Michigan, 1917–1945." In *Michigan: Visions of Our Past,* edited by Richard J. Hathaway. East Lansing: Michigan State University Press, 1989.

Faires, Nora, and Nancy Hanflik. "Jewish Life in Postwar Flint." *Michigan Jewish History* 41 (Fall 2001): 11–23.

Farley, Reynolds, and William H. Frey. "Changes in the Segregation of Whites from Blacks during the 1980s." *American Sociological Review* 59 (February 1994): 23–45.

Feingold, Henry L. *A Time for Searching: Entering the Mainstream, 1920–1945.* The Jewish People in America 4. Baltimore: Johns Hopkins University Press, 1992.

Fine, Lisa M. *The Story of Reo Joe: Work, Kin, and Community in Autotown, U.S.A.* Philadelphia: Temple University Press, 2004.

Fine, Sidney. "The General Motors Sit-Down Strike: A Re-examination." *American Historical Review* 70

(April 1965): 691–713.

———. *Sit-Down: The General Motors Strike of 1936–37*. Ann Arbor: University of Michigan Press, 1969.

Firey, Walter. *Social Aspects to Land Use Planning in the Country-City Fringe: The Case of Flint*. East Lansing: Michigan State College, Agricultural Experiment Station, Section of Anthropology, 1946.

Flint, Michigan, Polk City Directory. Taylor, Mich.: R. L. Polk and Company, 1905–6, 1909, 1910, 1913, 1916, 1919–20, 1930, 1934,. 1936, 1939, 1940, 1941, 1942, 1945, 1947, 1949, 1950, 1968, 1970, 1978, 1985–86, 1991.

Flint, Michigan: The Vehicle City. Flint, Mich.: Flint Chamber of Commerce, 1955.

"Flint—A City Fighting Back." *U.S. News and World Report*, 7 July 1975.

Flint Board of Education. "The Background Story of Flint and Transportation." *The World We Live By*. Rev. ed. Vol. 5, 1965.

———. "Buick Motor Division, General Motors Corporation." *The World We Live By*. Rev. ed. Vol. 12, 1964.

———. "Retailing in Flint." *The World We Live By*. Vol. 19, 1963.

———. "Your City Government." *The World We Live By*. Vol. 17, 1961.

———. "Your Public Schools." *The World We Live By*. Rev. ed. Vol. 11 , 1964.

Flint City and Genesee County Directory, 1881–1882. Flint, Mich.: W. I. Beardsley, 1882.

Flint: City of Industrial Peace. Flint, Mich.: Board of Commerce, 1910.

Fried, Carla, with Leslie M. Marable and Sheryl Nance-Nash. "Best Places to Live in America." *Money* 25 (July 1996).

Frisch, Michael. *A Shared Authority: Essays on the Craft and Meaning of Public History*. Albany: State University of New York Press, 1990.

Gabin, Nancy F. *Feminism in the Labor Movement: Women and the United Auto Workers* Ithaca, N.Y.: Cornell University Press, 1990.

General Motors Golden Carnival: Celebrating Its First 50 Million Cars. Flint, Mich..: Flint Journal, 1954.

Gentleman's Agreement. Produced by Darryl F. Zanuck. Directed by Elia Kazan. Twentieth Century Fox. 1947.

Glen V. Mills' Directory Map of Flint City, 1894. Ann Arbor, Mich.: G. V. Mills, 1894.

Godley, Andrew. *Jewish Immigrant Entrepreneurship in New York and London, 1880–1914*. New York: Palgrave, 2001.

Goodstein, Laurie. "Survey Finds Slight Rise in Jews' Intermarrying." *New York Times* 11 September 2003, Midwest edition.

Gordon, Milton. *Assimilation in American Life: The Role of Race, Religion, and National Origins*. New York: Oxford University Press, 1964.

Goss, Jon. "The 'Magic of the Mall': An Analysis of Form, Function, and Meaning in the Contemporary Retail Built Environment." *Annals of the Association of American Geographers* 83, no. 1 (March 1993): 18–47.

Green, Nancy L. *Ready-to-Wear and Ready-to-Work: A Century of Industry and Immigrants in Paris and New York*. Durham, N.C.: Duke University Press, 1997.

Gustin, Lawrence R. *Billy Durant: Creator of General Motors*. Grand Rapids, Mich.: Eerdmans, 1973.

———., ed. *The Flint Journal Centennial Picture History of Flint*. Flint, Mich.: William B. Eerdmans and Flint Bicentennial Commission, 1976.

Hakim, Danny. "G.M. Will Reduce Hourly Workers in U.S. by 25,000." *New York Times*, 8 June 2005.

Hakim, Danny, and Jeremy W. Peters. "Tough Times at U.S. Makers of Auto Parts." *New York Times*.12 December 2004.

Hammond, P. J. *Flint*. Flint, Mich.: P. J. Hammond , 1922. Flint Jewish History Collection, Sloan Museum, Flint, Michigan.

Hamper, Ben. *Rivethead: Tales from the Assembly Line*. New York: Warner Books, 1991.

Hanflik, Nancy. "150 Years of Jewish Life in Flint: 1850–2000." Master's thesis, University of Michigan–Flint, 2000.

"Happiest Town in Michigan." *Coronet*, June 1956.

"Harlow Curtice." *Time*, 2 January 1956.

Harvey, David. *The Condition of Postmodernity: An Enquiry into the Origins of Cultural Change.* Oxford: Basil Blackwell, 1989.

Hébert, Richard. "Flint: GM's Mark of Excellence." In *Highways to Nowhere: The Politics of City Transportation.* New York: Bobbs–Merrill, 1972.

Herberg, Will. *Protestant, Catholic, Jew: An Essay in Religious Sociology.* Garden City, N.Y.: Doubleday, 1955.

———. "The 'Triple Melting Pot.'" *Commentary* 20 (August 1955): 101–8.

High, Steven. *Industrial Sunset: The Making of North America's Rust Belt, 1969–1984.* Toronto: University of Toronto Press, 2003.

Hicks, Jay. "Houses Built by General Motors: The Flint Housing Crisis and GMC." *Michigan History* 71 (March/April 1987): 32–39.

Hughes Jr., I. Harding. *Local Government in the Fringe Area of Flint, Michigan.* Ann Arbor, Mich.: Institute for Social Adjustment, Social Sciences Research Project, University of Michigan, 1947.

Hyman, Paula. "Gender and the Immigrant Jewish Experience in the United States." In *Jewish Women in Historical Perspective*, edited by Judith R. Baskin. Detroit: Wayne State University Press, 1991.

Jackson, Kenneth T. *The Ku Klux Klan in the City, 1915–1930.* New York: Oxford University Press, 1967.

"Jews of Flint!" *Community Herald*, 12 September 1920.

Jones, Bryan D., and Lynn W. Bachelor. "Flint: Political Maneuvering and Buick City." In *The Sustaining Hand: Community Leadership and Corporate Control.* Lawrence: University of Kansas Press, 1986.

Kantner, John. *The Relationship between Accessibility and Socio-Economic Status of Residential Lands, Flint, Michigan.* Ann Arbor, Mich.: Institute for Social Adjustment, Social Sciences Research Project, University of Michigan, 1948.

Keats, John. *The Insolent Chariots.* Philadelphia: Lippincott, 1958.

Kennedy, Ruby Jo Reeves, "Single or Triple Melting Pot? Intermarriage Trends in New Haven, 1870–1940." *American Journal of Sociology*, 49 (January 1944): 331–39.

Kessler, E. J. "The Lubavitch Factor," *Forward*, 14 January 2000.

Kraus, Henry. *The Many and the Few: A Chronicle of the Dynamic Auto Workers.* 2d ed. Chicago: University of Illinois Press, 1985.

"Labor Peace: It's Wonderful," *U.S. News and World Report*, July 1950.

Lee, Steve. "Stag Reports on a Wide-Open Town." *Stag* 7 (March 1956): 11–15, 66–67.

Lenski, Gerhard. *The Religious Factor: A Sociologist's Inquiry.* New York: Anchor, 1963.

Lichtenstein, Nelson. *The Most Dangerous Man in Detroit: Walter Reuther and the Fate of American Labor.* New York: Basic Books, 1995.

"Life of Ald. Henry Brown" *Flint (Michigan) Sunday Democrat.* 10 February 1877.

Lord, George F., and Albert C. Price, "Growth Ideology in a Period of Decline: Deindustrialization and Restructuring, Flint Style," *Social Problems* 39 (May 1992): 155–69.

Magosci, Paul Robert. *Historical Atlas of East Central Europe.* Vol. 1. Seattle: University of Washington Press, 1995.

Manley, F. J., B. W. Reed, and R. K. Burns, *The Community School in Action: The Flint Program.* Chicago: University of Chicago Press, 1961.

Marcus, Jacob R. *A History of Jews in Michigan Before 1850.* Detroit: Wayne State University Press, 1955.

Maxwell, James A. "What's Bad for General Motors Is Bad for Flint," *Reporter*, 20 March 1958.

Mayer, Albert J. *Flint Jewish Population Study 1967.* Flint, Mich.: Flint Jewish Community Council, 1969.

Meyer, Stephen. "Work, Play, and Power: Masculine Culture on the Automotive Shop Floor, 1930–1960." *Men and Masculinities* 2 (October 1999): 115–34.

———. "Rough Manhood: The Aggressive and Confrontational Shop Culture of U.S. Auto Workers during World War II." *Journal of Social History* 36 (Fall 2002): 125–47.

Michigan, Governor's Task Force on Redlining. *Final Report of the Governor's Task Force on Redlining*. Lansing: State of Michigan, 1976.

Montgomery, David. *The Fall of the House of Labor: The Workplace, the State, and American Labor Activism*. New York: Cambridge University Press, 1987.

Moody, Kim. "On the Line in Flint." *Nation* 28 (13 July 1998).

Moore, Deborah Dash. *GI Jews: How World War II Changed a Generation*. Cambridge, Mass.: Harvard University Press, 2004.

———. "Jewish GIs and the Creation of the Judeo-Christian Tradition." *Religion and American Culture* 8 (Winter 1998): 31–53.

Moore, Michael. "Flint and Me." *Money* 25 (July 1996).

Morawska, Ewa. *Insecure Prosperity: Small-Town Jews in Industrial America, 1890–1940*. Princeton, N.J.: Princeton University Press, 1996.

Nader, Ralph. *Unsafe at Any Speed: The Designed-In Dangers of the American Automobile*. New York: Grossman Publishers, 1965.

Novick, Peter. *The Holocaust in American Life*. Boston: Houghton Mifflin, 1999.

Office of Planning, Michigan State Highway Department. *Freeways for Flint: A Statement of the Michigan State Highway Department. Proposals for Location of I-475, M78/21 Freeways in Flint*. Presented to the Flint City Commission by the Office of Planning, Michigan State Highway Department. 17 January 1963.

Penkower, Monty Noam. "The Genesis of the American Council for Judaism: A Quest for Identity in World War II." *American Jewish History* 86, no. 2 (1998): 167–94.

Perlmann, Joel. *Ethnic Differences: Schooling and Social Structure among the Irish, Italians, Jews, and Blacks in an American City, 1880–1935*. Cambridge: Cambridge University Press, 1988.

Retzloff, Tim. "Cars and Bars: Assembling Gay Men in Postwar Flint, Michigan." In *Creating a Place for Ourselves: Lesbian, Gay, and Bisexual Community Histories*, edited by Brett Beemyn. New York: Routledge, 1997.

Ringer, James B. *The Edge of Friendliness: A Study of Jewish-Gentile Relations*. New York: Basic Books, 1967.

Rockaway, Robert. *The Jews of Detroit*. Detroit: Wayne State University Press, 1986.

———. *Words of the Uprooted: Jewish Immigration in Early 20ᵗʰ Century America*. Ithaca, N.Y.: Cornell University Press, 1998.

Roger & Me. Produced and directed by Michael Moore. Dog Eat Dog Films. 1989.

Rogoff, Leonard. *Homelands: Southern Jewish Identity in Durham and Chapel Hill, North Carolina*. Tuscaloosa: University of Alabama Press, 2001.

Rosenthal, Gilbert S. *The Many Faces of Judaism: Orthodox, Conservative, Reconstructionist and Reform*. Edited by Seymour Rossel. New York: Behrman House, 1978.

Rottenberg, Dan, ed. *Middletown Jews: The Tenuous Survival of an American Jewish Community*. Bloomington: Indiana University Press, 1997.

Rouse, J. W. "Must Shopping Centers Be Inhuman?" *Architectural Forum* (June 1962)

"Salute to General Motors on the Completion of 50,000,000 Automobiles." Special edition. *Flint News-Advertiser*. 23 November 1954.

Sanders, Rhonda. *Bronze Pillars: An Oral History of African-Americans in Flint*. Flint, Mich.: Flint Journal and Alfred P. Sloan Museum, 1995.

Sarna, Jonathan D. "American Jewish History: A Chance to Reflect," *Chronicle of Higher Education* 51 (1 October 2004).

———. *American Judaism: A History*. New Haven, Conn.: Yale University Press, 2004.

Sawicki, D. S. "The Festival Marketplace as Public Policy: Guidelines for Future Policy Decisions." *American Planning Association Journal* (Summer 1989): 347–61.

Schafer, Robert. *Charles Stewart Mott of Applewood: A Memoir*. Flint, Mich..: University of Michigan-Flint Archives, in cooperation with the Genesee County Historical Society, 1984.

———. *Producing a Human Mosaic: Immigration and Economic Change in the Development of Genesee County's Population, 1820–1987.* Flint, Mich.: University of Michigan–Flint Archives in cooperation with the Genesee County Historical Society, 1989.

Schmitt, Robert C. *The Future Population of Metropolitan Flint.* Ann Arbor, Mich.: Institute for Social Adjustment, Social Sciences Research Project, University of Michigan, 1947.

Segal, Abraham. *One People: A Study in Comparative Judaism.* Edited by Bernard M. Zlotowitz. New York: Union of Hebrew Congregations, 1982.

Shapiro, Edward S. *A Time for Healing: American Jewry since World War II.* The Jewish People in America 5. Baltimore: Johns Hopkins University Press, 1992.

"Six-Year-Old Boy Shoots Classmate; Man, 19, Charged with Involuntary Manslaughter for Possessing the Gun." *Jet* 97 (20 March 2000).

Sklare, Marshall. *Conservative Judaism: An American Religious Movement.* 1955. Reprint, Glencoe, Ill.: Free Press, 1972.

———. "Protestant-Catholic-Jew: An Essay in Religious Sociology." *Commentary* 21 (February 1956).

Sorin, Gerald. *A Time for Building: The Third Migration, 1880–1920.* The Jewish People in America 3. Baltimore: Johns Hopkins University Press, 1992.

Sorscher, Sidell. *You're a Wonderful Person.* Detroit: Harlo Press, 1985.

Spencer v. Flint Memorial Park Association, 318 Mich. 4th (Mich. Ct. App. 1966).

Steinmetz, Daniel. *1990 and Beyond: Needs and Possibilities Facing the Greater Flint Area Jewish Communities.* Project for Urban and Regional Affairs, University of Michigan–Flint, July 1990.

Stodghill, Ron. "A Train Hop to Tragedy." *Time*, 21 July 1997.

"Sub-Committee Begins Planning." *Flint News-Advertiser.* 4 June 1954.

Sugrue, Thomas J. *The Origins of the Urban Crisis: Race and Inequality in Postwar Detroit.* Princeton, N.J.: Princeton University Press, 1996.

Swados, Harvey. "*Unsafe at Any Speed*, by Ralph Nader, and *Safety Last*, by Jeffrey O'Connell and Arthur Meyers," *Commentary* 41 (June 1966).

Swan, Tony. "Buick Celebrates 100 Years of Tasteful, Not Crass, Automobiles." *Detroit Free Press.* 17 July 2003.

Tableman, Betty. *Intra-Community Migration in the Flint Metropolitan District.* Ann Arbor, Mich.: Institute for Social Adjustment, Social Sciences Research Project, University of Michigan, 1948.

Teaford, Jon C. *Cities of the Heartland: The Rise and Fall of the Industrial Midwest.* Bloomington: Indiana University Press, 1993.

Tenenbaum, Shelley. *A Credit to Their Community: Jewish Loan Societies in the United States, 1880–1945.* Detroit: Wayne State University Press, 1993.

Terry, Don. "A City Where Hope Runs on Empty," *New York Times.* 26 February 1992.

Totten, William Fred, and Frank J. Manley, *The Community School: Basic Concepts, Function, and Organization.* Galien, Mich.: Allied Education Council, 1969.

U.S. Bureau of the Census. *Population Schedules of the Eighth Census of the United States, 1860. Michigan, Genesee County.* New Haven, Conn..: Research Publications, 197-?. Microform.

———. *Population Schedules of the Ninth Census of the United States, 1870. Michigan, Genesee County.* Washington, D.C.: National Archives and Records Services Administration, 1965. Microform.

———. *Population Schedules of the Seventh Census of the United States, 1850. Michigan, Genesee County.* Washington, D.C.: National Archives and Records Services Administration, 1963. Microform.

———. *Population Schedules of the Tenth Census of the United States, 1880. Michigan, Genesee County.* New Haven, Conn..: Research Publications, 197-?. Microform.

———. *Population Schedules of the Thirteenth Census of the United States, 1910. Michigan, Genesee County.* Washington, D.C.: Micro-film Lab, Bureau of the Census, 196-?. Microform.

———. *Population Schedules of the Twelfth Census of the United States, 1900. Michigan, Genesee County.* Washington, D.C.: Micro-film Lab, Bureau of the Census, 196-?. Microform.

U.S. Congress, House. Committee on Un-American Activities. *Investigation of Communist Activities in the State of Michigan. Hearings before the United States House Committee on Un-American Activities.* 83rd Cong., 2nd sess., parts 8 (12 May 1954), 9 (13 May 1954), 10 (14 May 1954), and 11 (17 November 1954).

U.S. Congress, Senate Committee on the Budget. *Regional Impact of an Economic Slowdown: The Michigan Picture. Hearings before the Committee on the Budget, United States Senate*, 96th Cong., 1st sess., February 1980. Washington, D.C.: U.S. Government Printing Office, 1980.

University of California Regents v. Bakke, 438 U.S. 265 (1978).

Vilma, Hastaoglou-Martinidis. "A Mediterranean City in Transition: Thessaloniki between the Two World Wars," *Facta Universitatus, Architecture and Civil Engineering* 1 (1997): 493–507.

Waltzer, Kenneth. "East European Jewish Detroit in the Early Twentieth Century," *Judaism* 49 (Summer 2000): 291–309.

———. "Picturing Flint Jewry at the Sloan Museum." Comments delivered at the exhibit "A Century of Jewish Life in Flint." Sloan Museum, Flint, Mich., 14 October 2001.

Weinberg, Sydney Stahl. "Jewish Mothers and Immigrant Daughters: Positive and Negative Role Models." *Journal of American Ethnic History* 9 (Spring 1987): 39–55.

Weissbach, Lee Shai. *Jewish Life in Small Town America: A History*. New Haven, Conn: Yale University Press, 2005.

Wenger, Beth S. "Jewish Women and Voluntarism: Beyond the Myth of Enablers." *American Jewish History* 79 (Autumn 1989): 16–36.

———. "Jewish Women of the Club: The Changing Public Role of Atlanta's Jewish Women (1870–1930)." *American Jewish History* 76 (March 1987): 311–33.

———. *New York Jews and the Great Depression: Uncertain Promise*. New Haven, Conn.: Yale University Press, 1996.

Werblowsky, R. J. Zwi, and Geoffrey Wigoder, eds. *Oxford Dictionary of the Jewish Religion*. New York: Oxford University Press, 1997.

Wertheimer, Jack. "Recent Trends in American Judaism." In *American Jewish Year Book, 1989*. Philadelphia: Jewish Publication Society of America, 89: 63–162.

West, Kenneth B. "'On the Line': Rank and File Reminiscences of Working Conditions and the General Motors Sit-Down Strike of 1936–37," *Michigan Historical Review* 12 (Spring 1986): 57–82.

———. "Standard Cotton Products and the General Motors Sit-Down Strike: Some 'Forgotten Men' Remembered," *Michigan Historical Review* 14 (Spring 1988): 57–73.

Wood, Edwin O. *History of Genesee County, Michigan: Her People, Industries and Institutions. With Biographical Sketches of Representative Citizens and Genealogical Records of Many of the Old Families*. Vol. 1. Indianapolis: Federal Publishing Company, 1916.

Wright, Dell S. *Central Business District of Flint, Michigan: Changes in the Assessed Valuation of Real Property, 1930-1951*. Ann Arbor, Mich.: Institute for Social Adjustment, Social Sciences Research Project, University of Michigan, 1953.

"Yankee Stores Now Prime Target of Group Seeking Free Enterprise Control." *Flint Weekly Review*. 20 December 1962.

Zimmer, Basil G. *Demographic Handbook of Flint Metropolitan Area*. Ann Arbor, Mich.: Institute for Social Adjustment, Social Sciences Research Project, University of Michigan, 1955.

Zunz, Olivier. *The Changing Face of Inequality: Urbanization, Industrial Development, and Immigrants in Detroit*. Chicago: University of Chicago Press, 1982.

Zwerdling, Daniel. "And Then There's the Disneyland Solution." *Progressive*, July 1982.

Index